ENGLISH PROSE, PROSE FICTION, and CRITICISM to 1660

AMERICAN LITERATURE, ENGLISH LITERATURE, AND WORLD LITERATURES IN ENGLISH: AN INFORMATION GUIDE SERIES

Series Editor: Theodore Grieder, Curator, Division of Special Collections, Fales Library, New York University, New York, New York

Associate Editor: Duane DeVries, Assistant Professor, Polytechnic Institute of New York, Brooklyn, New York

Other books on English Literature in this Series:

ENGLISH PROSE AND CRITICISM, 1660-1800—*Edited by John T. Shawcross***

ENGLISH PROSE AND CRITICISM IN THE NINETEENTH CENTURY—*Edited by Harris W. Wilson***

ENGLISH PROSE AND CRITICISM, 1900-1950—*Edited by Sondra Rosenberg***

ENGLISH FICTION, 1660-1800—*Edited by Jerry Beasley***

ENGLISH FICTION, 1800-1850—*Edited by Duane DeVries***

BRITISH FICTION, 1900-1950—*Edited by Thomas J. Rice***

CONTEMPORARY FICTION IN AMERICA AND ENGLAND—*Edited by A. F. Rosa and P. A. Eschholz***

ENGLISH DRAMA TO 1660—*Edited by F. Elaine Penninger**

ENGLISH DRAMA, 1660-1800—*Edited by Frederick M. Link***

ENGLISH DRAMA IN THE NINETEENTH CENTURY—*Edited by L. W. Conolly and J. P. Wearing***

BRITISH DRAMA, 1900-1950—*Edited by E. H. Mikhail***

CONTEMPORARY DRAMA IN AMERICA AND ENGLAND, 1950-1970—*Edited by Richard H. Harris***

*in press
**in preparation

The above series is part of the
GALE INFORMATION GUIDE LIBRARY

The Library consists of a number of separate Series of guides covering major areas in the social sciences, humanities, and current affairs.

General Editor: Paul Wasserman, Professor and former Dean, School of Library and Information Services, University of Maryland

ENGLISH PROSE, PROSE FICTION, and CRITICISM to 1660

A GUIDE TO INFORMATION SOURCES

Volume 2 in the American Literature, English Literature, and World Literatures in English Information Guide Series

S. K. Heninger, Jr.

Professor of English, University of British Columbia

Gale Research Company
Book Tower, Detroit, Michigan 48226

**Library of Congress
Cataloging in Publication Data**

Heninger, S   K
    English prose, prose fiction, and criticism to 1660.

    (American literature, English literature, and world
literatures in English: an information guide series; v.2)
(Gale information guide library)
    1. English prose literature--Early modern, 1500-1700
--Bibliography. 2. English prose literature--Early modern,
1500-1700--History and criticism--Bibliography. 3. English prose literature--Middle English, 1100-1500--Bibliog-
raphy. 4. English prose literature--Middle English, 1100-
1500--History and criticism--Bibliography. I. Title.
Z2014.P795H45   016.082   73-16980
ISBN 0-8103-1233-6

Copyright © 1975 by
Gale Research Company

Contents

Preface vii

Table of Abbreviations ix

I – General 3

II – Religious Writings 11

III – Historical Writings 43

IV – Travel Literature 61

V – Scientific and Technical Writings 79

VI – Ephemeral and Polemical Writings 91

VII – Essays 127

VIII – Narrative Fiction 143

IX – Literary Criticism 177

X – Writings on Education 185

XI – Translations 199

XII – Translations of the Bible 219

Index 225

Vita

S.K. Heninger, Jr., is currently professor of English at the University of British Columbia. He received his B.A. and M.A. from Tulane University; his B. Litt. from Oxford University, where he was a Fulbright scholar; and his Ph.D. from Johns Hopkins University. Heninger has been a professor of English at Duke University and the University of Wisconsin, Madison, where he was chairman of the department. Academic honors awarded him include a Guggenheim fellowship and a Huntington Library fellowship.

Heninger is the author of A HANDBOOK OF RENAISSANCE METEOROLOGY and TOUCHES OF SWEET HARMONY. He has edited SELECTIONS FROM THE POETICAL WORKS OF EDMUND SPENSER and Thomas Watson's HEKATOMPATHIA. At present, he is completing THE COSMOGRAPHICAL GLASS: RENAISSANCE DIAGRAMS OF THE UNIVERSE, to be published in 1975; and is at work on a reading of the major works of Philip Sidney and Edmund Spenser.

Preface

This bibliography is intended for the serious reader who seeks guidance among the major works in English prose from its beginnings to the Restoration in 1660. The coverage is comprehensive, including all types of prose written in English during the period. It is also balanced, so that each type receives attention proportional to its importance. All of the well-known writers are included, as well as some of the smaller fry who nonetheless produced notable works.

The items covered by this bibliography are categorized under the following headings:

    I.   General
    II.   Religious Writings
    III.   Historical Writings
    IV.   Travel Literature
    V.   Scientific and Technical Writings
    VI.   Ephemeral and Polemical Writings
    VII.   Essays
    VIII.   Narrative Fiction
    IX.   Literary Criticism
    X.   Writings on Education
    XI.   Translations
    XII.   Translations of the Bible

For each heading a brief comment defines the category, followed by a list of secondary works that are pertinent to it in a general way. Individual primary works are then enumerated.

For each primary work there is (a) an entry for its date of composition (if written before 1460) or its first date of publication (if written after 1460), (b) entries for the best modern editions if it has been reprinted, (c) entries for bibliographies pertaining to the author, and (d) entries for the published scholarship and criticism most helpful in understanding the work. Entries for primary works are numbered continuously throughout the volume and are indicated by arabic numerals (1, 2, 3. . .). Entries for modern editions are indicated by capital letters (A, B, C. . .). Entries for bibliographies are indicated by small roman numerals (i, ii, iii. . .). And entries for scholarship and criticism are indicated by small letters (a, b, c. . .).

Preface

Within each category the primary works are arranged chronologically according to the date of composition or publication. As a consequence, the usual division of this body of literature into periods--medieval, Tudor, and seventeenth-century--may be blurred. But chronological arrangement has the advantage of making clear the sequential development for each type of prose.

At the end of the bibliography there is a complete index of all authors and editors, comprising both primary and secondary materials.

Table of Abbreviations

The following abbreviations have been used for series and current periodicals:

ARCHIV	Archiv fur das Studium der Neueren Sprachen und Literaturen
3HR	Bibliotheque d'Humanisme et Renaissance
BJRL	Bulletin of the John Rylands Library
BNYPL	Bulletin of the New York Public Library
C&M	Classica et Mediaevalia
CARRELL	The Carrell: Journal of the Friends of the University of Miami (Fla.) Library
CCC	College Composition and Communication
CE	College English
CL	Comparative Literature
E&S	Essays and Studies by Members of the English Association
EETS ES	Early English Text Society, Extra Series
EETS OS	Early English Text Society, Original Series
EHR	English Historical Review
ELH	ELH: A Journal of English Literary History
ELR	English Literary Renaissance
ES	English Studies
ESA	English Studies in Africa (Johannesburg)
HLB	Harvard Library Bulletin
HLQ	Huntington Library Quarterly
HR	Hispanic Review
JEGP	Journal of English and Germanic Philology
JHI	Journal of the History of Ideas
KR	Kenyon Review

Table of Abbreviations

LeedsSE	Leeds Studies in English
LIBRARY	The Library
MAE	Medium AEvum
MiltonS	Milton Studies
MLN	Modern Language Notes
MLQ	Modern Language Quarterly
MLR	Modern Language Review
MP	Modern Philology
N&Q	Notes and Queries
NEOPHIL	Neophilologus (Groningen)
NM	Neuphilologische Mitteilungen
PBA	Proceedings of the British Academy
PBSA	Papers of the Bibliographical Society of America
PhR	Philosophical Review
PLL	Papers on Language and Literature
PMLA	PMLA: Publications of the Modern Language Association of America
PQ	Philological Quarterly
RenP	Renaissance Papers
RES	Review of English Studies
RLC	Revue de Litterature Comparee
RN	Renaissance News
SB	Studies in Bibliography: Papers of the Bibliographical Society of the University of Virginia
SEL	Studies in English Literature, 1500-1900
SOUNDINGS	Soundings: A Journal of Interdisciplinary Studies
SP	Studies in Philology
SQ	Shakespeare Quarterly
SRen	Studies in the Renaissance
SSF	Studies in Short Fiction
TSL	Tennessee Studies in Literature
TSLL	Texas Studies in Literature and Language
UTQ	University of Toronto Quarterly

I. GENERAL

I. General

A. Grein, Christian W. M., and Richard P. Wulker, eds. BIBLI-
OTHEK DER ANGELSACHSISCHEN PROSA. 13 vols. Kassel
and Hamburg, 1872-1933.

B. Saintsbury, George, ed. SPECIMENS OF ENGLISH PROSE
STYLE FROM MALORY TO MACAULAY. London, 1886.

C. Craik, Henry, ed. ENGLISH PROSE. 5 vols. London,
1893-96. Vols. I-III.

D. Cook, A. S., and C. B. Tinker, eds. SELECT TRANSLATIONS
FROM OLD ENGLISH PROSE. Boston, 1908.

E. Peacock, W., ed. ENGLISH PROSE. 5 vols. Oxford:
World's Classics, 1921-22. Vols. I-III.

F. Sedgefield, W. J., ed. AN ANGLO-SAXON PROSE BOOK.
Manchester University Press, 1928.

G. Moore, C. A., and Douglas Bush, eds. ENGLISH PROSE,
1600-1660. Garden City, New York, 1930.

H. Roberts, Michael, ed. ELIZABETHAN PROSE. London, 1933.

I. Brinkley, Roberta F., ed. ENGLISH PROSE OF THE XVII
CENTURY. New York, 1951.

J. Hebel, J. W., et al., eds. PROSE OF THE ENGLISH RE-
NAISSANCE. New York, 1952.

K. Holzknecht, K. J., ed. SIXTEENTH-CENTURY ENGLISH
PROSE. New York, 1954.

L. James, Eirian, ed. AN ANTHOLOGY OF ENGLISH PROSE 1400-1900. Cambridge University Press, 1956.

M. Muir, Kenneth, ed. ELIZABETHAN AND JACOBEAN PROSE, 1550-1620. Harmondsworth: Pelican, 1956.

N. Nugent, Elizabeth M., ed. THE THOUGHT AND CULTURE OF THE ENGLISH RENAISSANCE: AN ANTHOLOGY OF TUDOR PROSE, 1481-1555. Cambridge University Press, 1956.

O. Shaaber, M. A., ed. SEVENTEENTH-CENTURY ENGLISH PROSE. New York, 1957.

P. Matthews, William, ed. LATER MEDIEVAL ENGLISH PROSE. New York: Goldentree, 1963.

Q. Harris, Victor, and Itrat Husain, eds. ENGLISH PROSE, 1600-1660. New York: Rinehart Editions, 1965.

R. Novarr, David, ed. SEVENTEENTH-CENTURY ENGLISH PROSE. New York, 1967.

S. Mahl, Mary R., ed. SEVENTEENTH CENTURY ENGLISH PROSE. Philadelphia, 1968.

T. Creeth, E. H., ed. TUDOR PROSE, 1513-1570. Garden City, New York: Anchor, 1969.

i. Heusinkveld, Arthur H., and Edwin J. Bashe. "Prose," in A BIBLIOGRAPHICAL GUIDE TO OLD ENGLISH. University of Iowa Press, 1931.

ii. Bennett, James R. "An Annotated Bibliography of Selected Writings on English Prose Style," CCC, 16 (1965), 248-55.

iii. Renwick, W. L., and Harold Orton. THE BEGINNINGS OF ENGLISH LITERATURE TO SKELTON 1509. 3rd ed., rev. M. F. Wakelin. London, 1966.

iv. Sola Pinto, Vivian de. THE ENGLISH RENAISSANCE 1510-1688. Rev. ed. London, 1966.

v. Donovan, Dennis G., et al. ELIZABETHAN BIBLIOGRAPHIES SUPPLEMENTS. London, 1967- .

Intended to bring Tannenbaum's Elizabethan bibliographies up to date.

vi. Matthews, William. OLD AND MIDDLE ENGLISH LITERATURE. New York: Goldentree, 1968.

vii. Lievsay, John L. THE SIXTEENTH CENTURY: SKELTON THROUGH HOOKER. New York: Goldentree, 1968.

viii. Robinson, Fred C. OLD ENGLISH LITERATURE: A SELECT BIBLIOGRAPHY. University of Toronto Press, 1970.

a. Earle, John. ENGLISH PROSE: ITS ELEMENTS, HISTORY, AND USAGE. New York, 1891.

b. Tupper, J. W. TROPES AND FIGURES IN ANGLO-SAXON PROSE. Baltimore, 1897.

c. Greenwood, Alice D. "English Prose in the Fifteenth Century," in THE CAMBRIDGE HISTORY OF ENGLISH LITERATURE, ed. A. W. Ward and A. R. Waller. 15 vols. Cambridge University Press, 1907-27. II,286-309, 332-40.

d. Saintsbury, George. A HISTORY OF ENGLISH PROSE RHYTHM. London, 1912.

e. Clark, Albert C. PROSE RHYTHM IN ENGLISH. Oxford, 1913.

f. Krapp, George P. THE RISE OF ENGLISH LITERARY PROSE. Oxford University Press, 1915.

g. Croll, Morris W. " 'Attic Prose' in the Seventeenth Century," SP, 18 (1921), 79-128.

h. _____. "The Baroque Style in Prose," in STUDIES IN EN-GLISH PHILOLOGY: A MISCELLANY IN HONOR OF FRED-ERICK KLAEBER, ed. Kemp Malone and M. B. Ruud. University of Minnesota Press, 1929, pp. 427-56.

i. Chambers, R. W. "The Continuity of English Prose from Alfred to More and His School," in Nicholas Harpsfield, THE LIFE AND DEATH OF SIR THOMAS MOORE, ed. Chambers. EETS OS 186. London, 1932, pp. xlv-clxxiv. Also printed separately.

j. Knights, L. C. "Elizabethan Prose," SCRUTINY, 2 (1934), 427-38.

k. Crane, William G. WIT AND RHETORIC IN THE RENAIS-SANCE: THE FORMAL BASIS OF ELIZABETHAN PROSE STYLE. Columbia University Press, 1937.

l. Workman, Samuel K. FIFTEENTH CENTURY TRANSLATION AS AN INFLUENCE ON ENGLISH PROSE. Princeton University Press, 1940.

m. Daniells, Roy. "Baroque Form in English Literature," UTQ, 14 (1945), 393-408.

n. Bennett, H. S. "Fifteenth Century Secular Prose," RES, 21 (1945), 257-63.

o. _____. "Fifteenth-Century Prose," in CHAUCER AND THE FIFTEENTH CENTURY. Oxford, 1947, pp. 177-217.

p. Allen, Don C. "Style and Certitude," ELH, 15 (1948), 167-75.

q. Malone, Kemp. "Literary Prose [The Old English Period]," in A LITERARY HISTORY OF ENGLAND, ed. A. C. Baugh. New York, 1948, pp. 96-105.

r. Stedmond, John M. "English Prose of the Seventeenth Century," DALHOUSIE REVIEW, 30 (1950), 269-78.

s. Williamson, George. THE SENECAN AMBLE: A STUDY IN PROSE FORM FROM BACON TO COLLIER. University of Chicago Press, 1951.

t. Fisch, Harold. "The Puritans and the Reform of Prose Style," ELH, 19 (1952), 229-48.

u. Lewis, C. S. "Drab and Transitional Prose" and "Prose in the 'Golden' Period," in ENGLISH LITERATURE IN THE SIXTEENTH CENTURY. Oxford, 1954, pp. 272-317 and 394-463.

v. Thompson, James A. K. CLASSICAL INFLUENCES ON ENGLISH PROSE. London, 1956.

w. Howell, Wilbur S. LOGIC AND RHETORIC IN ENGLAND, 1500-1700. Princeton University Press, 1956.

x. Sutherland, James. ON ENGLISH PROSE. Alexander Lectures. University of Toronto Press, 1957.

y. Staton, Walter F., Jr. "The Characters of Style in Elizabethan Prose," JEGP, 57 (1958), 197-207.

z. Harris, Victor. "The Arts of Discourse in England, 1500-1700," PQ, 37 (1958), 484-94.

aa. Ohmann, Richard. "Prolegomena to Prose Style," in STYLE IN PROSE FICTION. New York: English Institute Essays, 1959, pp. 1-24.

bb. Wilson, R. M. "On the Continuity of English Prose," in MELANGES DE LINGUISTIC ET DE PHILOLOGIE FERNAND MOSSE IN MEMORIAM. Paris, 1959, pp. 486-94.

cc. Miller, Edwin H. THE PROFESSIONAL WRITER IN ELIZABE-THAN ENGLAND. Harvard University Press, 1959.

dd. Wilson, Frank P. SEVENTEENTH CENTURY PROSE: FIVE LECTURES. University of California Press, 1960.

    "A Survey," "Robert Burton," "Biography," "Sir Thomas Browne," "The Sermon."

ee. Barish, Jonas A. BEN JONSON AND THE LANGUAGE OF PROSE COMEDY. Harvard University Press, 1960.

ff. Davis, Norman. "Styles in English Prose of the Late Middle and Early Modern Period," LANGUE ET LITTERATURE, 21 (1961), 165-84.

gg. Heuston, R. F. V. "The Law Reports as Sources of English Prose," REVIEW OF ENGLISH LITERATURE, 2 (1961), 28-38.

hh. Beum, Robert. "The Scientific Affinities of English Baroque Prose," ENGLISH MISCELLANY, 13 (1962), 59-80.

ii. Hamilton, K. G. THE TWO HARMONIES: POETRY AND PROSE IN THE SEVENTEENTH CENTURY. Oxford, 1963.

jj. Ong, Walter J., S.J. "Oral Residue in Tudor Prose Style," PMLA, 80 (1965), 145-54.

kk. Croll, Morris W. STYLE, RHETORIC, AND RHYTHM, ed.

J. Max Patrick et al. Princeton University Press, 1966.

ll. Gordon, Ian A. THE MOVEMENT OF ENGLISH PROSE.
London, 1966.

mm. Colie, Rosalie. PARADOXIA EPIDEMICA: THE RENAISSANCE
TRADITION OF PARADOX. Princeton University Press, 1966.

nn. Webber, Joan. THE ELOQUENT "I": STYLE AND SELF IN
SEVENTEENTH-CENTURY PROSE. University of Wisconsin
Press, 1968.

oo. Adolph, Robert. THE RISE OF MODERN PROSE STYLE.
Massachusetts Institute of Technology Press, 1968.

pp. Carey, John. "Sixteenth and Seventeenth Century Prose," in
ENGLISH POETRY AND PROSE, 1540-1674, ed. Christopher
Ricks. London, 1970, pp. 339-431.

qq. Cope, Jackson I. "Modes of Modernity in Seventeenth-Century
Prose," MLQ, 31 (1970), 92-111.

rr. Miner, Earl. "Patterns of Stoicism in Thought and Prose Styles,
1530-1700," PMLA, 85 (1970), 1023-34.

ss. Fish, Stanley E. SELF-CONSUMING ARTIFACTS: THE EX-
PERIENCE OF SEVENTEENTH-CENTURY LITERATURE. University of California Press, 1972.

II. RELIGIOUS WRITINGS

II. Religious Writings

During the earlier portion of our period the preponderance of literary effort, like most artistic endeavor, was directed toward religious ends. Throughout the period, however, literary skill was freely expended in the Christian cause. This section includes homilies, sermons, manuals of devotion, treatises of religious or moral instruction, and occasionally prose allegories on religious topics. All of these works are didactic; some verge on the polemical.

See also entries I.dd, III.r, 130, 143, 153, 177, 179, 196, V.f, 320, 329, VI.M, VI.N, VI.S, VI.l, VI.q, VI.s, VI.w, VI.v, VI.z, 344-45, 358, 381, 405, 425-26, 443-53, 454-55, 457, 461, 471, 472, 473, 474-75, 489, 497, 498; VIII.g, VIII.s, 522, 523, 524, 525, 559, 685, 687, 688, 689, 692, 697, 706, 710, 713, 716, 721, 732, 735, 747, 752, 753, 756, 757, 762, 763, 765-78.

A. Jones, C. W., ed. SAINTS LIVES AND CHRONICLES IN EARLY ENGLAND. Cornell University Press, 1947.

B. Colledge, Eric, ed. THE MEDIAEVAL MYSTICS OF ENGLAND. New York, 1961.

C. Roberts, John R., ed. A CRITICAL ANTHOLOGY OF ENGLISH RECUSANT DEVOTIONAL PROSE, 1558-1603. Duquesne University Press, 1966.

D. Ferry, Anne D., ed. RELIGIOUS PROSE OF SEVENTEENTH-CENTURY ENGLAND. New York, 1967.

E. Blake, Norman F., ed. MIDDLE ENGLISH RELIGIOUS PROSE. London: York Medieval Texts, 1972.

a. Inge, William R. STUDIES OF ENGLISH MYSTICS. London, 1906.

b. Whitney, Rev. J. P. "Religious Movements in the Fourteenth
    Century," in THE CAMBRIDGE HISTORY OF ENGLISH LITERA-
    TURE, ed. A. W. Ward and A. R. Waller. 15 vols. Cambridge
    University Press, 1907-27. II, 43-69.

c. Hutchinson, Rev. F. E. "The English Pulpit from Fisher to
    Donne," in THE CAMBRIDGE HISTORY OF ENGLISH LITERA-
    TURE, ed. A. W. Ward and A. R. Waller. 15 vols. Cambridge
    University Press, 1907-27. IV, 224-41.

d. Owst, Gerald R. PREACHING IN MEDIEVAL ENGLAND.
    Cambridge University Press, 1926.

e. White, Helen C. ENGLISH DEVOTIONAL LITERATURE
    (PROSE) 1600-1640. Madison, Wisconsin, 1931.

f. Jones, Richard F. "The Attack on Pulpit Eloquence in the
    Restoration," JEGP, 30 (1931), 188-217.

g. Mitchell, William F. ENGLISH PULPIT ORATORY FROM
    ANDREWES TO TILLOTSON. London, 1932.

h. Owst, Gerald R. LITERATURE AND PULPIT IN MEDIEVAL
    ENGLAND. Cambridge University Press, 1933. Rev. ed.
    Oxford, 1961.

i. Coleman, T. W. ENGLISH MYSTICS OF THE FOURTEENTH
    CENTURY. London, 1938.

j. Herr, A. F. THE ELIZABETHAN SERMON: A SURVEY AND
    A BIBLIOGRAPHY. Philadelphia, 1940.

k. White, Helen C. "Some Continuing Traditions in English De-
    votional Literature," PMLA, 57 (1942), 966-80.

l. Morison, Stanley. ENGLISH PRAYER BOOKS: AN INTRODUC-
    TION TO THE LITERATURE OF CHRISTIAN PUBLIC WORSHIP.
    Cambridge University Press, 1943.

m. Darwin, F. D. S. THE ENGLISH MEDIEVAL RECLUSE.
    London, 1944.

n. Bush, Douglas. "Religion and Religious Thought," in ENGLISH
    LITERATURE IN THE EARLIER SEVENTEENTH CENTURY 1600-
    1660. Oxford, 1945, pp. 294-349.

o. Ratcliff, E. C. THE BOOKE OF COMMON PRAYER OF THE CHURCHE OF ENGLAND, ITS MAKING AND REVISIONS, M.D.XLIX–M.D.CLXI. London, 1949.

p. Bullett, G. W. THE ENGLISH MYSTICS. London, 1950.

q. White, Helen C. THE TUDOR BOOKS OF PRIVATE DEVOTION. University of Wisconsin Press, 1951.

r. Morgan, Margery M. "A TALKING OF THE LOVE OF GOD and the Continuity of Stylistic Tradition in Middle English Prose Meditations," RES, 3 (1952), 97–116.

s. Zeeman, Elizabeth. "Continuity in Middle English Devotional Prose," JEGP, 55 (1956), 417–22.

t. Pepler, Conrad. THE ENGLISH RELIGIOUS HERITAGE. London, 1958.

u. Maclure, Millar. THE PAUL'S CROSS SERMONS, 1534–1642. University of Toronto Press, 1958.

v. Janelle, Pierre. "English Devotional Literature in the Sixteenth and Seventeenth Centuries," in ENGLISH STUDIES TODAY: SECOND SERIES, ed. G. A. Bonnard. Bern, 1959, pp. 159–71.

w. Knowles, David. THE ENGLISH MYSTICAL TRADITION. London, 1961.

x. White, Helen C. TUDOR BOOKS OF SAINTS AND MARTYRS. University of Wisconsin Press, 1963.

y. Blench, John W. PREACHING IN ENGLAND IN THE LATE FIFTEENTH AND SIXTEENTH CENTURIES: A STUDY OF ENGLISH SERMONS, 1450–c.1600. Oxford, 1964.

z. Gatch, Milton McC. "Eschatology in the Anonymous Old English Homilies," TRADITIO, 21 (1965), 117–65.

aa. Murphy, James J. "Rhetoric in Fourteenth-Century Oxford," MAE, 34 (1965), 1–20.

bb. Walsh, James, S.J., ed. PRE-REFORMATION ENGLISH SPIRITUALITY. London, 1966.

cc. Allison, C. Fitz-Simons. THE RISE OF MORALISM: THE PROCLAMATION OF THE GOSPEL FROM HOOKER TO BAXTER. New York, 1966.

dd. Hodgson, Phyllis. THREE 14th CENTURY ENGLISH MYSTICS. London, 1967.

> Richard Rolle, CLOUD OF UNKNOWING, Walter Hilton, with useful bibliography.

1. Aelfric. CATHOLIC HOMILIES. 990-98.

   > Sermons, homilies, and saints' lives which illuminate the early Church in England; see also 277, 645, and 765.

   A. _____. SELECTED HOMILIES, ed. Henry Sweet. Oxford, 1885.

   B. _____. EARLY ENGLISH HOMILIES, ed. Rubie D.-N. Warner. EETS OS 152. London, 1917.

   C. _____. HOMILIES. . . A SUPPLEMENTARY COLLECTION, ed. John C. Pope. 2 vols. EETS OS 259-60. London, 1967-68.

   a. Halvorson, Nelius O. DOCTRINAL TERMS IN AELFRIC'S HOMILIES. University of Iowa Press, 1932.

   b. Smetana, Cyril L. "Aelfric and the Early Medieval Homiliary," TRADITIO, 15 (1959), 163-204.

   c. Cross, J. E. "More Sources for Two of Aelfric's CATHOLIC HOMILIES," ANGLIA, 86 (1968), 59-78.

   d. Godden, M. R. "The Sources for Aelfric's Homily on St. Gregory," ANGLIA, 86 (1968), 79-88.

2. Aelfric. LIVES OF THE SAINTS. 990-98.

   A. _____. LIVES OF SAINTS, ed. W. W. Skeat. EETS OS 76, 82, 94, 114. London, 1881-1900.

   B. _____. LIVES OF THREE ENGLISH SAINTS, ed. G. I. Needham. London, 1966.

a. White, Caroline L. AELFRIC. Boston, 1898.

b.. Gerould, Gordon H. "Abbot Aelfric's Rhythmic Prose," MP, 22 (1924-25), 353-66.

c. Bethurum, Dorothy. "The Form of Aelfric's LIVES OF THE SAINTS," SP, 29 (1932), 515-33.

d. Dubois, Marguerite-Marie. AELFRIC: SERMONNAIRE, DOC-TEUR ET GRAMMARIEN. Paris, 1943.

e. Reszkiewicz, Alfred. ORDERING OF ELEMENTS IN LATE OLD ENGLISH PROSE IN TERMS OF THEIR SIZE AND STRUCTURAL COMPLEXITY. Warsaw, 1966.

f. Lipp, Frances R. "Aelfric's Old English Prose Style," SP, 66 (1969), 689-718.

3. Wulfstan. HOMILIES. 1000-15.

A. _____. SAMMLUNG DER IHM ZUGESCHRIEBENEN HOMILIEN. I: TEXT UND VARIANTEN, ed. A. S. Napier. Berlin, 1883.

B. _____. THE HOMILIES, ed. Dorothy Bethurum. Oxford, 1957.

i. Becher, R. WULFSTANS HOMILIEN. Leipzig, 1910.

An annotated bibliography.

a. Kinard, J. P. A STUDY OF WULFSTAN'S HOMILIES: THEIR STYLE AND SOURCES. Baltimore, 1897.

b. Whitelock, Dorothy. "Archbishop Wulfstan, Homilist and Statesman," TRANSACTIONS OF THE ROYAL HISTORICAL SOCIETY, 24 (1942), 25-45.

c. McIntosh, Angus. "Wulfstan's Prose," PBA, 35 (1949), 109-42.

d. Jost, Karl T. WULFSTANSTUDIEN. Bern, 1950.

e. Levin, Samuel R. "On the Authenticity of Five 'Wulfstan' Homilies," JEGP, 60 (1961), 451-59.

f. Funke, Otto. "Some Remarks on Wulfstan's Prose Rhythms," ES, 43 (1962), 311-18.

4. Wulfstan. SERMO LUPI AD ANGLOS. 1014.

    The best known of Wulfstan's HOMILIES; a powerful
    sermon denouncing the moral laxity of the times.

    A. _____. SERMO LUPI AD ANGLOS, ed. Dorothy Whitelock.
    3rd ed. New York, 1966.

5. Anon. EARLY ENGLISH HOMILIES [ca.1125], ed. Rubie D.-N. Warner.
    EETS OS 152. London, 1917.

6. Anon. OLD ENGLISH HOMILIES OF THE TWELFTH CENTURY, ed. Rev.
    Richard Morris. EETS OS 53, 58, 63, 73. London, 1873.

7. Anon. TWELFTH CENTURY HOMILIES, ed. A. O. Belfour. EETS OS
    137. London, 1909.

8. Anon. OLD ENGLISH HOMILIES AND HOMILETIC TREATISES OF THE
    TWELFTH AND THIRTEENTH CENTURIES, ed. Rev. Richard Morris. EETS
    OS 29, 34. London, 1868.

9. Anon. VICES AND VIRTUES. ca.1200.

    A didactic dialogue that catalogues the vices and virtues.

    A. _____. VICES AND VIRTUES, ed. Ferdinand Holthausen.
    EETS OS 89. London, 1888.

10. Anon. THE ANCRENE RIWLE. ca.1200.

    A manual of religious instruction prepared for three
    sisters with delightful realism and a pleasing style.

    A. _____. THE ANCRENE RIWLE, ed. James Morton. London:
    Camden Society, 1853.

    B. Morton, James, tr. THE NUN'S RULE BEING THE ANCREN
    RIWLE MODERNISED. London: King's Classics, 1905.

    C. Anon. THE ENGLISH TEXT OF THE ANCRENE RIWLE, ed.
    A. C. Baugh. EETS OS 232. London, 1956.

    D. _____. ANCRENE WISSE: THE ENGLISH TEXT OF THE
    ANCRENE RIWLE, ed. J. R. R. Tolkien. EETS OS 249.
    London, 1962.

E. _____. THE ANCRENE RIWLE, tr. M. B. Salu. London, 1955.

a. Allen, Hope E. "The Origin of the ANCREN RIWLE," PMLA, 33 (1918), 474-546.

b. _____. "On the Author of the ANCREN RIWLE," PMLA, 44 (1929), 635-80.

c. Bogholm, N. "Vocabulary and Style of the Middle English ANCRENE RIWLE," ES, 19 (1937), 113-16.

d. Utley, Francis L. THE CROOKED RIB. Ohio State University Press, 1944.

e. Fisher, John H. "Continental Associations for the ANCRENE RIWLE," PMLA, 64 (1949), 1180-89.

f. Dobson, E. J. "The Date and Composition of ANCRENE WISSE," PBA, 52 (1966), 181-208.

11. Lorens d'Orleans. THE AYENBITE OF INWIT, tr. Dan Michel of Northgate. 1340.

> A translation of the SOMME DES VICES ET DES VERTUES, a tedious survey of vices and virtues for the benefit of man's soul.

A. _____. THE AYENBITE OF INWYT, tr. Dan Michel of Northgate, ed. Rev. Richard Morris. EETS OS 23. London, 1866.

B. _____. THE BOOK OF VICES AND VIRTUES, tr. anon., ed. W. N. Francis. EETS OS 217. London, 1942.

a. Wallenberg, J. K. THE VOCABULARY OF DAN MICHEL'S AYENBITE OF INWYT. Uppsala, 1923.

12. Rolle, Richard. THE FORM OF LIVING. ca.1345.

> Mystic regimen for a female recluse, Margaret Kirkby; see also II.dd, 22, 472.b.

A. _____. ENGLISH PROSE TREATISES, ed. George G. Perry. EETS OS 20. London, 1866.

B. _____. [ENGLISH WRITINGS] in YORKSHIRE WRITERS, ed. Carl Horstman. 2 vols. London, 1895-96.

C. _____. ENGLISH WRITINGS, ed. Hope E. Allen. Oxford, 1931.

D. _____. SELECTED WRITINGS, tr. J. G. Harrell. London, 1963.

a. Schneider, J. P. THE PROSE STYLE OF RICHARD ROLLE. Baltimore, 1906.

b. Hodgson, G. E. THE SANITY OF MYSTICISM: A STUDY OF RICHARD ROLLE. London, 1926.

c. Allen, Hope E. WRITINGS ASCRIBED TO RICHARD ROLLE. New York, 1927.

13. Anon. THE CLOUD OF UNKNOWING. ca.1360.

A spiritual exercise in contemptus mundi; see also II.dd.

A. Anon. THE CLOUD OF UNKNOWING AND THE BOOK OF PRIVY COUNSELLING, ed. Phyllis Hodgson. EETS OS 218. London, 1944.

B. Anon. DEONISE HID DIVINITE et al., ed. Phyllis Hodgson. EETS OS 231. London, 1955.

C. Anon. THE CLOUD OF UNKNOWING et al., with commentary of Father Augustine Baker, ed. J. McCann. London, 1924.

D. Anon. THE CLOUD OF UNKNOWING, tr. Clifton Wolters. Baltimore: Penguin, 1961.

a. Gardner, Helen L. "Walter Hilton and the Authorship of THE CLOUD OF UNKNOWING," RES, 9 (1933), 129-47.

b. Hodgson, Phyllis. "Walter Hilton and THE CLOUD OF UN- KNOWING: A Problem of Authorship Reconsidered," MLR, 50 (1955), 395-406.

14. Anon. MIDDLE ENGLISH SERMONS [ca.1370-1420], ed. Woodburn O. Ross. EETS OS 209. London, 1940.

15. Lavynham, Richard. A LITIL TRETYS ON THE SEVEN DEADLY SINS. ca.1375.

A. _____. A LITIL TRETYS ON THE SEVEN DEADLY SINS, ed. J. P. W. M. van Zutphen. Rome, 1956.

16. Wyclif, John. [Sermons, Homilies, Polemical Tracts.] ca.1350-84. See also 766.

A. _____. SELECT ENGLISH WORKS, ed. Thomas Arnold. 3 vols. Oxford, 1869-71.

B. _____. THE ENGLISH WORKS. . .HITHERTO UNPRINTED, ed. F. D. Matthew. EETS OS 74. London, 1880.

C. _____. SELECT ENGLISH WRITINGS, ed. Herbert E. Winn. Oxford University Press, 1929.

a. Workman, H. B. JOHN WYCLIF: A STUDY OF THE ENGLISH MEDIEVAL CHURCH. 2 vols. Oxford, 1926.

b. Hurley, Michael. " 'Scriptura Sola': Wyclif and His Critics," TRADITIO, 16 (1960), 275-352.

c. Robson, J. A. WYCLIF AND THE OXFORD SCHOOLS. Cambridge University Press, 1961.

d. Hargreaves, Henry. "Wyclif's Prose," E&S, 19 (1966), 1-17.

17. Anon. SPECULUM CHRISTIANI, tr. anon. ca.1380.

An English translation of a famous Latin manual of devotion, no doubt rendered by a Lollard.

A. Anon. SPECULUM CHRISTIANI, tr. anon., ed. Gustaf Holmstedt. EETS OS 182. London, 1933.

18. Hilton, Walter. THE SCALE OF PERFECTION. ca.1375.

A mystic's account of the soul's ascent by means of meditation. Printed by Wynken de Worde in 1494, and oft-reprinted thereafter; see also II.dd.

A. _____. THE SCALE OF PERFECTION, ed. Evelyn Underhill. London, 1923.

B. _____. THE SCALE OF PERFECTION, tr. G. Sitwell. London, 1953.

C. _____. THE LADDER OF PERFECTION, tr. Leo Sherley-Price.
Baltimore: Penguin, 1957.

D. _____. THE PARIS MANUSCRIPT OF WALTER HILTON'S
EIGHT CHAPTERS ON PERFECTION, ed. F. Kuriyagawa.
Tokyo, 1958.

a. Gardner, Helen L. "Walter Hilton and the Mystical Tradition
in England," E&S, 22 (1936), 103-27.

b. Hussey, S. S. "The Text of THE SCALE OF PERFECTION,
Book II," NM, 65 (1964), 75-92.

c. Lawler, T. M. C. "Some Parallels Between Walter Hilton's
SCALE OF PERFECTION and St. John Fisher's PENITENTIAL
PSALMS," MOREANA, 9 (1966), 13-27.

d. Milosh, Joseph E. THE SCALE OF PERFECTION AND THE
ENGLISH MYSTICAL TRADITION. University of Wisconsin
Press, 1966.

19. Usk, Thomas. THE TESTAMENT OF LOVE. ca.1385.

A prose dream-allegory written in prison and imitative
of Boethius.

A. _____. THE TESTAMENT OF LOVE, in CHAUCERIAN AND
OTHER PIECES, ed. W. W. Skeat. Oxford, 1897.

a. Schaar, Claes. NOTES ON THOMAS USK'S TESTAMENT OF
LOVE. Lund, 1950.

b. Heninger, S. K., Jr. "The Margarite-Pearl Allegory in Thomas
Usk's TESTAMENT OF LOVE," SPECULUM, 32 (1957), 92-98.

20. Mirk, John. THE FESTIAL. ca.1403.

A collection of sermons and homilies based on the
LEGENDA AUREA; printed by Caxton in 1483, twelve
editions by 1500.

A. _____. MIRK'S FESTIAL, ed. Theodor Erbe. EETS ES 96.
London, 1905.

a. Long, Mary McD. "Undetected Verse in Mirk's FESTIAL,"
MLN, 70 (1955), 13-15.

b. Wakelin, Martyn F. "The Manuscripts of John Mirk's FESTIAL," LeedsSE, 1 (1967), 93-118.

21. Anon. THE LANTERN OF LIGHT. ca.1410.

A Lollard treatise of religious instruction, sometime attributed to Wyclif; printed ca.1532.

A. Anon. THE LANTERNE OF LIGHT, ed. Lilian M. Swinburn. EETS OS 151. London, 1917.

22. Rolle, Richard. THE FIRE OF LOVE and THE MENDING OF LIFE, tr. Richard Misyn. 1434-35.

See also 12.

A. _____. THE FIRE OF LOVE, AND THE MENDING OF LIFE, tr. Richard Misyn, ed. Rev. Ralph Harvey. EETS OS 106. London, 1896.

23. Anon. JACOB'S WELL. ca.1440.

A collection of exempla for pulpit use in an allegorical framework of cleansing a well.

A. Anon. JACOB'S WELL, ed. Arthur Brandeis. EETS OS 115. London, 1900.

24. Pecock, Reginald. THE RULE OF CHRISTIAN RELIGION. 1443.

An exposition of theology for everyday use.

A. _____. THE REULE OF CRYSTEN RELIGIOUN, ed. W. C. Greet. EETS OS 171. London, 1927.

25. _____. THE DONET. ca.1445.

A guide to the Christian life in the form of a dialogue between father and son.

A. _____. THE DONET, ed. Elsie V. Hitchcock. EETS OS 156. London, 1921.

26. _____. THE FOLLOWER TO THE DONET. ca.1454.

A sequel to THE DONET, likewise in dialogue form.

A. _____. THE FOLEWER TO THE DONET, ed. Elsie V. Hitchcock. EETS OS 164. London, 1924.

27. _____. THE REPRESSOR OF OVER MUCH BLAMING OF THE CLERGY.
ca.1455.

A vigorous refutation of the Lollards, outstanding for its
clarity of diction.

A. _____. THE REPRESSOR OF OVER MUCH BLAMING OF THE
CLERGY, ed. Churchill Babington. 2 vols. Rolls Series.
London, 1860.

28. _____. THE BOOK OF FAITH. ca.1456.

A defence of the Church's authority.

A. _____. BOOK OF FAITH, ed. J. L. Morison. Glasgow,
1909.

a. Blackie, E. M. "Reginald Pecock," EHR, 26 (1911), 448-68.

b. Green, Vivian H. H. BISHOP REGINALD PECOCK. Cambridge University Press, 1945.

c. Emerson, Everett H. "Reginald Pecock: Christian Rationalist,"
SPECULUM, 31 (1956), 235-42.

d. Ferguson, Arthur B. "Reginald Pecock and the Renaissance
Sense of History," SRen, 13 (1966), 147-65.

e. Jacob, Ernest F., ed. ESSAYS IN LATER MEDIEVAL HISTORY.
Manchester University Press, 1968.

29. Anon. SPECULUM HUMANAE SALVATIONIS, tr. anon. ca.1450.

An English rendition of a well-known Latin devotional.

A. Anon. THE MIROURE OF MANS SALVACIONNE, tr. anon.,
ed. A. H. Huth. London: Roxburghe Club, 1888.

30. Alcock, John. MONS PERFECTIONIS, IN ENGLISH: HILL OF PERFEC-
TION. Westminster: Wynken de Worde, 1496.

More moral instruction.

31. Thomas a Kempis. A FULL DEVOUT AND GOSTELY TREATYSE OF THE
IMYTACION AND FOLLOWYNGE THE BLESSED LYFE OF OURE SAV-
YOURE CRISTE, tr. William Atkynson. 2 vols. London, 1503-04.

At least four more editions of this translation by 1525,

and another in 1585; Thomas a Kempis' DE IMITATIONE
CHRISTI was rendered into English by several other translators in the sixteenth century.

A. _____. THE EARLIEST PRINTED TRANSLATION [De imitatione
Christi], tr. William Atkynson, ed. John K. Ingram. EETS ES
63. London, 1893.

32. St. Catherine of Siena. THE ORCHARDE OF SYON, tr. anon. London:
Wynken de Worde, 1519.

An early fifteenth-century translation of the DIALOGO
DELLA DIVINA PROVIDENZA by St. Catherine, an
Italian mystic who died in 1380.

A. _____. THE ORCHARD OF SYON, tr. anon., ed. Phyllis
Hodgson and Gabriel M. Liegey. EETS OS 258. London,
1966.

a. Sister Mary Denise. "THE ORCHARD OF SYON: An Introduction," TRADITIO, 14 (1958), 269-93.

33. Fisher, St. John. [Sermons, etc.] ca.1508.

A new concern with rhetoric in the humanist tradition;
see also 18.c.

34. _____. A GODLIE TREATISSE DECLARYNG THE BENEFITES OF PRAYER.
London, 1560.

Another edition in 1577.

A. _____. THE ENGLISH WORKS, ed. J. E. B. Mayor.
EETS ES 27. London, 1876.

a. Surtz, Edward L., S.J. THE WORKS AND DAYS OF JOHN
FISHER. Harvard University Press, 1967.

b. _____. "John Fisher and the Nature of Man," MOREANA,
21 (1968), 69-84.

35. Anon. THE MYRROURE OF OURE LADY. London, 1530.

A compilation of devotional tracts prepared for the
sisters of a religious community on the Thames in the
fifteenth century.

A. Anon. THE MYROURE OF OURE LADYE, ed. John H. Blunt.
EETS ES 19. London, 1873.

36. Tyndale, William. THE PARABLE OF THE WICKED MAMMON. Antwerp,
1528.

Part of Tyndale's simple campaign for public morality,
apparently the earliest of Tyndale's controversial pamphlets; at least seven more editions by 1560. For Tyndale's controversy with Sir Thomas More, see also 340,
767-769.

37. _____. THE OBEDIENCE OF A CHRISTEN MAN. Antwerp, 1528.

A forthright statement of belief propounding Luther's
extollment of faith over works, supporting the authority
of scripture, and attacking papal authority; at least
seven more editions by 1561.

A. _____. THE OBEDIENCE OF A CHRISTIAN MAN, ed.
Richard Lovett. London: Christian Classics, 1886.

38. _____. THE PRACTYSE OF PRELATES. Antwerp, 1530.

Advice (unwanted) to Henry VIII against Wolsey's administration and against divorce.

A. _____. EXPOSITIONS AND NOTES ON SUNDRY PORTIONS
OF THE HOLY SCRIPTURES; TOGETHER WITH THE PRACTICE
OF PRELATES, ed. Rev. Henry Walter. Cambridge University
Press: Parker Society, 1849.

39. _____. THE SOUPER OF THE LORDE. Antwerp, 1533.

Skeptical queries about transubstantiation, attributed to
Tyndale.

A. _____. THE WHOLE WORKES OF W. TYNDALE, JOHN
FRITH AND DOCT. BARNES, ed. John Foxe. 2 vols., London,
1572-73.

The only complete edition of Tyndale's works.

B. _____. DOCTRINAL TREATISES AND INTRODUCTIONS TO
DIFFERENT PORTIONS OF THE HOLY SCRIPTURES, ed. Rev.
Henry Walter. Cambridge University Press: Parker Society,
1848.

C. _____. THE WORK OF WILLIAM TINDALE, ed. Rev. S. L.
Greenslade. London, 1938.

D. _____. THE WORK OF WILLIAM TYNDALE, ed. G. E.
Duffield. Philadelphia, 1965.

a. Mozley, James F. WILLIAM TYNDALE. London, 1937.

b. Pineas, Rainer. "William Tyndale: Controversialist," SP, 60 (1963), 117-32.

c. Williams, Charles H. WILLIAM TYNDALE. London, 1969.

40. Colet, John. THE SERMON OF DOCTOR COLETE MADE TO THE CONVOCATION AT PAUL'S. London, ca.1530.

An English translation (perhaps by Thomas Lupset; see also 42-45) of a famous sermon delivered in Latin.

41. _____. A RYGHT FRUTEFULL MONYCION, CONCERNYNG THE ORDRE OF A GOOD CHRYSTEN MANNES LYFE. London, 1534.

A brief treatise inducing piety; other editions in 1563, 1577.

i. Meyer, Carl S. A JOHN COLET BIBLIOGRAPHY. University of Missouri Press, 1963.

a. Duhamel, P. Albert. "The Oxford Lectures of John Colet," JHI, 14 (1953), 493-510.

b. Hunt, Ernest W. DEAN COLET AND HIS THEOLOGY. London, 1956.

c. Miles, Leland. JOHN COLET AND THE PLATONIC TRADITION. LaSalle, Illinois, 1961.

d. Jayne, Sears. JOHN COLET AND MARSILIO FICINO. Oxford University Press, 1963.

e. Miles, Leland. "John Colet: An Appreciation," MOREANA, 22 (1969), 5-11.

f. Peters, Robert. "John Colet's Knowledge and Use of Patristics," MOREANA, 22 (1969), 45-59.

42. Lupset, Thomas. A TREATISE OF CHARITIE. London, 1533.

43. _____. A COMPENDIOUS AND A VERY FRUTEFUL TREATYSE, TEACHYNGE THE WAYE OF DYENGE WELL. London, 1534.

a. Beaty, Nancy L. THE CRAFT OF DYING: A STUDY IN THE

LITERARY TRADITION OF THE ARS MORIENDI IN ENGLAND.
Yale University Press, 1970.

44. Lupset, Thomas. AN EXHORTATION TO YONGE MEN. London, 1535.

45. _____. WORKES. London, 1546.

    A. _____. THE LIFE AND WORKS, ed. John A. Gee. Yale
    University Press, 1928.

46. Coverdale, Miles. THE CHRISTEN RULE, OR STATE OF ALL THE WORLDE.
London, ca.1547.

    See also 770, 772.

47. _____. AN EXHORTACION TO THE CAREINGE OF CHRYSTES CROSSE.
London(?), ca.1550.

    A. _____. WRITINGS AND TRANSLATIONS, ed. Rev. George
    Pearson. Cambridge University Press: Parker Society, 1844.

    B. _____. REMAINS, ed. Rev. George Pearson. Cambridge
    University Press: Parker Society, 1846.

48. Cranmer, Thomas. CATHECHISMUS. . .A SHORTE INSTRUCTION INTO
CHRISTIAN RELIGION. London, 1548.

    See also 774.

49. _____. A DEFENCE OF THE TRUE AND CATHOLIKE DOCTRINE OF
THE SACRAMENT. London, 1550.

    A. _____. THE WORKS, ed. Rev. John E. Cox. 2 vols.
    Cambridge University Press: Parker Society, 1844–46.

    B. _____. SELECTED WRITINGS, ed. Carl S. Meyer. London,
    1961.

    C. _____. THE WORKS, ed. G. E. Duffield. Philadelphia,
    1965.

    a. Bromley, G. W. THOMAS CRANMER, THEOLOGIAN.
    Oxford University Press, 1956.

50. Latimer, Hugh. A NOTABLE SERMON. . .PREACHED IN THE SHROUDS
AT PAULES CHURCHE IN LONDON. London, 1548.

The famous sermon on the plough, written in a colloquial
style and with a direct approach to scripture that bespeaks
the new Protestant literalness.

A. _____. SERMON ON THE PLOUGHERS, ed. Edward Arber.
London: English Reprints, 1869.

51. _____. 27 SERMONS. London, 1562.

52. _____. FRUTEFULL SERMONS. 3 pts. London, 1571-75.

A large collection of Latimer's best sermons.

A. _____. THE WORKS, ed. Rev. George E. Corrie. 2 vols.
Cambridge University Press: Parker Society, 1844-45.

B. _____. SERMONS, ed. Henry C. Beeching. London: Everyman's, 1906.

C. _____. SELECTED SERMONS, ed. Allan G. Chester. University of Virginia Press: Folger Documents, 1968.

a. Darby, Harold S. HUGH LATIMER. London, 1953.

b. Chester, Allan G. HUGH LATIMER, APOSTLE TO THE EN-
GLISH. University of Pennsylvania Press, 1954.

c. Marc'hadour, Germain. "Hugh Latimer (ca.1492-1555) and
Thomas More," MOREANA, 18 (1968), 29-48.

53. Calvin, John. THE INSTITUTION OF CHRISTIAN RELIGION, tr. Thomas
Norton. London, 1561.

The enormously influential tract that underlay English
Puritanism; at least ten editions by 1634.

A. _____. INSTITUTES OF THE CHRISTIAN RELIGION, tr. F. L.
Battles, ed. J. T. McNeill. London, 1961.

B. _____. SELECTIONS FROM HIS WRITINGS, ed. John Dillenberger. Garden City, New York: Anchor, 1971.

54. Foxe, John. ACTES AND MONUMENTS OF THESE LATTER AND PERIL-
LOUS DAYES. London, 1563.

An inflammatory account of the Protestant martyrs during
Bloody Mary's reign, known popularly as "Foxe's Book of

Martyrs"; first published in Latin at Strasbourg, 1554.

A. _____. THE ACTS AND MONUMENTS, ed. Rev. Stephen R. Cattley and Rev. George Townsend. 8 vols. London, 1837–41.

B. _____. THE ACTS AND MONUMENTS, rev. Rev. Josiah Pratt. 4th ed. 8 vols. London, 1877.

a. Mozley, James F. JOHN FOXE AND HIS BOOK. New York, 1940.

b. Haller, William. THE ELECT NATION: THE MEANING AND RELEVANCE OF FOXE'S BOOK OF MARTYRS. New York, 1963.

55. Foxe, John. A SERMON OF CHRIST CRUCIFIED. London, 1570.

Several later editions into the seventeenth century.

56. Northbrooke, John. A BREEFE AND PITHIE SUMME OF THE CHRISTIAN FAITH. London, 1571.

Incipient puritanism; see also 365.

57. _____. THE POOR MANS GARDEN. London, 1573.

Incipient evangelicalism; several later editions until 1606.

58. Jewel, John. CERTAINE SERMONS PREACHED BEFORE THE QUEENES MAJESTIE, AND AT PAULES CROSSE. London, 1583.

See also 351–352.

A. _____. THE WORKS. London, 1609.

B. _____. THE WORKS, ed. Rev. John Ayre. 4 vols. Cambridge University Press: Parker Society, 1845–50.

59. Parsons, Robert. THE FIRST BOOKE OF THE CHRISTIAN EXERCISE. Rouen, 1582.

A devotional by the Jesuit who led the Catholic resistance in England; after 1585 entitled A CHRISTIAN DIRECTORY, and revised and reprinted continually for the benefit of Protestants as well as Catholics.

60. Dent, Arthur. A SERMON OF REPENTAUNCE. London, 1583.

61. _____. THE PLAINE MANS PATH-WAY TO HEAVEN. London, 1601.

    Twenty-five editions of this popular manual of devotion
    by 1640.

    a. Hussey, Maurice. "Arthur Dent's PLAINE MANS PATH-WAY
    TO HEAVEN," MLR, 44 (1949), 26-34.

62. Dent, Arthur. THE RUINE OF ROME: OR, AN EXPOSITION UPON
    THE WHOLE REVELATION. London, 1603.

    St. John's Revelation as Protestant progaganda.

63. _____. A PASTIME FOR PARENTS. . .CONTAYNING THE MOST
    PRINCIPALL GROUNDS OF CHRISTIAN RELIGION. London, 1606.

64. Norden, John. A PENSIVE MANS PRACTISE. London, 1584.

    One of the most popular expressions of personal piety.

65. _____. A MIRROR FOR THE MULTITUDE. London, 1586.

    An attempt at godly moderation in an era of religious
    intolerance.

66. Mornay, Philippe de. THE TREWNESSE OF THE CHRISTIAN RELIGION,
    tr. Sir Philip Sidney and Arthur Golding. London, 1587.

    The masterwork of an eminent French Protestant; other
    editions in 1592, 1604, and 1617.

    a. Robinson, Forrest G. "A Note on the Sidney-Golding Trans-
    lation of Philippe de Mornay's DE LA VERITE DE LA RELIGION
    CHRESTIENNE," HLB, 17 (1969), 98-102.

67. Smith, Henry. THE WEDDING GARMENT. London, 1590.

68. _____. THE PRIDE OF KING NEBUCHADNEZZAR. London, 1591.

69. _____. THE TRUMPET OF THE SOULE, SOUNDING TO JUDGEMENT.
    London, 1591.

70. _____. THE SINFULL MANS SEARCH. London, 1592.

71. _____. GODS ARROWE AGAINST ATHEISTS. London, 1593.

72. _____. THE SERMONS. . .GATHERED INTO ONE VOLUME. London, 1593.

    A. _____. THE WORKS, ed. Thomas Fuller. 2 vols. Edinburgh, 1866-67.

    a. Lievsay, John L. " 'Silver-tongued Smith,' Paragon of Elizabethan Preachers," HLQ, 11 (1947-48), 13-36.

73. Stubbes, Philip. A CHRISTAL GLASSE FOR CHRISTIAN WOMEN. London, 1591.

    Extremely popular, with at least twenty editions by 1660; see also 372.

74. Southwell, Robert. MARIE MAGDALENS FUNERAL TEARES. London, 1591.

    Meditative essays by a prominent Catholic poet; other editions in 1594, 1602, and 1609.

75. _____. THE TRIUMPHS OVER DEATH. London, 1595.

    Two other editions in 1596.

76. Andrewes, Lancelot. THE WONDERFULL COMBATE. . .BETWEENE CHRIST AND SATAN. OPENED IN SEVEN SERMONS. London, 1592.

77. _____. XCVI SERMONS, ed. William Laud and John Buckeridge. London, 1629.

    Sermons by the Bishop (successively) of Chichester, Ely, and Winchester; see also II.g.

    A. _____. [WORKS], ed. J. P. Wilson and James Bliss. 11 vols. Oxford, 1841-54.

    B. _____. SERMONS, ed. G. M. Story. Oxford, 1967.

    a. Eliot, T. S. "Lancelot Andrewes," in SELECTED ESSAYS. 2nd ed. London, 1934, pp. 331-43.

    b. Reidy, Maurice F. BISHOP LANCELOT ANDREWES, JACOBEAN COURT PREACHER. Loyola University Press, 1955.

    c. Welsby, Paul A. LANCELOT ANDREWES, 1555-1626. London, 1958.

d. Webber, Joan. "Celebration of Word and World in Lancelot Andrewes' Style," JEGP, 64 (1965), 255-69.

e. McCutcheon, Elizabeth. "Lancelot Andrewes' PRECES PRIVATAE: A Journey Through Time," SP, 65 (1968), 223-41.

78. Napier, John. A PLAINE DISCOVERY OF THE WHOLE REVELATION OF SAINT JOHN. Edinburgh, 1593.

A Protestant's progagandistic interpretation of St. John's Revelation; reprinted in 1594, 1611, and 1645.

79. Sandys, Sir Edwin. A RELATION OF THE STATE OF RELIGION. . .IN THE SEVERALL STATES OF THESE WESTERNE PARTS OF THE WORLD. London, 1605.

A moderate's attempt to induce Christian unity; oft-reprinted.

80. Hall, Joseph. MEDITATIONS AND VOWES DIVINE AND MORALL. London, 1605.

Enlarged in 1609 and 1621.

81. _____. HEAVEN UPON EARTH: OR OF TRUE PEACE AND TRANQUIL-LITIE OF MIND. London, 1606.

A. _____. HEAVEN UPON EARTH, AND CHARACTERS OF VERTUES AND VICES, ed. Rudolf Kirk. Rutgers University Press, 1948.

82. _____. CONTEMPLATIONS UPON THE PRINCIPALL PASSAGES OF THE HOLY STORIE. 8 vols. London, 1612-26.

A. _____. CONTEMPLATIONS ON THE HISTORICAL PASSAGES OF THE OLD AND NEW TESTAMENTS, ed. Charles Wordsworth. London, 1871.

83. _____. THE WORKS. London, 1625.

One of the most learned and influential men of the period.

a. Kinloch, Tom F. THE LIFE AND WORKS OF JOSEPH HALL, 1574-1656. London, 1951.

84. Bayly, Lewis. THE PRACTISE OF PIETIE. London, ca.1612.

A famous devotional tract of Puritan persuasion; over

fifty editions in England and abroad by 1660.

85. Goodman, Godfrey. THE FALL OF MAN, OR THE CORRUPTION OF NA-
TURE, PROVED BY THE LIGHT OF OUR NATURALL REASON. London, 1616.

A philosophical look at man's place in the universe by
a religious conservative.

a. Soden, Geoffrey I. GODFREY GOODMAN, BISHOP OF
GLOUCESTER, 1583-1656. London, 1953.

b. Hepburn, Ronald W. "Godfrey Goodman: Nature Vilified,"
CAMBRIDGE JOURNAL, 7 (1953-54), 424-34.

86. St. Augustine. THE CONFESSIONS, tr. Sir Tobie Matthews. St. Omer,
1620.

87. Hakewill, George. KING DAVIDS VOW. . .DELIVERED IN TWELVE
SERMONS. London, 1621.

88. _____. AN APOLOGIE OF THE POWER AND PROVIDENCE OF GOD
IN THE GOVERNMENT OF THE WORLD. Oxford, 1627.

Hakewill's respectful reply to Goodman's FALL OF MAN,
and a massive antidote for Jacobean pessimism about the
decay of the world; revised 1630 and 1635.

89. Donne, John. THREE SERMONS. London, 1623. FOURE SERMONS.
London, 1625. FIVE SERMONS. London, 1626. SIX SERMONS. London, 1634. LXXX SERMONS. London, 1640. FIFTY SERMONS. London, 1649. XXVI SERMONS. London, 1660.

The sermon in its most literary form; see also I.ss.

A. _____. SERMONS, ed. George R. Potter and Evelyn M.
Simpson. 10 vols. University of California Press, 1953-62.

a. Umbach, Herbert H. "The Rhetoric of Donne's Sermons,"
PMLA, 52 (1937), 354-58.

b. _____. "The Merit of Metaphysical Style in Donne's Easter
Sermons," ELH, 12 (1945), 108-29.

c. Lowe, Irving. "John Donne: The Middle Way: The Reason-
Faith Equation in Donne's Sermons." JHI, 22 (1961), 389-97.

d. Mueller, William R. JOHN DONNE: PREACHER. Princeton
University Press, 1962.

e. Krueger, Robert. "The Publication of John Donne's Sermons," RES, 15 (1964), 151–60.

f. Rowe, Frederick A. I LAUNCH AT PARADISE: A CONSIDERATION OF JOHN DONNE, POET AND PREACHER. London, 1964.

g. Gifford, William. "Time and Place in Donne's Sermons," PMLA, 82 (1967), 388–98.

h. Schleiner, Winfried. THE IMAGERY OF JOHN DONNE'S SERMONS. Brown University Press, 1970.

i. Carrithers, Gale H. DONNE AT SERMONS: A CHRISTIAN EXISTENTIAL WORLD. State University of New York Press, 1972.

90. Donne, John. DEVOTIONS UPON EMERGENT OCCASIONS. London, 1624.

A minute and intimate record of Donne's thoughts during a serious illness.

A. _____. DEVOTIONS UPON EMERGENT OCCASIONS, ed. John Sparrow. Cambridge University Press, 1923.

a. Shapiro, I. A. "Walton and the Occasion of Donne's DEVOTIONS," RES, 9 (1958), 18–22.

b. Webber, Joan. "The Prose Styles of John Donne's DEVOTIONS UPON EMERGENT OCCASIONS," ANGLIA, 79 (1961), 138–52.

c. Andreasen, Nancy J. C. "Donne's DEVOTIONS and the Psychology of Assent," MP, 62 (1964–65), 207–16.

d. Harding, D. W. "The DEVOTIONS Now," in JOHN DONNE: ESSAYS IN CELEBRATION, ed. A. J. Smith. London, 1972, pp. 385–403.

91. Donne, John. ESSAYES IN DIVINITY. London, 1651.

Written 1611–15; private meditations largely upon passages in Genesis and Exodus.

A. _____. ESSAYS IN DIVINITY, ed. Evelyn M. Simpson. Oxford, 1952.

B. _____. SELECTED PROSE, ed. Helen L. Gardner and T. S. Healy, S.J. Oxford, 1967.

i. Keynes, Geoffrey L. BIBLIOGRAPHY OF THE WORKS OF DR. JOHN DONNE. Cambridge, 1914.

a. Simpson, Evelyn M. A STUDY OF THE PROSE WORKS OF JOHN DONNE. Second ed. Oxford, 1948.

b. Webber, Joan. CONTRARY MUSIC: THE PROSE STYLE OF JOHN DONNE. University of Wisconsin Press, 1963.

c. LeComte, Edward. GRACE TO A WITTY SINNER: A LIFE OF DONNE. New York, 1965.

d. Bald, R. C. JOHN DONNE: A LIFE. Oxford, 1970.

92. Sanderson, Robert. TEN SERMONS. London, 1627.

Sermons by a casuist famous for preaching and for determining cases of conscience.

a. Walton, Izaak. LIFE OF DR. SANDERSON. London, 1678.

See also 515.A.

b. Lewis, Rev. George. ROBERT SANDERSON. London, 1924.

93. Cosin, John. A COLLECTION OF PRIVATE DEVOTIONS. London, 1627.

A fifth edition by 1638.

A. _____. A COLLECTION OF PRIVATE DEVOTIONS, ed. Paul G. Stanwood. Oxford University Press, 1967.

94. King, Henry. AN EXPOSITION UPON THE LORDS PRAYER. DELIVERED IN CERTAINE SERMONS. London, 1628.

a. Berman, Ronald. HENRY KING & THE SEVENTEENTH CENTURY. London, 1964.

95. Burton, Henry. THE SEVEN VIALS OR A BRIEFE AND PLAINE EXPOSITION UPON THE 15. AND 16. CHAPTERS OF THE REVELATION. London, 1628.

A Puritan divine still using the Revelation as a platform for abuse of conservatives.

96. Sibbes, Richard. THE BRUISED REEDE AND SMOAKING FLAX. London, 1630.

> A collection of sermons.

97. _____. THE SOULES CONFLICT WITH IT SELFE. London, 1635.

98. _____. BEAMES OF DIVINE LIGHT. BREAKING FORTH FROM SEV-
ERALL PLACES OF HOLY SCRIPTURE. . .IN XXI SERMONS. London, 1639.

99. _____. BOWELS OPENED, OR, A DISCOVERY OF THE NEERE AND
DEERE LOVE, UNION AND COMMUNION BETWIXT CHRIST AND THE CHURCH. London, 1639.

> A. _____. COMPLETE WORKS, ed. Rev. A. B. Grosart. 7
> vols. Edinburgh, 1862-64.

100. Fletcher, Phineas. JOY IN TRIBULATION. OR, CONSOLATIONS FOR AFFLICTED SPIRITS. London, 1632.

101. _____. THE WAY TO BLESSEDNES, A TREATISE. . .ON THE FIRST
PSALME. London, 1632.

> a. Langdale, Abram B. PHINEAS FLETCHER, MAN OF LETTERS,
> SCIENCE AND DIVINITY. Columbia University Press, 1937.

102. Fuller, Thomas. [SERMONS.] ca.1630-1660.

> See also 177-180, 273, 507-508.

> A. _____. THE COLLECTED SERMONS, ed. John E. Bailey and
> William E. A. Axon. 2 vols. London, 1891.

103. Gill, Alexander. THE SACRED PHILOSOPHIE OF THE HOLY SCRIPTURE. London, 1635.

> An attempt to rationalize Christian theology.

104. Chillingworth, William. THE RELIGION OF PROTESTANTS A SAFE WAY TO SALVATION. London, 1638.

> A. _____. THE WORKS. 11th ed. 3 vols. Oxford University
> Press, 1838.

> a. Orr, Robert R. REASON AND AUTHORITY: THE THOUGHT
> OF WILLIAM CHILLINGWORTH. Oxford University Press, 1967.

105. Brinsley, John. THE HEALING OF ISRAELS BREACHES IN SIX SERMONS. London, 1642.

106. Cudworth, Ralph. THE UNION OF CHRIST AND THE CHURCH. London, 1642.

> An early theological tract by one of the best-known Cambridge Platonists; see also 123.i.

107. Wilkins, John. ECCLESIASTES; OR, A DISCOURSE CONCERNING THE GIFT OF PREACHING. London, 1646.

> A popular book about preaching; oft-reprinted.

108. _____. A DISCOURSE CONCERNING THE GIFT OF PRAYER. London, 1651.

> A devotional tract; oft-reprinted.

109. Taylor, Jeremy. THEOLOGIA ECLECTICA. A DISCOURSE OF THE LIBERTY OF PROPHESYING. London, 1647.

> A plea for tolerance in an age when feelings on religious matters ran high.

110. _____. THE RULE AND EXERCISES OF HOLY LIVING. London, 1650.

> Another manual for the Christian in his daily life.

A. _____. THE RULE AND EXERCISES OF HOLY LIVING, ed. T. S. Kepler. Cleveland, 1956.

111. _____. THE RULE AND EXERCISES OF HOLY DYING. London, 1651.

> An exercise in contemptus mundi which assumes that this life is largely preparation for the next; at least seventeen editions before the end of the century.

A. _____. HOLY LIVING AND HOLY DYING. London: Bohn's, 1850.

112. _____. XXVIII SERMONS. London, 1651; XXV SERMONS. London, 1653.

> Effective sermons with popular appeal combining piety, charity, and rhetoric.

113. _____. THE GOLDEN GROVE; OR A MANUALL OF DAILY PRAYERS AND LETANIES. London, 1655.

> A handbook of personal devotions, as the subtitle indicates;

oft-reprinted.

A. _____. THE GOLDEN GROVE, ed. Logan Pearsall Smith. Oxford, 1930.

B. _____. THE WHOLE WORKS, ed. Rev. Charles P. Eden. 10 vols. London, 1862-65.

i. Gathorne-Hardy, Robert. "Some Notes on the Bibliography of Jeremy Taylor," LIBRARY, 5th series, 2 (1948), 233-49.

a. Stranks, Charles J. THE LIFE AND WRITINGS OF JEREMY TAYLOR. London, 1952.

b. Elmen, Paul. "Jeremy Taylor and the Fall of Man," MLQ, 14 (1953), 139-48.

c. Bolton, Frederick R. THE CAROLINE TRADITION OF THE CHURCH OF IRELAND, WITH PARTICULAR REFERENCE TO BISHOP JEREMY TAYLOR. London, 1958.

d. Hughes, Henry T. THE PIETY OF JEREMY TAYLOR. London, 1960.

e. Huntley, Frank L. JEREMY TAYLOR AND THE GREAT REBEL-LION. University of Michigan Press, 1970.

114. Baxter, Richard. THE SAINTS EVERLASTING REST. London, 1650.

A Puritan book of devotion; oft-reprinted.

A. _____. THE SAINTS' EVERLASTING REST, ed. William Young. London, 1907.

B. _____. THE SAINTS' EVERLASTING REST, ed. John T. Wilkinson. Westwood, New Jersey, 1962.

115. _____. A CALL TO THE UNCONVERTED TO TURN AND LIVE AND ACCEPT OF MERCY. London, 1658.

An appeal for conversion by one of the most active and most influential Puritan divines.

i. Matthews, Arnold G. THE WORKS OF RICHARD BAXTER. AN ANNOTATED LIST. London, 1933.

a. Ladell, Arthur R. RICHARD BAXTER, PURITAN AND MYSTIC. London, 1925.

b. Martin, Hugh. PURITANISM AND RICHARD BAXTER. London, 1954.

c. Nuttall, Geoffrey F. RICHARD BAXTER. London, 1965.

116. Laud, William. SEVEN SERMONS. London, 1651.

Some closely argued sermons by the royalist Archbishop of Canterbury.

A. _____. THE WORKS, ed. William Scott and James Bliss. 7 vols. Oxford, 1847-60.

a. Prynne, William. A BREVIATE OF THE LIFE, OF WILLIAM LAUD. London, 1644.

Contemporary extracts from Laud's diary and other private papers.

b. Trevor-Roper, H. R. ARCHBISHOP LAUD, 1573-1645. London, 1940.

117. Culverwel, Nathanael. SPIRITUAL OPTICKS. Cambridge, 1651.

A learned tract with Puritan leanings by an early Cambridge Platonist.

118. _____. AN ELEGANT AND LEARNED DISCOURSE OF THE LIGHT OF NATURE. London, 1652.

An original essay precursing deism; oft-reprinted.

A. _____. THE LIGHT OF NATURE, ed. John Brown. Edinburgh, 1857.

119. Herbert, George. A PRIEST TO THE TEMPLE. London, 1652.

A handbook to guide gently the country parson in his duties.

120. More, Henry. AN ANTIDOTE AGAINST ATHEISME. London, 1653.

A contribution to the effort of the Cambridge Platonists in combatting the materialism of Hobbes (see also 463-465); another edition in 1655.

121. _____. CONJECTURA CABBALISTICA. London, 1653.

> An esoteric interpretation of Genesis according to the
> three-fold cabala.

a. Brown, C. C. "The Mere Numbers of Henry More's Cabbala,"
   SEL, 10 (1970), 143-53.

122. More, Henry. ENTHUSIASMUS TRIUMPHATUS. London, 1656.

> An expose of fashionable religions during the Common-
> wealth, and an anatomy of "enthusiasm."

A. _____. ENTHUSIASMUS TRIUMPHATUS, 1662, ed. M. V.
   DePorte. Los Angeles: Augustan Reprints, 1966.

123. _____. THE IMMORTALITY OF THE SOUL. London, 1659.

> A rational argument on a familiar but difficult theme.

A. _____. PHILOSOPHICAL WRITINGS, ed. Flora I. MacKinnon.
   Oxford University Press, 1925.

i. Guffey, George R. ELIZABETHAN BIBLIOGRAPHIES SUPPLE-
   MENTS, XI: TRAHERNE AND THE SEVENTEENTH-CENTURY
   ENGLISH PLATONISTS. London, 1969.

> Includes Ralph Cudworth, Nathanael Culverwel,
> Henry More, John Norris, George Rust, John Smith,
> Peter Sterry, Thomas Traherne, Benjamin Whichcote,
> and John Worthington.

a. Colie, Rosalie L. LIGHT AND ENLIGHTENMENT: A STUDY
   OF THE CAMBRIDGE PLATONISTS AND THE DUTCH ARMIN-
   IANS. Cambridge University Press, 1957.

b. Lichtenstein, Aharon. HENRY MORE. THE RATIONAL THE-
   OLOGY OF A CAMBRIDGE PLATONIST. Cambridge, 1962.

124. Ross, Alexander. PANSEBEIA: OR, A VIEW OF ALL RELIGIONS IN
THE WORLD. London, 1653.

> A fascinating early effort at comparative religion; see
> also 644.

125. Vane, Sir Henry. THE RETIRED MANS MEDITATIONS. London, 1655.

126. Wright, Abraham. FIVE SERMONS, IN FIVE SEVERAL STYLES. London,
1656.

A sermon in the style of Bishop Andrewes and another in
the style of Bishop Hall, and three parodies of others.

127. Hierocles, UPON THE GOLDEN VERSES OF PYTHAGORAS, tr. John Hall.
London, 1657.

A reverential translation of a late classical text which
moralized Pythagoras and made him a proto-Christian;
several other translations of Hierocles before the end of
the century.

128. Allestree, Richard. THE WHOLE DUTY OF MAN. London, 1658.

An extremely popular Anglican royalist devotional tract
published anonymously, but most probably the work of
Allestree, Chaplain to Charles II, Regius Professor of
Divinity at Oxford, and Provost of Eton.

a. Elmen, Paul. "Richard Allestree and THE WHOLE DUTY OF
MAN," LIBRARY, 5th Series, 6 (1951-52), 19-27.

III. HISTORICAL WRITINGS

III. Historical Writings

The writing of history in English began as an attempt to chronicle events of national importance. Historians usually assumed a providential view of their subject. Often in the Tudor period chroniclers intended to propagandize, so that history became an instrument of nationalism. Prominent in this movement was the legend of Brut and Troynovant. The ultimate development in this direction was the sophisticated topography of the antiquaries.

Complementary to the writing of history was the writing of biography, and eventually autobiography. First there were saints' lives in the spirit of hagiography, but later there were secular lives and even biographies with the intention of defaming.

See also I.dd, II.A, 2, 28.d, 28.e, 92.a, 206, 238, 255, 269, 438, 470, 684, 686, 690, 692, 693, 697, 705, 707, 708, 715, 717, 723, 728, 729, 734, 738, 739, 742, 743, 745, 748, 749, 751, 755, 759, 760, 761.

i. Read, Conyers. BIBLIOGRAPHY OF BRITISH HISTORY, TUDOR PERIOD, 1485-1603. 2nd ed. Oxford, 1959.

a. Whibley, Charles. "Chroniclers and Antiquaries," in THE CAMBRIDGE HISTORY OF ENGLISH LITERATURE, ed. A. W. Ward and A. R. Waller. 15 vols. Cambridge University Press, 1907-27, III,313-38.

b. Saintsbury, George. "Antiquaries," in THE CAMBRIDGE HISTORY OF ENGLISH LITERATURE, ed. A. W. Ward and A. R. Pollard. 15 vols. Cambridge University Press, 1907-27, VII, 232-58.

c. Kingsford, Charles L. ENGLISH HISTORICAL LITERATURE IN THE FIFTEENTH CENTURY. Oxford, 1913.

d. Smith, D. Nichol. CHARACTERS FROM THE HISTORIES & MEMOIRS OF THE SEVENTEENTH CENTURY. Oxford, 1929.

e. Stauffer, Donald A. ENGLISH BIOGRAPHY BEFORE 1700. Harvard University Press, 1930.

f. Walters, Henry B. THE ENGLISH ANTIQUARIES OF THE SIX-TEENTH, SEVENTEENTH, AND EIGHTEENTH CENTURIES. London, 1934.

g. Thompson, James W. A HISTORY OF HISTORICAL WRITING. 2 vols. New York, 1942.

h. Bush, Douglas, "History and Biography" in ENGLISH LITERA-TURE IN THE EARLIER SEVENTEENTH CENTURY 1600-1660. Oxford, 1945, pp. 209-31.

i. Dean, Leonard F. TUDOR THEORIES OF HISTORY WRITING. University of Michigan Press, 1947.

j. Trimble, William R. "Early Tudor Historiography, 1485-1548," JHI, 11 (1950), 30-41.

k. Sola Pinto, Vivian de. ENGLISH BIOGRAPHY IN THE SEVEN-TEENTH CENTURY. London, 1951.

l. Buford, Albert H. "History and Biography: The Renaissance Distinction," in A TRIBUTE TO GEORGE COFFIN TAYLOR, ed. Arnold Williams. University of North Carolina Press, 1952, pp. 100-12.

m. Wheeler, Thomas. "The New Style of the Tudor Chroniclers," TSL, 7 (1962), 71-77.

n. Moir, Esther. THE DISCOVERY OF BRITAIN. London, 1964.

o. Hanning, Robert W. THE VISION OF HISTORY IN EARLY BRITAIN: FROM GILDAS TO GEOFFREY OF MONMOUTH. Columbia University Press, 1966.

p. Baker, Herschel. THE RACE OF TIME: THREE LECTURES ON RENAISSANCE HISTORIOGRAPHY. University of Toronto Press, 1967.

q. Delany, Paul. BRITISH AUTOBIOGRAPHY IN THE SEVEN-TEENTH CENTURY. London, 1969.

r. Patrides, C. A. THE GRAND DESIGN OF GOD. University of Toronto Press, 1973.

129. THE ANGLO-SAXON CHRONICLE. ca. 890 ff.

A record of national events in several versions by a
succession of compilers until 1155.

A. THE ANGLO-SAXON CHRONICLE, ed. Benjamin Thorpe.
2 vols. Rolls Series. London, 1861.

B. Plummer, Charles, ed. TWO OF THE SAXON CHRONICLES
PARALLEL. 2 vols. Oxford, 1892-99.

C. THE PARKER CHRONICLE, 832-900, ed. Albert H. Smith.
London, 1935.

D. THE PETERBOROUGH CHRONICLE, tr. Harry A. Rositzke.
Columbia University Press, 1951.

E. THE ANGLO-SAXON CHRONICLE, tr. G. N. Garmonsway.
London: Everyman's, 1953.

F. THE ANGLO-SAXON CHRONICLE, ed. Dorothy Whitelock.
Rutgers University Press, 1961.

G. THE PETERBOROUGH CHRONICLE, 1070-1145, ed. Cecily
Clark. 2nd ed. Oxford, 1970.

130. Capgrave, John. THE LIVES OF ST. AUGUSTINE AND ST. GILBERT OF
SEMPRINGHAM. ca.1450.

A. _____ . LIVES OF ST. AUGUSTINE AND ST. GILBERT OF
SEMPRINGHAM AND A SERMON, ed. J. J. Munro. EETS
OS 140. London, 1910.

131. _____ . THE CHRONICLE OF ENGLAND. 1464.

English history to 1417.

A. _____ . THE CHRONICLE OF ENGLAND, ed. Rev. Francis
C. Hingeston. Rolls Series. London, 1858.

132. _____ . et al. THE NEWE LEGENDE OF ENGLANDE, tr. anon. London, 1516.

A collection of English saints' lives abridged and translated from Capgrave's NOVA LEGENDA ANGLIAE.

133. Anon. THE BRUT OF ENGLAND. ca.1480.

An extensive history of England from the legendary time
of Brutus to 1479; in part a translation of the French
BRUT D'ANGLETERRE.

A. Anon. THE BRUT, OR THE CHRONICLES OF ENGLAND, ed.
Friedrich W. D. Brie. EETS OS 131, 136. London, 1906-08.

134. Froissart, Jean. THE CRONYCLES OF ENGLANDE, tr. Sir John Bourchier,
Lord Berners. 2 vols. London, 1523-25.

An English rendering of Froissart's important chronicle,
covering the period 1326-1400.

A. _____. THE CHRONICLE, tr. Sir John Bourchier, Lord
Berners, ed. William P. Ker. 6 vols. London: Tudor
Translations, 1901-03.

B. _____. THE CHRONICLES, tr. Sir John Bourchier, Lord
Berners, ed. Gillian and William Anderson. Southern Illinois
University Press, 1963.

a. Benson, Larry D. "The Use of a Physical Viewpoint in Berners'
FROISSART," MLQ, 20 (1959), 333-38.

135. Fabyan, Robert. CHRONICLE. London, 1516.

A free-wheeling account of the English nation from Brut
to the Battle of Bosworth (1485); reprinted in 1533, 1542,
and 1559.

A. _____. THE NEW CHRONICLES OF ENGLAND AND FRANCE,
ed. Sir Henry Ellis. London, 1811.

136. Boece, Hector. THE HYSTORY AND CRONIKLIS OF SCOTLAND, tr.
John Bellenden. Edinburgh, 1540(?).

A patriotic history by the greatest of Scotland's early
humanists.

137. Bale, John. A BREFE CHRONYCLE CONCERNYNGE. . .SYR JOHAN
OLDECASTELL. Antwerp(?), 1544.

The Protestant polemicist writing martyrology for an
ulterior purpose.

138. _____. THE LABORYOUSE JOURNEY & SERCHE OF JOHAN LEYLANDE,
FOR ENGLANDES ANTIQUITEES. London, 1549.

Bale's heavily annotated publication of some of Leland's
notes, not fully published until 1710 by Thomas Hearne.

A. Leland, John. THE ITINERARY OF JOHN LELAND THE ANTI-
QUARY, ed. Thomas Hearne. 2nd ed. 9 vols. Oxford, 1745.

B. _____. THE ITINERARY, ed. Lucy T. Smith. 5 vols. London,
1907-10.

139. Hall, Edward. THE UNION OF THE TWO NOBLE AND ILLUSTRE FAM-
ELIES OF LANCASTRE & YORK. London, 1548.

A Protestant writing history to further the Tudor cause,
but nonetheless of historical value, especially on the
reign of Henry VIII; an earlier edition of 1542 exists
in a unique fragment.

A. _____. CHRONICLE, ed. Sir Henry Ellis. London, 1809.

a. Smith, Robert M. "The Date and Authorship of Hall's CHRON-
ICLE," JEGP, 17 (1918), 252-66.

b. Holmes, Martin. "Edward Hall and His CHRONICLE," E&S,
20 (1967), 15-28.

140. Proctor, John. THE HISTORIE OF WYATES REBELLION. London, 1554.

A contemporary account of a notorious incident; another
edition in 1555.

141. More, Sir Thomas. THE HISTORY OF KING RICHARD THE THIRDE, in
THE WORKES, ed. William Rastell. London, 1557.

Not accurate, but a stylish and lively report of a trou-
blous period in English politics; written ca.1513; see also
172.a, 339-342, 474-476.

A. _____. THE HISTORY OF KING RICHARD III, ed. Richard
S. Sylvester. Yale University Press, 1963.

A volume in the Yale edition of THE COMPLETE
WORKS of Sir Thomas More.

a. Heath, T. G. "Another Look at Thomas More's RICHARD,"
MOREANA, 19 (1968), 11-19.

142. Cavendish, George. THE LIFE AND DEATH OF CARDINAL WOLSEY.
ca.1557.

A moving biography by a former member of Wolsey's
household; in manuscript only, but widely known.

A. _____. THE LIFE AND DEATH OF CARDINAL WOLSEY, ed. Richard S. Sylvester. EETS OS 243. London, 1959.

B. Sylvester, Richard S., and Davis P. Harding, eds. TWO EARLY TUDOR LIVES: THE LIFE AND DEATH OF CARDINAL WOLSEY, BY GEORGE CAVENDISH, THE LIFE OF SIR THOMAS MORE, BY WILLIAM ROPER. Yale University Press, 1962.

a. Wiley, Paul L. "Renaissance Exploitation of Cavendish's LIFE OF WOLSEY," SP, 43 (1946), 121-46.

b. Sylvester, Richard S. "Cavendish's LIFE OF WOLSEY: The Artistry of a Tudor Biographer," SP, 57 (1960), 44-71.

143. Bede. THE HISTORY OF THE CHURCH OF ENGLANDE, tr. Thomas Stapleton. Antwerp, 1565.

The Anglo-Saxon classic made available to the common man; other editions in 1622 and 1626.

144. Stow, John. A SUMMARIE OF ENGLYSHE CHRONICLES. London, 1565.

A chronological epitome of English history, continuously brought up to date by a rapid succession of editions until 1618.

145. Grafton, Richard. A CHRONICLE AT LARGE. . .UNTO THE FIRST YERE OF THE REIGNE OF. . .QUEENE ELIZABETH. London, 1569.

A derivative compilation from earlier chronicles.

A. _____. GRAFTON'S CHRONICLE, ed. Sir Henry Ellis. 2 vols. London, 1809.

146. Llwyd, Humphrey. THE BREVIARY OF BRITAYNE. London, 1573.

A chorographical description of Britain.

147. Parker, Matthew. THE LIFE OFF THE 70. ARCHBISHOPP OFF CANTER-BURY, tr. John Stubs(?). Zurich, 1574.

148. Lambarde, William. A PERAMBULATION OF KENT. London, 1576.

A chorographical description of Kent.

A. _____. A PERAMBULATION OF KENT, ed. Richard Church. Bath, 1970.

149. Holinshed, Raphael. THE CHRONICLES OF ENGLAND, SCOTLANDE,

AND IRELANDE. London, 1577.

The most readable of the English chronicles with a wealth
of concrete detail that made it a treasure-chest for Shakespeare and many others; enlarged edition in 1587.

A. _____. CHRONICLES OF ENGLAND, SCOTLAND, AND
IRELAND, ed. Sir Henry Ellis. 6 vols. London, 1807-08.

B. _____. HOLINSHED'S CHRONICLE AS USED IN SHAKE-
SPEARE'S PLAYS, ed. Allardyce and Josephine Nicoll. London: Everyman's, 1927.

C. Hosley, Richard, ed. SHAKESPEARE'S HOLINSHED. New
York, 1968.

a. Fellheimer, Jeanette. "Geoffrey Fenton's HISTORY OF GUIC-
CIARDIN and Holinshed's CHRONICLES of 1587," MLQ, 6
(1945), 285-98.

b. Benbow, R. Mark. "The Providential Theory of Historical Causa-
tion in Holinshed's CHRONICLES, 1577 and 1587," TSLL, 1
(1959), 264-76.

c. Booth, Stephen. THE BOOK CALLED HOLINSHED'S CHRON-
ICLES: AN ACCOUNT OF ITS INCEPTION, PURPOSE, CON-
TRIBUTORS, CONTENTS, PUBLICATION, REVISION, AND IN-
FLUENCE ON WILLIAM SHAKESPEARE. San Francisco, 1968.

150. Guicciardini, Francesco. THE HISTORIE. . .CONTEINING THE WARRES
OF ITALIE, tr. Geoffrey Fenton. London, 1579.

a. Gottfried, Rudolf B. GEOFFREY FENTON'S HISTORIE OF
GUICCIARDIN. Indiana University Press, 1940.

151. Stow, John. THE CHRONICLES OF ENGLAND, FROM BRUTE UNTO
THIS PRESENT YEARE OF CHRIST. 1580. London, 1580.

Retitled ANNALES in 1592, and kept up to date by a
succession of editions until 1631.

a. Dorsch, T. S. "Two English Antiquaries: John Leland and
John Stow," E&S, 12 (1959), 18-35.

152. Caradog of Llancarvan. THE HISTORIE OF CAMBRIA, NOW CALLED
WALES, tr. Humphrey Llwyd. London, 1584.

153. Knox, John. THE HISTORIE OF THE REFORMATION OF THE CHURCH OF SCOTLAND. London, 1587.

    A. _____. HISTORY OF THE REFORMATION IN SCOTLAND, ed. William C. Dickinson. 2 vols. New York: Philosophical Library, 1950.

154. Harrison, William. "The description of England," in Raphael Holinshed, CHRONICLES. 2nd ed. London, 1587.

    A dependable account of England on the eve of the Spanish Armada.

    A. _____. THE DESCRIPTION OF ENGLAND, ed. Georges Edelen. Cornell University Press: Folger Documents, 1968.

    a. Edelen, Georges. "William Harrison (1535-1593)," SRen, 9 (1962), 256-72.

    b. McCollum, John I., Jr. "William Harrison: A Sixteenth-Century Mind," in SWEET SMOKE OF RHETORIC, ed. Natalie G. Lawrence and J. A. Reynolds. University of Miami Press, 1964, pp. 53-67.

155. Harvey, Richard. PHILADELPHUS, OR A DEFENCE OF BRUTES, AND THE BRUTAN HISTORY. London, 1593.

    A sympathetic study of the legendary history of Albion.

156. Norden, John. SPECULUM BRITANNIAE. THE FIRST PARTE. AN HISTORICALL & CHOROGRAPHICALL DISCRIPTION OF MIDDLESEX. London, 1593.

    A thorough chorographical description of Middlesex, with a map of the county and maps of the cities of London and Westminster; the first fruit of Norden's project to map all of Britain.

157. _____. NORDENS PREPARATIVE TO HIS SPECULUM BRITANNIAE. London, 1596.

    A brief exposition of the principles to underlie his monumental atlas, the SPECULUM BRITANNIAE.

158. _____. SPECULI BRITANNIAE PARS. THE DESCRIPTION OF HARTFORDSHIRE. London, 1598.

    A chorographical description of Hartfordshire with a map of the country; this with items 156-157 is all that was completed of Norden's project for an atlas of England.

159. Machiavelli, Niccolo. THE FLORENTINE HISTORIE, tr. Thomas Bedingfield. London, 1595.

    A. _____. THE FLORENTINE HISTORY, tr. Thomas Bedingfield,
    ed. Henry Cust. London: Tudor Translations, 1905.

160. Commines, Philippe de. THE HISTORIE, tr. Thomas Danett. London,
1596.

    An account of European affairs from 1464 to the end of
    the century.

    A. _____. THE HISTORY, tr. Thomas Danett, ed. Charles Whib-
    ley. 2 vols. London: Tudor Translations, 1897.

161. Hayward, Sir John. THE FIRST PART OF THE LIFE AND RAIGNE OF
KING HENRIE THE IIII. London, 1599.

162. _____. THE LIFE AND RAIGNE OF KING EDWARD THE SIXT. London,
1630.

163. Verstegan (i.e., Rowlands), Richard. A RESTITUTION OF DECAYED IN-
TELLIGENCE: IN ANTIQUITIES. CONCERNING THE MOST NOBLE
AND RENOWNED ENGLISH NATION. Antwerp, 1605.

    A Catholic writing English history in exile; reprinted in
    London in 1628, 1634, etc.

164. Camden, William. REMAINES OF A GREATER WORKE, CONCERNING
BRITAINE. London, 1605.

    Learned essays on a variety of subjects having to do with
    British social history; enlarged in 1614, 1623, 1629,
    1636, 1637, and 1657.

165. _____. BRITAIN, OR A CHOROGRAPHICALL DESCRIPTION OF. . .ENG-
LAND, SCOTLAND, AND IRELAND, tr. Philemon Holland. London, 1610.

    A monumental county-by-county description of England,
    Scotland, and Ireland, compiled by the greatest of the
    Elizabethan antiquaries; first published in Latin in 1586.

    A. _____. BRITANNIA, ed. Richard Gough. 2nd ed. London,
    1806.

    a. Powicke, Sir Maurice. "William Camden," E&S, 1 (1948),
    67–84.

    b. Piggott, Stuart. WILLIAM CAMDEN AND THE BRITANNIA.

London, 1953.

    c. Levy, F. J. "The Making of Camden's BRITANNIA," BHR, 26 (1964), 70-97.

166. Grimestone, Edward. A GENERALL HISTORIE OF THE NETHERLANDS. London, 1608.

    Corrected edition in 1627.

167. Speed, John. THE THEATRE OF THE EMPIRE OF GREAT BRITAINE. 2 vols. London, 1611-12.

    Primarily an atlas of maps, but the accounts of each county are replete with antiquarian information.

168. _____. THE HISTORIE OF GREAT BRITAINE. . .FROM JULIUS CAESAR, TO. . .KING JAMES. London, 1611.

    An outgrowth of Speed's THEATRE which makes a stately progress through British history; oft-reprinted.

169. Raleigh, Sir Walter. THE HISTORY OF THE WORLD. London, 1614.

    A magnificent and enormous compilation, though unfinished (it goes from the beginnings only to 130 B.C.), held together by Raleigh's acknowledgment of divine providence; frequently reprinted despite its size; see also 229-230.

    A. _____. THE HISTORY OF THE WORLD, ed. C. A. Patrides. Temple University Press, 1972.

        Selections with an attempt at epitomization.

    a. Racin, John, Jr. "The Early Editions of Sir Walter Ralegh's THE HISTORY OF THE WORLD," SB, 17 (1964), 199-209.

    b. McCollum, John I., Jr. "Ralegh's THE HISTORY OF THE WORLD," CARRELL, 5 (1964), 1-6.

170. Gainsford, Thomas. THE TRUE AND WONDERFULL HISTORY OF PERKIN WARBECK. London, 1618.

    An account of a famous political imposter, the source of Ford's play; see also 615.

171. _____. THE TRUE EXEMPLARY, AND REMARKABLE HISTORY OF THE EARLE OF TIRONE. London, 1619.

    A contemporary report by someone who knew Ireland well.

172. Bacon, Francis. THE HISTORIE OF THE RAIGNE OF KING HENRY THE SEVENTH. London, 1622.

> A psychological inquiry into the character of the first Tudor monarch with a decidedly modern cast; see also 194.a, 482.

   a. Schuster, Sister Mary Faith, O.S.B. "Philosophy of Life and Prose Style in Thomas More's RICHARD III and Francis Bacon's HENRY VII," PMLA, 70 (1955), 474-87.

   b. Wheeler, Thomas. "Sir Francis Bacon's Concept of the Historian's Task," RenP 1955. Columbia, South Carolina, 1955, pp. 40-46.

   c. _____. "The Purpose of Bacon's HISTORY OF HENRY THE SEVENTH," SP, 54 (1957), 1-13.

   d. Kirkwood, James J. "Bacon's HENRY VII: A Model of a Theory of Historiography," RenP 1965. Durham, North Carolina, 1966, pp. 51-55.

173. Heywood, Thomas. GYNAIKEION: OR, NINE BOOKES OF VARIOUS HISTORY, CONCERNINGE WOMEN. London, 1624.

> A tribute to famous women of antiquity; see also 755.

174. _____. ENGLANDS ELIZABETH HER LIFE AND TROUBLES. London, 1631.

175. Camden, William. ANNALES. THE TRUE AND ROYALL HISTORY OF THE FAMOUS EMPRESSE ELIZABETH, tr. Abraham Darcy. London, 1625.

> A history of England under Elizabeth by the most learned of the Elizabethan antiquaries; first published in Latin in 1615 and 1627.

176. Roper, William. THE MIRROUR OF VERTUE IN WORLDLY GREATNES. OR THE LIFE OF SYR THOMAS MORE, KNIGHT. Paris, 1626.

> A son-in-law's tribute to a great man, most notable for intimate anecdotes reported with a flair for characterization and dialogue; written ca.1555; see also 339-342.

   A. _____. THE LYFE OF SIR THOMAS MOORE, ed. Elsie V. Hitchcock. EETS OS 197. London, 1935.

   B. Sylvester, Richard S., and Davis P. Harding, eds. TWO EARLY TUDOR LIVES: THE LIFE AND DEATH OF CARDINAL

WOLSEY, BY GEORGE CAVENDISH, THE LIFE OF SIR THOMAS MORE, BY WILLIAM ROPER. Yale University Press, 1962.

    a. Maguire, John. "William Roper's LIFE OF MORE: The Working Methods of a Tudor Biographer," MOREANA, 23 (1969), 59-65.

177. Fuller, Thomas. THE HISTORIE OF THE HOLY WARRE. London, 1639.

    A partisan but lively account of the Crusades in Palestine; see also 102, 273, 507-508.

178. _____. ABEL REDEVIVUS; OR, THE DEAD YET SPEAKING. THE LIVES AND DEATHS OF THE MODERNE DIVINES. London, 1651.

    A. _____. ABEL REDEVIVUS; OR, THE DEAD YET SPEAKING, ed. William Nichols. London, 1867.

179. _____. THE CHURCH-HISTORY OF BRITAIN: FROM THE BIRTH OF JESUS CHRIST UNTILL THE YEAR M.DC.XLVIII. London, 1655.

    An account of the Christian Church in England, told with learning yet with an eye on its present-day relevance.

    A. _____. THE CHURCH HISTORY OF BRITAIN, ed. Rev. J. S. Brewer. Oxford University Press, 1845.

180. _____. THE HISTORY OF THE WORTHIES OF ENGLAND. London, 1662.

    A curious compilation of all sorts of facts about England, biographical as well as topographical, arranged alphabetically by counties.

    A. _____. THE HISTORY OF THE WORTHIES OF ENGLAND, ed. P. Austin Nuttall. London, 1840.

    i. Gibson, Strickland. A BIBLIOGRAPHY OF THE WORKS OF THOMAS FULLER. Oxford, 1936.

    a. Lyman, Dean B. THE GREAT TOM FULLER. University of California Press, 1935.

    b. Addison, William. WORTHY DR. FULLER. London, 1951.

181. Lupton, Donald. THE GLORY OF THEIR TIMES, OR THE LIVES OF THE PRIMITIVE FATHERS. London, 1640.

A compendious treatment of all those who have written
in the Christian tradition, from Philo Judaeus to Thomas
Aquinas.

182. Somner, William. THE ANTIQUITIES OF CANTERBURY. London, 1640.

183. Walton, Izaak. LIFE OF JOHN DONNE, in John Donne, LXXX SERMONS.
London, 1640.

Written as a preface to Donne's LXXX SERMONS; revised
in 1658, and later; see also 515.A.

184. _____. THE LIFE OF SIR HENRY WOTTON, in RELIQUIAE WOTTON-
IANAE. London, 1651.

An edition of Wotton's remains by Walton with a biography
included; revised 1654, and later; see also 515.A.

A. _____. THE LIVES OF JOHN DONNE, SIR HENRY WOTTON,
RICHARD HOOKER, GEORGE HERBERT, & ROBERT SANDERSON,
ed. George Saintsbury. Oxford University Press: World's Classics, 1927.

The text of the fourth edition, 1675, and the 1678
text of Sanderson's LIFE.

a. Novarr, David. THE MAKING OF WALTON'S "LIVES".
Cornell University Press, 1958.

185. Habington, William. THE HISTORIE OF EDWARD THE FOURTH. London,
1640.

186. _____. OBSERVATIONS UPON HISTORIE. London, 1641.

187. Naunton, Sir Robert. FRAGMENTA REGALIA, OR OBSERVATIONS ON
THE LATE QUEEN ELIZABETH, HER TIMES AND FAVORITES. London,
1641.

Especially interesting for the thumbnail accounts of Elizabeth's most powerful advisers, originally written ca.1630;
other editions in 1642, 1650, 1653.

A. _____. FRAGMENTA REGALIA, ed. Edward Arber. London:
English Reprints, 1870.

188. Baker, Sir Richard. A CHRONICLE OF THE KINGS OF ENGLAND.
London, 1643.

Perhaps the most useful of the seventeenth-century histories of England; oft-reprinted.

189. Wilson, Arthur. THE FIVE YEARES OF KING JAMES. London, 1643.

Erroneously attributed to Fulke Greville.

190. _____. THE HISTORY OF GREAT BRITAIN, BEING THE LIFE AND REIGN OF KING JAMES THE FIRST. London, 1653.

191. May, Thomas. THE HISTORY OF THE PARLIAMENT OF ENGLAND: WHICH BEGAN NOVEMBER THE THIRD M.DC.XL. London, 1647.

An official history.

192. Edward, Lord Herbert of Cherbury. THE LIFE AND RAIGNE OF KING HENRY THE EIGHTH. London, 1649.

193. Weldon, Sir Anthony. THE COURT AND CHARACTER OF KING JAMES. London, 1650.

History as personal observation; see also 271.

194. Greville, Fulke. THE LIFE OF THE RENOWNED SIR PHILIP SIDNEY. London, 1652.

Memoirs of a warm and fruitful friendship; written ca. 1610-12.

A. _____. LIFE OF SIR PHILIP SIDNEY, ed. Nowell Smith. Oxford: Tudor and Stuart Library, 1907.

B. _____. THE WORKS IN VERSE AND PROSE, ed. Rev. A. B. Grosart. 4 vols. Blackburn, 1870.

a. Maclean, Hugh N. "Bacon, Greville, History, and Biography," N&Q, 201 (1956), 95-97.

b. Rees, Joan. FULKE GREVILLE, LORD BROOKE. 1554-1628: A CRITICAL BIOGRAPHY. University of California Press, 1971.

195. Johnson, Edward. A HISTORY OF NEW-ENGLAND. London, 1654.

An important history by a man who settled in America in 1630.

A. _____. A HISTORY OF NEW-ENGLAND, in COLLECTIONS OF THE MASSACHUSETTS HISTORICAL SOCIETY, SECOND SERIES. Boston, 1814-23. Vols. 2, 3, 4, 7, 8.

196. Spottiswood, John. THE HISTORY OF THE CHURCH OF SCOTLAND. London, 1655.

An authoritative history written by a clergyman close to
James I and Charles I, and sometime Archbishop of St.
Andrews; published posthumously, and four editions by
1678.

A. _____. THE HISTORY OF THE CHURCH OF SCOTLAND,
ed. M. Russell and M. Napier. 3 vols. Edinburgh: Bannatyne
Club, 1850-51.

197. Stanley, Thomas. THE HISTORY OF PHILOSOPHY. 4 vols. London,
1655-62.

A triumph of compilation and a new type of history;
four editions by 1741.

198. Dugdale, Sir William. THE ANTIQUITIES OF WARWICKSHIRE. London,
1656.

The high-point of topographical studies--accurate, fully
documented, handsome.

199. _____. THE HISTORY OF ST. PAULS CATHEDRAL. London, 1658.

A carefully researched and beautifully illustrated volume,
given added importance because the Cathedral it describes
was destroyed in the great fire of 1666.

IV. TRAVEL LITERATURE

IV. Travel Literature

As we know from Chaucer, Englishmen delighted in travel. And next to travel itself, they delighted in reports from far-away places. The earliest travelling reporters were on pilgrimages to holy sites, such as Jerusalem, Rome, and St. James of Compostella. But gradually interest in the secular world also produced accounts of foreign nations, with Italy and the Near East being especial favorites. Discovery of the New World and its consequent exploration produced a spate of exotic and exciting accounts of unknown lands.

See also entries 124; III.a, III.b, III.f, III.n, 138, 146, 148, 152, 154, 156, 158, 165, 166, 167, 180, 182, 198, 437, 438, 470, 731, 743, 751.

A. Bent, J. Theodore, ed. EARLY VOYAGES AND TRAVELS IN THE LEVANT. London: Hakluyt Society, 1893.

B. Beazley, Charles R., ed. VOYAGES AND TRAVELS MAINLY DURING THE 16th AND 17th CENTURIES. 2 vols. Westminster: English Garner, 1903.

C. Winny, James, ed. THE ELIZABETHAN VOYAGES. London, 1956.

D. Wright, Louis B., ed. THE ELIZABETHANS' AMERICA: A COLLECTION OF EARLY REPORTS BY ENGLISHMEN ON THE NEW WORLD. Harvard University Press, 1965.

E. Boxer, C. R., ed. and tr. FURTHER SELECTIONS FROM THE TRAGIC HISTORY OF THE SEA, 1559-1565. Cambridge University Press: Hakluyt Society, 1968.

F. Berry, Lloyd E., and Robert O. Crummey, eds. RUDE & BARBAROUS KINGDOM: RUSSIA IN THE ACCOUNTS OF SIXTEENTH-CENTURY ENGLISH VOYAGERS. University of Wisconsin Press, 1968.

a. Jusserand, Jean J. ENGLISH WAYFARING LIFE IN THE MIDDLE AGES, tr. Lucy T. Smith. 4th ed. London, 1892.

b. Raleigh, Sir Walter A. THE ENGLISH VOYAGES OF THE SIXTEENTH CENTURY. Glasgow, 1906.

c. Robinson, Charles N. "The Literature of the Sea," in THE CAMBRIDGE HISTORY OF ENGLISH LITERATURE, ed. A. W. Ward and A. R. Waller. 15 vols. Cambridge University Press, 1907-27, IV,66-85.

d. Howard, Clare M. ENGLISH TRAVELLERS OF THE RENAIS-SANCE. London, 1914.

e. Parkes, Joan. TRAVEL IN ENGLAND IN THE SEVENTEENTH CENTURY. Oxford University Press, 1925.

f. Newton, Arthur P. TRAVEL AND TRAVELLERS OF THE MIDDLE AGES. New York, 1926.

g. Lambert, Richard S., ed. GRAND TOUR. London, 1935.

h. Chew, Samuel C. THE CRESCENT AND THE ROSE: ISLAM AND ENGLAND DURING THE RENAISSANCE. New York, 1937.

   Largely a chronicle of early English travelers to the Near East.

i. Braaksma, Michiel H. TRAVEL AND LITERATURE: AN AT-TEMPT AT A LITERARY APPRECIATION OF ENGLISH TRAVEL-BOOKS ABOUT PERSIA. Groningen, 1938.

j. Cawley, Robert R. UNPATHED WATERS: STUDIES IN THE INFLUENCE OF THE VOYAGERS ON ELIZABETHAN LITERA-TURE. Princeton University Press, 1940.

k. Penrose, Boise. URBANE TRAVELERS, 1591-1635. University of Pennsylvania Press, 1942.

l. Bush, Douglas. "The Literature of Travel," in ENGLISH LIT-ERATURE IN THE EARLIER SEVENTEENTH CENTURY 1600-1660. Oxford, 1945, pp. 170-80.

m. Penrose, Boise. TRAVEL AND DISCOVERY IN THE RENAIS-SANCE, 1420-1620. Harvard University Press, 1952.

n. Stoye, J. W. ENGLISH TRAVELLERS ABROAD, 1604-1667: THEIR INFLUENCE IN ENGLISH SOCIETY AND POLITICS. London, 1952.

o. Parks, George B. THE ENGLISH TRAVELER TO ITALY. Rome, 1954.

p. _____. "The First Italianate Englishmen," SRen, 8 (1961), 197-216.

q. Penrose, Boise. TUDOR AND EARLY STUART VOYAGING. Cornell University Press: Folger Booklets, 1962.

r. Jewkes, W. T. "The Literature of Travel and the Mode of Romance in the Renaissance," BNYPL, 67 (1963), 219-36.

s. Osborn, James M. "Travel Literature and the Rise of Neo-Hellenism in England," BNYPL, 67 (1963), 279-300.

t. Lievsay, John L. THE ELIZABETHAN IMAGE OF ITALY. Cornell University Press: Folger Booklets, 1964.

u. Sells, Arthur L. THE PARADISE OF TRAVELLERS: THE ITALIAN INFLUENCE ON ENGLISHMEN IN THE SEVENTEENTH CEN-TURY. Indiana University Press, 1964.

v. Trease, Geoffrey. THE GRAND TOUR. New York, 1967.

w. Parks, George B. "The Decline and Fall of the English Re-naissance Admiration of Italy," HLQ, 31 (1967-68), 341-57.

x. Jones, Eldred D. THE ELIZABETHAN IMAGE OF AFRICA. University of Virginia Press: Folger Booklets, 1971.

200. Mandeville, Sir John. TRAVELS, tr. anon. ca.1370.

Arm-chair travels by a fourteenth-century Englishman who set out for Jerusalem; written in French, soon trans-lated into English, and printed by Richard Pynson in 1496.

A. _____. THE BUKE OF JOHN MAUNDEVILL, tr. anon., ed. George F. Warner. Westminster: Roxburghe Club, 1889.

B. _____. TRAVELS, tr. anon., ed. Paul Hamelius. EETS OS 153-54. London, 1919, 1923.

C. _____. TRAVELS, tr. anon., ed. Malcolm H. I. Letts. 2 vols.
London: Hakluyt Society, 1953.

D. _____. MANDEVILLE'S TRAVELS, ed. Maurice C. Seymour.
Oxford, 1967.

a. Steiner, Arpad. "The Date of Composition of MANDEVILLE'S
TRAVELS," SPECULUM, 9 (1934), 144-47.

b. Letts, Malcolm H. I. SIR JOHN MANDEVILLE: THE MAN
AND HIS BOOK. London, 1949.

c. Bennett, Josephine W. THE REDISCOVERY OF SIR JOHN
MANDEVILLE. New York, 1954.

d. Thomas, J. D. "The Date of MANDEVILLE'S TRAVELS," MLN,
72 (1957), 165-69.

e. Seymour, M. C. "The English Epitome of MANDEVILLE'S
TRAVELS," ANGLIA, 84 (1966), 27-58.

201. Capgrave, John. THE SOLACE OF PILGRIMS. ca.1450.

A guide-book to the holy city of Rome.

A. _____. YE SOLACE OF PILGRIMES, ed. C. A. Mills.
Oxford University Press, 1911.

202. Wey, William. THE ITINERARIES. 1458-62.

A fellow of Eton College on Pilgrimages to St. James
of Compostella and Jerusalem.

A. _____. THE ITINERARIES, ed. B. Bandinel. London: Roxburghe Club, 1857.

203. Anon. INFORMACION FOR PYLGRYMES UNTO THE HOLY LONDE, tr.
anon. London: Wynken de Worde, ca.1498.

An English translation of a Latin guide-book; STC 14081.

204. Langton, Robert. THE PYLGRIMAGE OF M. ROBERT LANGTON CLERKE
TO SAYNT JAMES IN COMPOSTELL. London, 1522.

A. _____. THE PYLGRIMAGE, ed. Ernest M. Blackie. Harvard
University Press, 1924.

205. Boorde, Andrew. THE FYRST BOKE OF THE INTRODUCTION OF KNOWL-EDGE. London, 1548.

For the most part a description of the geography and man-ners of the European and Near Eastern nations; another edition ca.1562.

A. _____. THE FYRST BOKE OF THE INTRODUCTION OF KNOWLEDGE, ed. F. J. Furnivall. EETS ES 10. London, 1870.

206. Thomas, William. THE HISTORIE OF ITALIE. London, 1549.

A. _____. THE HISTORY OF ITALY, ed. George B. Parks. Cornell University Press: Folger Documents, 1963.

207. Peter Martyr (Anglerius). THE DECADES OF THE NEWE WORLDE OR WEST INDIA, tr. Richard Eden. London, 1555.

A translation of a famous Latin work dealing with the discovery of America.

208. Peter Martyr (Anglerius) et al. THE HISTORY OF TRAVAYLE IN THE WEST AND EAST INDIES, AND OTHER COUNTREYS, tr. Richard Eden, ed. Richard Willes. London, 1577.

A. Arber, Edward, ed. THE FIRST THREE ENGLISH BOOKS ON AMERICA. Birmingham, 1885.

a. Wagner, Henry R. PETER MARTYR AND HIS WORKS. Wor-cester, Massachusetts, 1947.

209. Hawkins, Sir John. A TRUE DECLARATION OF THE TROUBLESOME VOYADGE OF M. JOHN HAUKINS TO THE PARTIES OF GUYNEA AND THE WEST-INDIES, IN THE YEARES OF OUR LORD 1567. AND 1568. London, 1569.

A. _____. THE HAWKINS' VOYAGES, ed. Clements R. Markham. London: Hakluyt Society, 1878.

a. Williamson, James A. HAWKINS OF PLYMOUTH. 2nd ed. London, 1969.

210. Dionysius Periegetes. THE SURVEYE OF THE WORLD, tr. Thomas Twyne. London, 1572.

The classical handbook of popular geography.

211. Turler, Jerome. THE TRAVEILER. London, 1575.

> In two parts: the first on travelling in general, the second an account of Naples.

    A. _____. THE TRAVEILER, ed. Denver E. Baughan. Gainesville, Florida: Scholars' Facsimiles, 1951.

212. Rowlands, Richard. THE POST OF THE WORLD. London, 1576.

> A description of the cities of Europe.

213. Gilbert, Sir Humphrey. A DISCOURSE OF A DISCOVERIE FOR A NEW PASSAGE TO CATAIA. London, 1576.

> The arguments for a northwest passage to Cathay.

    A. Quinn, David B., ed. THE VOYAGES AND COLONIZING ENTERPRISES OF SIR HUMPHREY GILBERT. London: Hakluyt Society, 1940.

214. Monardes, Nicholas. JOYFULL NEWES OUT OF THE NEWE FOUNDE WORLDE, tr. John Frampton. London, 1577.

> A report on matters, largely medicinal, from America.

    A. _____. JOYFULL NEWES OUT OF THE NEWE FOUNDE WORLDE, tr. John Frampton, ed. Stephen Gaselee. 2 vols. London: Tudor Translations, 1925.

215. Best, George. A TRUE DISCOURSE OF THE THREE VOYAGES OF DISCOVERIE [by Martin Frobisher] FOR THE FINDING OF A PASSAGE TO CATHAYA. London, 1578.

    A. _____. THE THREE VOYAGES OF MARTIN FROBISHER, ed. Rear-Admiral Richard Collinson. London: Hakluyt Society, 1867.

    B. _____. THE THREE VOYAGES OF MARTIN FROBISHER, ed. Vilhjalmur Stefansson. London, 1938.

216. Polo, Marco. THE MOST NOBLE AND FAMOUS TRAVELS OF MARCUS PAULUS, tr. John Frampton. London, 1579.

> The classic of travels in the East.

217. Peckham, Sir George. A TRUE REPORTE, OF THE LATE DISCOVERIES, AND POSSESSION, TAKEN IN THE RIGHT OF THE CROWNE OF ENGLANDE, OF THE NEWFOUND LANDES: BY. . .SIR HUMFREY GILBERT. London, 1583.

A. _____. A TRUE REPORTE. . .OF THE NEWFOUND LANDES. Tarrytown, New York, 1920.

218. Cartier, Jacques. THE TWO NAVIGATIONS AND DISCOVERIES TO THE NORTHWEAST PARTES CALLED NEWE FRAUNCE, tr. John Florio. London, 1580.

219. Hakluyt, Richard, ed. DIVERS VOYAGES TOUCHING THE DISCOVERIE OF AMERICA, AND THE ILANDS ADJACENT UNTO THE SAME. London, 1582.

A. _____. ed. DIVERS VOYAGES TOUCHING THE DISCOVERY OF AMERICA AND THE ISLANDS ADJACENT, ed. John W. Jones. London: Hakluyt Society, 1850.

220. _____. THE PRINCIPALL NAVIGATIONS, VOIAGES AND DISCOVERIES OF THE ENGLISH NATION. London, 1589.

A. _____. THE PRINCIPALL NAVIGATIONS, VOIAGES, AND DISCOVERIES OF THE ENGLISH NATION, ed. David B. Quinn and Raleigh A. Skelton. 2 vols. Cambridge: Hakluyt Society, 1965.

221. _____. THE PRINCIPAL NAVIGATIONS, VOYAGES, TRAFFIQUES, AND DISCOVERIES OF THE ENGLISH NATION, MADE BY SEA OR OVER LAND, WITHIN THE COMPASS OF THESE 1500 YEARS. 3 vols. London, 1598-1600.

A monumental collection of the most stirring firsthand accounts of adventurous exploration ever written.

A. _____. THE PRINCIPAL NAVIGATIONS, VOYAGES, TRAF-FIQUES & DISCOVERIES OF THE ENGLISH NATION. 12 vols. Glasgow: Hakluyt Society, 1903-05.

B. _____. THE PRINCIPAL NAVIGATIONS, ed. John Masefield. 10 vols. London: Everyman's, 1927-28.

C. _____. HAKLUYT'S VOYAGES. SELECTED AND ARRANGED, ed. Adrian S. Mott. Oxford, 1929.

D. Blacker, Irwin R. R., ed. THE PORTABLE HAKLUYT'S VOY-AGES. New York, 1967.

a. Parks, George B. RICHARD HAKLUYT AND THE ENGLISH VOYAGES. New York, 1928.

b. Quinn, David B. RICHARD HAKLUYT, EDITOR. Amsterdam, 1968.

222. Saunders, Thomas. A TRUE DISCRIPTION. . .OF A MOST LAMENTABLE VOIAGE, MADE LATELIE TO TRIPOLIE IN BARBARIE. London, 1587.

A blood-and-guts story of the high seas demonstrating the brutishness of infidels.

223. Laudonniere, Rene de. A NOTABLE HISTORIE CONCERNING FOURE VOYAGES MADE BY CERTAYNE FRENCH CAPTAYNES UNTO FLORIDA, tr. Richard Hakluyt. London, 1587.

224. Harriot, Thomas. A BRIEFE AND TRUE REPORT OF THE NEW FOUND LAND OF VIRGINIA. London, 1588.

The report of a trip that Harriot undertook for Sir Walter Raleigh.

A. _____. A BRIEF AND TRUE REPORT OF THE NEW FOUND LAND OF VIRGINIA, ed. Randolph G. Adams. Ann Arbor, Michigan, 1951.

225. Bigges, Walter. A SUMMARIE AND TRUE DISCOURSE OF SIR FRANCES DRAKES WEST INDIAN VOYAGE. London, 1589.

226. Devereux, Robert. A TRUE COPPIE OF A DISCOURSE WRITTEN BY A GENTLEMAN, EMPLOYED IN THE LATE VOYAGE OF SPAINE AND PORTINGALE. London, 1589.

The young Essex who won Elizabeth's heart.

227. Webbe, Edward. THE RARE AND MOST WONDERFUL THINGES WHICH EDWARD WEBBE. . .HATH SEENE. London, 1590.

Travels mainly in the Near East and Russia.

A. _____. HIS TRAVAILES, 1590, ed. Edward Arber. London: English Reprints, 1869.

228. Fletcher, Giles. OF THE RUSSE COMMON WEALTH. London, 1591.

See also IV.f.

A. _____. OF THE RUSSE COMMONWEALTH, ed. Richard Pipes. Harvard University Press, 1966.

B. _____. OF THE RUS COMMONWEALTH, ed. Albert J. Schmidt. Cornell University Press: Folger Documents, 1966.

229. Raleigh, Sir Walter. A REPORT OF THE TRUTH OF THE FIGHT ABOUT THE ILES OF ACORES, THIS LAST SOMMER. BETWIXT THE REVENGE, ONE OF HER MAJESTIES SHIPPES, AND AN ARMADA OF THE KING OF SPAINE. London, 1591.

> A classic of eye-witness reporting that preserves the patriotism of Elizabethan England; see also 169.

A. _____. THE LAST FIGHT OF THE REVENGE AT SEA, ed. Edward Arber. London: English Reprints, 1871.

230. _____. THE DISCOVERIE OF THE LARGE, RICH, AND BEWTIFUL EMPIRE OF GUIANA. London, 1596.

> An accomplished account of Raleigh's first expedition to the New World.

A. _____. THE DISCOVERY OF. . .GUIANA, ed. Sir Robert H. Schomburgk. London: Hakluyt Society, 1848.

B. _____. THE DISCOVERIE OF THE LARGE AND BEWTIFUL EMPIRE OF GUIANA, ed. Vincent T. Harlow. London, 1928.

C. _____. THE WORKS, ed. William Oldys and Thomas Birch. 8 vols. Oxford University Press, 1829.

i. Brushfield, Thomas N. A BIBLIOGRAPHY OF SIR WALTER RALEIGH. 2nd ed. Exeter, 1908.

ii. Tonkin, Humphrey, comp. ELIZABETHAN BIBLIOGRAPHIES SUPPLEMENTS, XVII: SIR WALTER RALEGH. London, 1971.

a. Strathmann, Ernest A. SIR WALTER RALEIGH: A STUDY IN ELIZABETHAN SKEPTICISM. Columbia University Press, 1951.

b. Wallace, Willard M. SIR WALTER RALEIGH. Princeton University Press, 1959.

c. Irwin, Margaret. THAT GREAT LUCIFER: A PORTRAIT OF SIR WALTER RALEGH. London, 1960.

d. Lefranc, Pierre. SIR WALTER RALEGH ECRIVAIN: L'OEUVRE ET LES IDEES. Paris, 1968.

e. Greenblatt, Stephen J. SIR WALTER RALEGH: THE RENAISSANCE MAN AND HIS ROLES. Yale University Press, 1973.

231. Hasleton, Richard. STRANGE AND WONDERFULL THINGS HAPPENED TO RICHARD HASLETON. . .IN HIS TEN YEARES TRAVAILES. London, 1595.

   The journal of an observant adventurer.

232. Davis, John. THE WORLDES HYDROGRAPHICAL DISCRIPTION. London, 1595.

   The report of a famous sea-captain.

233. Abbott, George. A BRIEFE DESCRIPTION OF THE WHOLE WORLDE. London, 1599.

   An academic exercise in arm-chair travel; oft-reprinted.

   i. Christophers, Richard A. GEORGE ABBOTT, ARCHBISHOP OF CANTERBURY, 1562-1633: A BIBLIOGRAPHY. University of Virginia Press, 1967.

234. Kemp, William. NINE DAIES WONDER. London, 1600.

   A fascinating account of a journey from London to Norwich by the clownish actor who danced every step of the way on a bet.

   A. _____. NINE DAIES WONDER 1600, and Henry Chettle. KIND-HARTES DREAME 1592, ed. G. B. Harrison. London: Bodley Head Quartos, 1923.

235. Johnson, Robert. THE TRAVELLERS BREVIAT, OR AN HISTORICAL DE-SCRIPTION OF THE MOST FAMOUS KINGDOMES. London, 1601.

   Essentially a redaction of Giovanni Botero's RELAZIONI UNIVERSALI; see also 486.

236. Parry, William. THE TRAVELS OF SIR ANTHONY SHERLEY KNIGHT, BY SEA AND OVER LAND, TO THE PERSIAN EMPIRE. London, 1601.

   A. _____. THE TRAVELS OF SIR ANTHONY SHERLEY, ed. John P. Collier. London, 1864.

237. Carew, Richard. THE SURVEY OF CORNWALL. London, 1602.

238. Knolles, Richard. THE GENERALL HISTORIE OF THE TURKES. London, 1603.

   Revised in 1610, 1621, 1631, and 1638.

239. Dallington, Sir Robert. A METHOD FOR TRAVELL. SHEWED BY TAKING

THE VIEW OF FRANCE. London, ca.1604.

First printed in a pirated edition as THE VIEW OF FRANCE (London, 1604).

A. _____. THE VIEW OF FRANCE, 1604, ed. W. P. Barrett. Oxford University Press: Shakespeare Association Facsimiles, 1936.

240. _____. A SURVEY OF THE GREAT DUKES STATE OF TUSCANY, IN. . . 1596. London, 1605.

241. Smith, Sir Thomas. VOIAGE AND ENTERTAINMENT IN RUSHIA. London, 1605.

242. Day, John. THE TRAVAILES OF THE THREE ENGLISH BROTHERS. SIR THOMAS/SIR ANTHONY/MR. ROBERT/SHIRLEY. London, 1607.

243. Sherley, Sir Anthony. HIS RELATION OF HIS TRAVELS INTO PERSIA. London, 1613.

a. Davies, David W. ELIZABETHANS ERRANT: THE STRANGE FORTUNES OF SIR THOMAS SHERLEY AND HIS THREE SONS. Cornell University Press, 1967.

244. Smith, John. A TRUE RELATION OF SUCH OCCURENCES AND ACCIDENTS OF NOATE AS HATH HAPPENED IN VIRGINIA. London, 1608.

A report by the great colonizer of America.

A. _____. A TRUE RELATION OF VIRGINIA, ed. Charles Deane. Boston, 1866.

245. _____. A DESCRIPTION OF NEW ENGLAND. London, 1616.

A. _____. A DESCRIPTION OF NEW ENGLAND. Rochester, 1898.

246. _____. THE GENERALL HISTORIE OF VIRGINIA, NEW-ENGLAND, AND THE SUMMER ISLES. London, 1624.

Oft-reprinted.

A. _____. THE GENERALL HISTORIE OF VIRGINIA, NEW-ENGLAND, AND THE SUMMER ISLES. London, 1966.

247. _____. THE TRUE TRAVELS, ADVENTURES, AND OBSERVATIONS OF

CAPTAINE JOHN SMITH, IN EUROPE, ASIA, AFFRICA, AND AMERICA. London, 1630.

A. _____ . TRAVELS AND WORKS, ed. Edward Arber, rev. A. G. Bradley. 2 vols. Edinburgh, 1910.

i. Eames, Wilberforce. A BIBLIOGRAPHY OF CAPTAIN JOHN SMITH. New York, 1927.

248. Jourdain, Silvester. A DISCOVERY OF THE BARMUDAS. London, 1610.

An influence upon Shakespeare's TEMPEST; second edition in 1613.

A. _____ . A DISCOVERY OF THE BARMUDAS, ed. J. Q. Adams. New York: Scholars' Facsimiles, 1940.

249. Coryate, Thomas. CORYATS CRUDITIES. London, 1611.

A journal recording the famous travels through Western Europe of a favorite Jacobean buffoon.

A. _____ . CORYAT'S CRUDITIES. Glasgow, 1905.

a. Strachan, Michael. THE LIFE AND ADVENTURES OF THOMAS CORYATE. Oxford University Press, 1962.

250. Whitaker, Alexander. GOOD NEWES FROM VIRGINIA. London, 1613.

Another report from the New World.

251. Purchas, Samuel. PURCHAS HIS PILGRIMAGE. OR, RELATIONS OF THE WORLD AND THE RELIGIONS OBSERVED IN ALL AGES AND PLACES. London, 1613.

Augmented in 1614, 1617, and 1626.

252. _____ . PURCHAS HIS PILGRIM. MICROCOSMUS, OR THE HISTORIE OF MAN. London, 1619.

253. _____ . PURCHAS HIS PILGRIMES. 4 vols. London, 1625.

A continuation of Hakluyt's VOYAGES; see also 219-221.

A. _____ . HAKLUYTUS POSTHUMUS, OR PURCHAS HIS PIL-GRIMES. 20 vols. Glasgow, 1905-07.

B. Rawlinson, Hugh G., ed. NARRATIVES FROM PURCHAS HIS

PILGRIMES. Cambridge University Press, 1931.

254. Lithgow, William. AN ADMIRED AND PAINEFULL PEREGRINATION FROM SCOTLAND, TO THE MOST FAMOUS KINGDOMES IN EUROPE, ASIA AND AFFRICKE. London, 1614.

Successively enlarged until 1632.

A. _____ . THE TOTALL DISCOURSE OF THE RARE ADVENTURES & PAINEFULL PEREGRINATIONS. Glasgow, 1906.

255. Godwin, Thomas. ROMANAE HISTORIAE ANTHOLOGIA. AN ENGLISH EXPOSITION OF THE ROMANE ANTIQUITIES. Oxford, 1614.

256. Sandys, George. A RELATION OF A JOURNEY BEGUN AN: DOM: 1610. . . .CONTAINING A DESCRIPTION OF THE TURKISH EMPIRE, OF AEGYPT, OF THE HOLY LAND, OF THE REMOTE PARTS OF ITALY, AND ILANDS ADJOYNING. London, 1615.

Other editions in 1621, 1632, and 1637.

257. Moryson, Fynes. AN ITINERARY. . .CONTAINING HIS TEN YEERES TRAVELL THROUGH. . .GERMANY, BOHMERLAND, SWEITZERLAND, NETHERLAND, DENMARKE, POLAND, ITALY, TURKY, FRANCE, ENG-LAND, SCOTLAND, AND IRELAND. London, 1617.

A. _____ . AN ITINERARY. . . 4 vols. Glasgow, 1907-08.

258. Taylor, John. THREE WEEKES, THREE DAIES, AND THREE HOURES OBSERVATION AND TRAVEL, FROM LONDON TO HAMBURGH. London, 1617.

The Water-Poet reporting on the sights beyond his native London; see also 432-435.

259. _____ . THE PENNYLES PILGRIMAGE, OR THE MONEYLESSE PERAM-BULATION OF JOHN TAYLOR, FROM LONDON TO EDENBOROUGH. London, 1618.

260. _____ . TAYLOR HIS TRAVELS: FROM LONDON TO PRAGUE. London, 1620.

261. Heylen, Peter. MICROCOSMUS, OR A LITTLE DESCRIPTION OF THE GREAT WORLD. Oxford, 1621.

An inclusive gallimaufry; oft-reprinted.

262. Hawkins, Sir Richard. THE OBSERVATIONS OF SIR RICHARD HAWKINS KNIGHT, IN HIS VOIAGE INTO THE SOUTH SEA. ANNO DOMINI

1593. London, 1622.

A. _____. THE OBSERVATIONS, ed. James A. Williamson.
London, 1933.

263. Nichols, Philip. SIR FRANCIS DRAKE REVIVED. . . .IN A THIRD VOY-
AGE. . .INTO THE WEST INDIES. London, 1626.

A. Upcott, John D., ed. THREE VOYAGES OF DRAKE. London,
1936.

264. Drake, Sir Francis. THE WORLD ENCOMPASSED BY SIR FRANCIS DRAKE.
London, 1628.

An account of drake's voyage around the world.

A. _____. THE WORLD ENCOMPASSED, ed. G. E. Hollingsworth.
London, 1933.

265. Higginson, Francis. NEW-ENGLANDS PLANTATION. London, 1630.

A very early report from Massachusetts by a clergyman
settler.

266. Spenser, Edmund. "A view of the state of Ireland," in Sir James Ware,
THE HISTORIE OF IRELAND. Dublin, 1633.

A report written ca.1598 by a devoted civil servant who
lived in Ireland for almost twenty years.

267. Herbert, Sir Thomas. A RELATION OF SOME YEARES TRAVAILE, BE-
GUNNE ANNO 1626. INTO AFRIQUE AND THE GREATER ASIA. London, 1634.

268. Blount, Sir Henry. A VOYAGE INTO THE LEVANT. London, 1636.

Reprinted in 1637 and 1638, and eight editions by 1671.

269. Rous, Francis. ARCHAEOLOGICAE ATTICAE LIBRI TRES. THREE BOOKES
OF THE ATTICK ANTIQUITIES. Oxford, 1637.

Oft-reprinted.

270. Howell, James. INSTRUCTIONS FOR FORREINE TRAVELL. London, 1642.

A guidebook for the young Englishman on the grand tour,
enlarged 1650; see also 441, 470.

A. _____. INSTRUCTIONS FOR FORREINE TRAVELL, ed. Edward

Arber. London: English Reprints, 1869.

271. Weldon, Sir Anthony. A PERFECT DESCRIPTION OF THE PEOPLE AND COUNTRY OF SCOTLAND. London, 1649.

See also 193.

272. Raymond, John. AN ITINERARY: CONTAYNING A VOYAGE MADE THROUGH ITALY, IN THE YEARE 1646, and 1647. London, 1648.

273. Fuller, Thomas. A PISGAH-SIGHT OF PALESTINE. London, 1650.

A Christian arm-chair traveler looks at the Holy Land; see also 102, 177-180, 507-508.

274. Clarke, Samuel. A GEOGRAPHICALL DESCRIPTION OF ALL THE COUNTRIES IN THE KNOWNE WORLD. London, 1657.

275. Lupton, Donald. FLANDERS. London, 1658.

See also 181.

276. Porter, Thomas. A COMPENDIOUS VIEW, OR COSMOGRAPHICAL, AND GEOGRAPHICAL DESCRIPTION OF THE WHOLE WORLD. London, 1659.

V. SCIENTIFIC AND TECHNICAL WRITINGS

V. Scientific and Technical Writings

The world is always too much with us, and therefore treatises explaining the things of this world were in demand. Some of them dealt with the macrocosm, and concentrated on problems of time and space; others dealt with the microcosm, and purveyed rules for health. In the mid-sixteenth century Robert Recorde produced an unprecedented series of textbooks in English which brought up to date the science of Proclus and Boethius and Sacrobosco. In the early seventeenth century there was a notable efflorescence of works dealing with the occult.

See also I.hh, 157, 353, 458, 511, 691, 696, 727, 731, 733, 746, 747, 752, 753.

A. Davy, Norman, ed. BRITISH SCIENTIFIC LITERATURE IN THE SEVENTEENTH CENTURY. London, 1953.

i. Russell, K. F. "A Check List of Medical Books Published in England Before 1600," BULLETIN OF THE HISTORY OF MEDICINE, 21 (1947), 922-58.

a. Payne, J. F. ENGLISH MEDICINE IN THE ANGLO-SAXON TIMES. Oxford, 1904.

b. Smith, David E. RARA ARITHMETICA. Boston, 1908; ADDENDA. Boston, 1939.

c. Rohde, E. S. THE OLD ENGLISH HERBALS. London, 1922.

d. Johnson, Francis R. ASTRONOMICAL THOUGHT IN RENAISSANCE ENGLAND. Johns Hopkins Press, 1937.

e. Bush, Douglas. "Science and Scientific Thought," in ENGLISH LITERATURE IN THE EARLIER SEVENTEENTH CENTURY 1600-1660. Oxford, 1945, pp. 258-93.

f. Kocher, Paul H. SCIENCE AND RELIGION IN ELIZABETHAN ENGLAND. Huntington Library, 1953.

g. Jones, H. W. "Literary Problems in Seventeenth-Century Scientific Manuscripts," SB, 14 (1961), 69-80.

h. Webb, Henry J. ELIZABETHAN MILITARY SCIENCE: THE BOOKS AND THE PRACTICE. University of Wisconsin Press, 1965.

i. O'Malley, C. D. "Tudor Medicine and Biology," HLQ, 32 (1968-69), 1-27.

j. Heninger, S. K., Jr. "Tudor Literature of the Physical Sciences," HLQ, 32 (1968-69), 101-33, 249-70.

k. Meadows, Arthur J. THE HIGH FIRMAMENT: A SURVEY OF ASTRONOMY IN ENGLISH LITERATURE. Leicester University Press, 1969.

l. McLean, Antonia. HUMANISM AND THE RISE OF SCIENCE IN TUDOR ENGLAND. New York, 1972.

277. Aelfric. DE TEMPORIBUS ANNI. ca. 995.

A short treatise in the tradition of de rerum natura with emphasis upon time; see also 1-2.

A. _____. DE TEMPORIBUS ANNI, ed. Heinrich Henel. EETS OS 213. London, 1942.

278. Byrhtferth. MANUAL. 1011.

A treatise on the calendar and astronomy.

A. _____. MANUAL, ed. S. J. Crawford. EETS OS 177. London, 1929.

a. Forsey, George F. "Byrhtferth's PREFACE," SPECULUM, 3 (1928), 505-22.

279. ENGLISH MEDIAEVAL LAPIDARIES, ed. Joan Evans and Mary S. Serjeantson. EETS OS 190. London, 1933.

280. Lanfranco of Milan. SCIENCE OF CIRURGIE, tr. anon. ca. 1380.

A. ____ . SCIENCE OF CIRURGIE, tr. anon., ed. Robert von Fleischhacker. EETS OS 102. London, 1894.

281. Chaucer. A TREATISE ON THE ASTROLABE. 1391.

> Based upon an earlier Arabic treatise, but clearly demonstrating Chaucer's mastery of the instrument and knowledge of the science of astronomy.

A. ____ . A TREATISE ON THE ASTROLABE, ed. Rev. W. W. Skeat. EETS ES 6. London, 1872.

B. Gunther, Robert T., ed. CHAUCER ON THE ASTROLABE. 2nd ed. Oxford, 1931.

282. Guy de Chauliac. CYRURGIE, tr. anon. ca. 1425.

> A translation of the comprehensive treatise on surgical medicine, the INVENTARIUM SEU COLLECTORIUM IN PARTE CYRURGICALI MEDICINE, written by Guy de Chauliac in 1363.

A. ____ . THE CYRURGIE, tr. anon., ed. Margaret S. Ogden. EETS OS 265. Oxford University Press, 1971.

283. Hermes Trismegistus. THE BOOK OF QUINTE ESSENCE, tr. anon. ca. 1460.

> Actually, a treatise on wine-making.

A. ____ . THE BOOK OF QUINTE ESSENCE, ed. F. J. Furnivall. EETS OS 16. London, 1866.

284. THE EARLIEST ARITHMETICS IN ENGLISH, ed. Robert Steele. EETS ES 118. London, 1922.

285. Aristotle. THE SECRETE OF SECRETES, tr. Robert Copland. London, 1528.

> The miscellanea pertaining to kingship and health spuriously ascribed to Aristotle.

A. ____ . THREE PROSE VERSIONS OF THE SECRETA SECRETORUM, ed. Robert Steele. EETS ES 74. London, 1898.

286. Elyot, Sir Thomas. THE CASTEL OF HELTH. London, 1539.

> A lively discussion of medicine in general written for laymen; very popular, with at least fourteen editions

before the end of the century; see also 652–653.

A. _____. THE CASTEL OF HELTH, 1541, ed. S. A. Tannenbaum. New York: Scholars' Facsimiles, 1936.

287. Recorde, Robert. THE GROUNDE OF ARTES. London, 1542.

The standard textbook of arithmetic in England throughout
the century, with successive revised editions.

288. _____. THE URINAL OF PHYSICK. London, 1547.

A medical manual by the greatest writer of English
textbooks in the sixteenth century, reprinted in 1548,
1567, and 1599.

289. _____. THE PATHWAY TO KNOWLEDG. London, 1551.

A textbook of geometry, reprinted 1574 and 1602.

290. _____. THE CASTLE OF KNOWLEDGE. London, 1556.

A textbook of cosmography that mentions, but does not
follow, Copernicus; second ed., 1596.

a. Patterson, Louise D. "Recorde's Cosmography, 1556," ISIS,
42 (1951), 208-18.

291. Recorde, Robert. THE WHETSTONE OF WITTE. London, 1557.

A textbook of algebra, then in its infancy.

292. Boorde, Andrew. THE BREVIARY OF HEALTHE. London, 1552.

Other editions in 1557, 1575, 1587, 1598.

293. Proclus. THE DESCRIPCION OF THE SPHERE OR FRAME OF THE WORLDE,
tr. William Salesbury. London: Robert Wyer, 1550.

The standard textbook of astronomy in the schools.

294. Turner, William. A NEW HERBALL. London, 1551.

A second part, 1562; both parts reprinted, 1568.

295. Caius, John. A BOKE, OR COUNSEILL AGAINST THE DISEASE COM-
MONLY CALLED THE SWEATE. London, 1552.

A medical treatise by a famous physician who reformed
Gonville Hall in Cambridge to Gonville and Caius College.

A. _____ . A BOKE OR COUNSEILL AGAINST THE DISEASE
CALLED THE SWEATE, ed. Archibald Malloch. New York:
Scholars' Facsimiles, 1937.

296. Digges, Leonard. A PROGNOSTICATION OF RIGHT GOOD EFFECT.
London, 1555.

A perpetual almanac that remained popular throughout
the period, an earlier edition of 1553 no longer extant;
augmented by Thomas Digges (son of Leonard) in 1576
with an exposition of the Copernican astronomy, then oft-
reprinted.

297. Gesner, Conrad. THE TREASURE OF EUONYMUS, tr. Peter Morwyng.
London, 1559.

An authoritative treatise on distillation; another edition
in 1565.

298. Cuningham, William. THE COSMOGRAPHICAL GLASSE. London, 1559.

A handsome folio setting forth the discipline of cosmography, prepared by a young physician from Norwich.

299. Maplet, John. A GREENE FOREST, OR A NATURALL HISTORIE. London,
1567.

The lore accruing to stones, plants, and animals that
formed the natural history underlying Euphuism.

A. _____ . A GREENE FOREST, ed. W. H. Davies. London,
1930.

300. _____ . THE DIALL OF DESTINY. London, 1581.

An academic compilation of astrological lore arranged
according to the seven planets.

301. Baker, Humphrey. THE WELL-SPRYNG OF SCIENCES. London, 1568.

Perhaps the most popular of arithmetic textbooks.

302. Euclid. THE ELEMENTS OF GEOMETRIE, tr. Henry Billingsley. London,
1570.

A monumental edition of the basic text in geometry with
John Dee's important "Mathematical Praeface."

303. Dee, John. GENERAL AND RARE MEMORIALS PERTAYNING TO THE
PERFECT ARTE OF NAVIGATION. London, 1577.

A preliminary volume to a major work that never materialized.

a. Fell-Smith, Charlotte. JOHN DEE (1527-1608). London, 1909.

b. Deacon, Richard. JOHN DEE: SCIENTIST, GEOGRAPHER, ASTROLOGER AND SECRET AGENT TO ELIZABETH I. London, 1968.

304. Vicary, Thomas. THE ANATOMIE OF MANS BODY. London, 1577.

An extremely popular physiology which seems to have been first printed ca. 1548; kept in print into the seventeenth century.

A. _____ . THE ANATOMIE OF THE BODIE OF MAN, ed. F. J. Furnivall and Percy Furnivall. EETS ES 53. London, 1888.

305. Digges, Leonard, and Thomas Digges. AN ARITHMETICALL MILITARE TREATISE, NAMED STRATIOTICOS. London, 1579.

A manual of mathematics useful in soldiering; revised in 1590.

306. Bartholomaeus Anglicus. BATMAN UPPON BARTHOLOME HIS BOOKE DE PROPRIETATIBUS RERUM, tr. Stephen Batman. London, 1582.

The encyclopedia used by Shakespeare, compiled in the fourteenth century and therefore terribly old-fashioned.

a. Parish, Verna. "Batman's Additions from Elyot and Boorde to His English Edition of Bartholomaeus Anglicus," in STUDIES IN LANGUAGE, LITERATURE, AND CULTURE OF THE MIDDLE AGES AND LATER, ed. E. B. Atwood and A. A. Hill. University of Texas Press, 1969, pp. 337-46.

307. La Primaudaye, Pierre de. THE FRENCH ACADEMIE, tr. Thomas Bowes. London, 1586.

An influential French Protestant encyclopedia, enlarged and reprinted in English until well into the seventeenth century.

308. Bright, Timothy. A TREATISE OF MELANCHOLIE. London, 1586.

A medical manual for this common sickness.

A. Bright, Timothy. A TREATISE OF MELANCHOLIE, ed. Hardin Craig. Columbia University Press: Facsimile Text Society, 1940.

a. Keynes, Sir Geoffrey. DR. TIMOTHIE BRIGHT, 1550-1615: A SURVEY OF HIS LIFE WITH A BIBLIOGRAPHY OF HIS WRIT-INGS. London, 1962.

309. Blundeville, Thomas. EXERCISES. London, 1594.

Six treatises on cosmography, astronomy, and navigation, augmented to eight treatises in 1597, and oft-reprinted.

310. Gerard, John. THE HERBALL OR GENERALL HISTORIE OF PLANTES. London, 1597.

A massive folio with numerous woodcuts; greatly enlarged in 1633.

311. Vaughan, William. NATURALL AND ARTIFICIAL DIRECTIONS FOR HEALTH. London, 1600.

Many later editions.

312. Walkington, Thomas. THE OPTICK GLASSE OF HUMORS. London, 1607.

A learned examination of the microcosm; several later editions.

313. Topsell, Edward. THE HISTORIE OF FOURE-FOOTED BEASTES. London, 1607.

Essentially a translation of a natural history by Conrad Gesner.

314. _____. THE HISTORIE OF SERPENTS. London, 1608.

a. _____. THE ELIZABETHAN ZOO, ed. Muriel S. Byrne. London, 1926.

315. Bacon, Francis. THE WISDOME OF THE ANCIENTS, tr. Sir Arthur Gorges. London, 1619.

A rationalization of myths to produce symbolical interpretations, first published in Latin (1609); see also 482, 673.

316. _____. SYLVA SYLVARUM: OR, A NATURALL HISTORIE. London, 1626.

Essays in natural history. This volume includes THE NEW ATLANTIS, a fantasy that describes a college with the aim of subjecting nature to man's needs, in the tradition of More's UTOPIA and complementary to Bacon's ADVANCE-MENT OF LEARNING (673), unfinished; kept continuously in print throughout the seventeenth century.

A. _____. NEW ATLANTIS, ed. A. B. Gough. Oxford, 1915.

317. Burton, Robert. THE ANATOMY OF MELANCHOLY. Oxford, 1621.

A digressive journey through Jacobean psychology which
meanders interminably, dropping erudite quotations all
along the way; revised and augmented in 1624, 1628,
1632, 1638, and 1651; see also l.dd, l.ss.

A. _____. THE ANATOMY OF MELANCHOLY, ed. Floyd Dell
and Paul Jordan-Smith. New York, 1929.

B. _____. THE ANATOMY OF MELANCHOLY, ed. Holbrook
Jackson. 3 vols. London: Everyman's, 1932.

C. _____. THE ANATOMY OF MELANCHOLY: A SELECTION,
ed. Lawrence Babb. Michigan State University Press, 1965.

i. Donovan, Dennis G. ELIZABETHAN BIBLIOGRAPHIES SUP-
PLEMENTS, X: SIR THOMAS BROWNE AND ROBERT BURTON.
London, 1968.

ii. _____. "Recent Studies in Burton and Walton," ELR, 1 (1971),
294-303.

a. Patrick, J. Max. "Robert Burton's Utopianism," PQ, 27 (1948),
345-58.

b. Babb, Lawrence. THE ELIZABETHAN MALADY: A STUDY OF
MELANCHOLIA IN ENGLISH LITERATURE FROM 1580 TO 1642.
Michigan State University Press, 1951.

c. Browne, Robert M. "Robert Burton and the New Cosmology,"
MLQ, 13 (1952), 131-48.

d. Mueller, William R. THE ANATOMY OF ROBERT BURTON'S
ENGLAND. University of California Press, 1952.

e. Babb, Lawrence. SANITY IN BEDLAM: A STUDY OF ROBERT
BURTON'S ANATOMY OF MELANCHOLY. Michigan State
University Press, 1959.

f. Simon, Jean R. ROBERT BURTON (1577-1640) ET L'ANATOMIE
DE LA MELANCHOLIE. Paris, 1964.

318. Wotton, Sir Henry. THE ELEMENTS OF ARCHITECTURE. London, 1624.

A clear and complete account of the noble art of architecture based on Vitruvius and Alberti.

319. Person, David. VARIETIES. London, 1635.

A retrospective seventeenth-century encyclopedia.

320. Swan, John. SPECULUM MUNDI. OR, A GLASSE REPRESENTING THE
FACE OF THE WORLD. Cambridge, 1635.

A late example of an encyclopedia in the hexaemeral
tradition.

321. Wilkins, John. THE DISCOVERY OF A WORLD IN THE MOONE. London, 1638.

An imaginative argument for life on the moon.

322. _____. MATHEMATICALL MAGICK. London, 1648.

Geometry for fun and profit; oft-reprinted.

323. Brugis, Thomas. THE MARROW OF PHYSICKE. London, 1640.

A conservative textbook of anatomy and medicine.

324. Digby, Sir Kenelm. TWO TREATISES. . .THE NATURE OF BODIES. . .
THE NATURE OF MANS SOULE. Paris, 1644.

The translation of scientific investigation into the realm
of metaphysics.

325. Ross, Alexander. THE PHILOSOPHICALL TOUCH-STONE. London, 1645.

A response to Digby's TWO TREATISES (324); see also
124, 466, 644.

326. Browne, Sir Thomas. PSEUDODOXIA EPIDEMICA: OR, ENQUIRIES INTO
VERY MANY RECEIVED TENETS, AND COMMONLY PRESUMED TRUTHS.
London, 1646.

An extensive compilation of popular beliefs with an account of their origin and a look at their veracity, which
shows how the time-honored authorities were being re-
viewed in the light of empiricism, oft-reprinted; see also
509-511

327. Hermes Trismegistus. THE DIVINE PYMANDER, tr. John Everard. London,
1650.

The sacred writing of the hermetists.

328. Agrippa, Heinrich Cornelius. THREE BOOKS OF OCCULT PHILOSOPHY, tr. John Freake. London, 1651.

> The most complete compendium of occult lore in Western Europe; first printed in Latin, 1531.

329. Lilly, William. CHRISTIAN ASTROLOGY. London, 1647.

> The most helpful exposition of astrology for the modern reader; see also 458-460.

330. Vaughan, Thomas. ANIMA MAGICA ABSCONDITA: OR, A DISCOURSE OF THE UNIVERSALL SPIRIT OF NATURE. London, 1650.

331. _____. MAGIA ADAMICA: OR, THE ANTIQUITIE OF MAGIC. London, 1650.

332. _____. LUMEN DE LUMINE: OR, A NEW MAGICALL LIGHT DIS-COVERED. London, 1651.

A. _____. THE WORKS OF THOMAS VAUGHAN: EUGENIUS PHILALETHES, ed. A. E. Waite. London, 1919.

333. Ross, Alexander. ARCANA MICROCOSMI: OR, THE HID SECRETS OF MANS BODY DISCLOSED. London, 1651.

> Against Browne's PSEUDODOXIA EPIDEMICA (326) and others; augmented 1652; see also 124, 325, 466, 644.

334. Culpeper, Nicholas. THE ENGLISH PHYSITIAN: OR, AN ASTROLOGO-PHYSICAL DISCOURSE OF THE VULGAR HERBS OF THIS NATION. London, 1652.

> A pharmacopoeia that was successively enlarged and kept in print until far into the nineteenth century.

335. Boyle, Robert. NEW EXPERIMENTS PHYSICO-MECHANICALL, TOUCH-ING THE SPRING OF THE AIR. Oxford, 1660.

> Reports from the new science.

A. Boyle, Robert. THE WORKS, ed. Thomas Birch. 6 vols. Hildesheim: 1965-66. Reprint of London, 1772, edition.

VI. EPHEMERAL AND POLEMICAL WRITINGS

VI. Ephemeral and Polemical Writings

As might be expected, ephemeral and polemical writings appeared in great variety and great quantity. In fact, they ran the complete gamut from the serious and even vituperative in religio-political debate through the realistic and grim in the literature of roguery to the delightful and merely frivolous in descriptions of pastimes. They all share, however, a sense of immediacy, with the resultant vivacity of thought and language.

See also I.t, II.C, 4, 36-39, 54, 78, 79, 140, 249, 254, 257, 258-260, 515, VIII.d, 592, 632, 647, 714, 727, 733.

A. Collier, John P., ed. ILLUSTRATIONS OF EARLY ENGLISH POPULAR LITERATURE. 4 vols. London, 1863-64.

B. Hazlitt, W. C., ed. INEDITED TRACTS, ILLUSTRATING THE MANNERS, OPINIONS, AND OCCUPATIONS OF ENGLISHMEN DURING THE SIXTEENTH AND SEVENTEENTH CENTURIES. London: Roxburghe Club, 1868.

C. Collier, John P., ed. MISCELLANEOUS TRACTS. 5 vols. London, 1870.

> Especially important for the Nashe-Harvey quarrel.

D. Saintsbury, George, ed. ELIZABETHAN & JACOBEAN PAMPHLETS. London, 1892.

E. Pollard, A. F., ed. TUDOR TRACTS 1532-1588. Westminster: English Garner, 1903.

F. Firth, C. H., ed. STUART TRACTS 1603-1693. Westminster: English Garner, 1903.

G. Wilson, J. Dover, ed. LIFE IN SHAKESPEARE'S ENGLAND. Cambridge University Press, 1926.

H. Harrison, George B., ed. ENGLAND IN SHAKESPEARE'S DAY. London, 1928.

I. Judges, Arthur V., ed. THE ELIZABETHAN UNDERWORLD. London, 1930. 2nd ed. London, 1965.

   Contains pamphlets on roguery.

J. Chambers, R. W. and Marjorie Daunt, eds. A BOOK OF LONDON ENGLISH, 1384-1425. Oxford, 1931.

K. Gebert, Clara, ed. AN ANTHOLOGY OF ELIZABETHAN DEDICATIONS & PREFACES. University of Pennsylvania Press, 1933.

L. Haller, William, ed. TRACTS ON LIBERTY IN THE PURITAN REVOLUTION, 1638-47. 3 vols. Columbia University Press, 1934.

M. Dunham, William H., and Stanley Pargellis, eds. COMPLAINT AND REFORM IN ENGLAND, 1436-1714. Oxford University Press, 1938.

N. Woodhouse, A. S. P., ed. PURITANISM AND LIBERTY: BEING THE ARMY DEBATES (1647-9) FROM THE CLARKE MANUSCRIPTS. London, 1938.

O. Haller, William, and Godfrey Davies, eds. THE LEVELLER TRACTS. Columbia University Press, 1944.

P. Orwell, George, and Reginald Reynolds, eds. BRITISH PAM-PHLETEERS. 2 vols. London, 1948-51.

   Pamphlets from the sixteenth century to the French Revolution.

Q. Hibbard, George R., ed. THREE ELIZABETHAN PAMPHLETS. London, 1951.

   Contains Greene, THIRD PART OF CONY-CATCHING; Nashe, PIERCE PENNILESS; Dekker, WONDERFUL YEAR.

R. Peterson, Spiro, ed. THE COUNTERFEIT LADY UNVEILED AND OTHER CRIMINAL FICTION OF SEVENTEENTH CEN-TURY ENGLAND. New York: Anchor, 1961.

S. Trinterud, Leonard J., ed. ELIZABETHAN PURITANISM.

Oxford University Press, 1971.

Sixteen Puritanical tracts.

a. Routh, Harold V. "London and the Development of Popular Literature," in THE CAMBRIDGE HISTORY OF ENGLISH LITERATURE, ed. A. W. Ward and A. R. Waller. 15 vols. Cambridge University Press, 1907-27. IV,316-65.

b. Chandler, Frank W. THE LITERATURE OF ROGUERY. 2 vols. Boston, 1907.

c. Aydelotte, Frank. ELIZABETHAN ROGUES AND VAGABONDS. Oxford, 1913.

d. Bosanquet, Eustace F. ENGLISH PRINTED ALMANACKS AND PROGNOSTICATIONS: A BIBLIOGRAPHICAL HISTORY TO THE YEAR 1600. London, 1917. CORRIGENDA AND ADDENDA. London, 1928. NOTES ON FURTHER ADDENDA. London, 1937.

e. _____. "English Seventeenth-Century Almanacks," LIBRARY, 10 (1929-30), 361-97.

f. Wilson, Frank P. THE PLAGUE IN SHAKESPEARE'S LONDON. Oxford, 1927.

g. Head, Richard, and Francis Kirkman. THE ENGLISH ROGUE. New York, 1928.

h. Shaaber, Matthias A. SOME FORERUNNERS OF THE NEWSPAPER IN ENGLAND, 1476-1622. University of Pennsylvania Press, 1929.

i. Camden, Carroll, Jr. "Elizabethan Almanacs and Prognostications," LIBRARY, 4th series, 12 (1931-32), 83-108, 194-207.

j. Morison, Stanley. THE ENGLISH NEWSPAPER. . .BETWEEN 1622 & THE PRESENT DAY. Cambridge, 1932.

k. Wright, Louis B. MIDDLE-CLASS CULTURE IN ELIZABETHAN ENGLAND. University of North Carolina Press, 1935.

l. Haller, William. THE RISE OF PURITANISM. Columbia University Press, 1938.

m. Wilson, Frank P. "Some English Mock-Prognostications,"

LIBRARY, 4th series, 19 (1938-39), 6-43.

n. Lievsay, John L. "Newgate Penitents: Further Aspects of Elizabethan Pamphlet Sensationalism," HLQ, 7 (1943-44), 47-69.

o. White, Helen C. SOCIAL CRITICISM IN POPULAR RELIGIOUS LITERATURE OF THE SIXTEENTH CENTURY. New York, 1944.

p. Bush, Douglas. "Popular Literature and Translations," and "Political Thought," in ENGLISH LITERATURE IN THE EARLIER SEVENTEENTH CENTURY 1600-1660. Oxford, 1945, pp. 39-75 and 232-57, respectively.

q. Southern, A. C. ELIZABETHAN RECUSANT PROSE, 1559-1582. A HISTORICAL AND CRITICAL ACCOUNT OF THE BOOKS OF THE CATHOLIC REFUGEES. London, 1950.

r. Wright, Herbert G. "Some Sixteenth and Seventeenth Century Writers on the Plague," E&S, 6 (1953), 41-55.

s. Holden, William P. ANTI-PURITAN SATIRE 1572-1642. Yale University Press, 1954.

t. Ferguson, Arthur B. "Renaissance Realism in the 'Commonwealth' Literature of Early Tudor England," JHI, 16 (1955), 287-305.

u. Peter, John. COMPLAINT AND SATIRE IN EARLY ENGLISH LITERATURE. Oxford, 1956.

v. Marsh, T. N. "Humor and Invective in Early Tudor Polemic Prose," RICE INSTITUTE PAMPHLETS, 44 (1957-58), 79-89.

w. Sasek, Lawrence A. THE LITERARY TEMPER OF THE ENGLISH PURITANS. Louisiana State University Press, 1961.

x. Frank, Joseph. THE BEGINNINGS OF THE ENGLISH NEWS-PAPER, 1620-1660. Harvard University Press, 1961.

y. New, John F. H. ANGLICAN AND PURITAN: THE BASIS OF THEIR OPPOSITION, 1558-1640. Stanford University Press, 1964.

z. Clancy, Thomas H. PAPIST PAMPHLETEERS: THE ALLEN-PERSONS PARTY AND THE POLITICAL THOUGHT OF THE COUNTER-REFORMATION IN ENGLAND, 1572-1615. Loyola

University Press, 1964.

336. Fortescue, Sir John. THE GOVERNANCE OF ENGLAND. ca. 1470.

A forward-looking plan for the government of England
by a constitutional lawyer who advocated limitation of
the monarchy; see also 356.

A. _____. THE GOVERNANCE OF ENGLAND, ed. Charles
Plummer. Oxford University Press, 1926.

a. Arrowood, Charles F. "Sir John Fortescue on the Education
of Rulers," SPECULUM, 10 (1935), 404-10.

337. Berners, Dame Juliana. THE BOKYS OF HAUKYNG AND HUNTYNG.
St. Albans, 1486.

An early manual from an unexpected source on various
sports; kept in print throughout the sixteenth century.

A. _____. THE BOOK OF ST. ALBANS, ed. Joseph Haslewood.
New York, 1966.

338. Fish, Simon. A SUPPLICACYON FOR THE BEGGERS. London, ca. 1529.

A harsh critique of the administration of England under
Henry VIII; another edition in 1546.

A. _____. A SUPPLICACYON FOR THE BEGGERS et al., ed.
F. J. Furnivall. EETS ES 13. London, 1871.

B. _____. A SUPPLICATION FOR THE BEGGARS, ed. Edward
Arber. Westminster: English Scholar's Library, 1895.

339. More, Sir Thomas. A DYALOGE OF SYR THOMAS MORE. . .WHERIN
BE TREATYD DYVERS MATERS, AS OF THE VENERACYON & WORSHYP
OF YMAGYS. London, 1529.

340. Tyndale, William. AN ANSWERE UNTO SIR T. MORES DIALOGE.
Antwerp(?), 1530.

See also 36-39, 767-769.

A. _____. AN ANSWER TO SIR THOMAS MORE'S DIALOGUE,
ed. Rev. Henry Walker. Cambridge University Press: Parker
Society, 1850.

341. More, Sir Thomas. THE CONFUTACYON OF TYNDALES ANSWERE.

London, 1532.

a. Campbell, William E. ERASMUS, TYNDALE, AND MORE. London, 1949.

b. Pineas, Rainer. "Thomas More's Use of the Dialogue Form as a Weapon of Religious Controversy," SRen, 7 (1960), 193-206.

c. _____. "More versus Tyndale: A Study of Controversial Technique," MLQ, 24 (1963), 144-50.

342. More, Sir Thomas. UTOPIA, tr. Ralph Robynson. London, 1551.

A spirited rendition of More's humanistic classic in political science, first published abroad in Latin in 1516; reprinted in 1556, 1597, 1624, and 1639; see also 141, 474-476.

A. _____. UTOPIA, ed. J. H. Lupton. Oxford, 1895.

Contains both the original Latin text (Louvain, 1516) and Robynson's English translation (London, 1551).

B. _____. UTOPIA, tr. Ralph Robynson, ed. Robert Steele. London: King's Classics, 1908.

C. _____. UTOPIA, tr. Ralph Robynson, ed. Right Rev. Mgr. Philip E. Hallett. London, 1937.

D. _____. THE ENGLISH WORKS. . .REPRODUCED IN FACSIMILE FROM WILLIAM RASTELL'S EDITION OF 1557, ed. W. E. Campbell. 2 vols. London, 1931.

E. _____. THE COMPLETE WORKS, ed. Louis Martz, R. S. Sylvester, E. L. Surtz, J. H. Hexter, et al. Yale University Press, in progress.

i. Gibson, R. W. ST. THOMAS MORE: A PRELIMINARY BIBLIOGRAPHY OF HIS WORKS AND OF MOREANA TO THE YEAR 1750. Yale University Press, 1961.

a. Adams, Robert P. "The Philosophic Unity of More's UTOPIA," SP, 38 (1941), 45-65.

b. Donner, Henry W. INTRODUCTION TO UTOPIA. Uppsala, 1945.

c. Binder, James. "More's UTOPIA in English: A Note on Translation," MLN, 62 (1947), 370-76.

d. Ames, Russell A. CITIZEN THOMAS MORE AND HIS UTOPIA. Princeton University Press, 1949.

e. Hexter, Jack H. MORE'S UTOPIA: THE BIOGRAPHY OF AN IDEA. Princeton University Press, 1952.

f. Duhamel, P. Albert. "Medievalism of More's UTOPIA," SP, 52 (1955), 99-126.

g. Surtz, Edward L. THE PRAISE OF PLEASURE: PHILOSOPHY, EDUCATION, AND COMMUNISM IN MORE'S UTOPIA. Harvard University Press, 1957.

h. Bevington, David M. "The Dialogue in UTOPIA: Two Sides to the Question," SP, 58 (1961), 496-509.

i. Elliott, Robert C. "The Shape of Utopia," ELH, 30 (1963), 317-34.

j. Heiserman, A. R. "Satire in the UTOPIA," PMLA, 78 (1963), 163-74.

k. Allen, Peter R. "UTOPIA and European Humanism: The Function of the Prefatory Letters and Verses," SRen, 10 (1963), 91-107.

l. Pineas, Rainer. "Thomas More's 'Utopia' and Protestant Polemics," RN, 17 (1964), 197-201.

m. Schoeck, Richard J. "Sir Thomas More, Humanist and Lawyer," UTQ, 34 (1964-65), 1-14.

n. Reynolds, E. E. THOMAS MORE AND ERASMUS. Fordham University Press, 1965.

o. Dorsch, T. S. "Sir Thomas More and Lucian: An Interpretation of UTOPIA," ARCHIV, 203 (1966-67), 345-63.

p. Sylvester, Richard S. "A Part of His Own: Thomas More's Personality in His Early Works," MOREANA, 15-16 (1967), 29-42.

q. _____. " 'Si Hythlodaeo Credimus': Vision and Revision in Thomas More's UTOPIA," SOUNDINGS, 51 (1968), 272-89.

r. Pineas, Rainer. THOMAS MORE AND TUDOR POLEMICS. Indiana University Press, 1968.

s. Johnson, Robbin S. MORE'S UTOPIA: IDEAL AND ILLUSION. Yale University Press, 1969.

343. Starkey, Thomas. AN EXHORTATION TO THE PEOPLE INSTRUCTYNGE THEYM TO UNITIE AND OBEDIENCE. London, ca. 1540.

A forthright critique of social evils and needed reform.

a. _____. ENGLAND IN THE REIGN OF KING HENRY THE EIGHTH: PART I. STARKEY'S LIFE AND LETTERS, ed. Sidney J. Herrtage. EETS ES 12, 32. London, 1878.

344. Bale, John. THE IMAGE OF BOTHE CHURCHES. London, ca. 1548.

An invidious comparison of the Catholic and Protestant churches, to the shame of Rome.

345. _____. THE APOLOGY OF JOHAN BALE AGAYNSTE A RANKE PAPYST. London, ca. 1550.

The papist as Antichrist.

A. _____. SELECT WORKS, ed. Rev. Henry Christmas. Cambridge University Press: Parker Society, 1849.

i. Davies, W. T. A BIBLIOGRAPHY OF JOHN BALE. Oxford, 1940.

a. Harris, Jesse W. JOHN BALE: A STUDY IN THE MINOR LITERATURE OF THE REFORMATION. University of Illinois Press, 1940.

b. Pineas, Rainer. "Some Polemical Techniques in the Nondramatic Works of John Bale," BHR, 24 (1962), 583-88.

c. _____. "John Bale's Nondramatic Works of Religious Controversy," SRen, 9 (1962), 218-33.

346. Cheke, Sir John. THE HURT OF SEDICION. London, 1549.

An establishment tract on law and order.

347. Ponet, John. A SHORTE TREATISE OF POLITIKE POWER. Strasbourg(?), 1556.

> Politics as played by the Bishop of Winchester, with the expected call for obedience to authority.

    a. Hudson, Winthrop S. JOHN PONET (1516?-1556), ADVOCATE OF LIMITED MONARCHY. University of Chicago Press, 1942.

348. Knox, John. THE FIRST BLAST OF THE TRUMPET AGAINST THE MONSTRUOUS REGIMENT OF WOMEN. Geneva, 1558.

> The ardent Calvinist at his fieriest; see also 153.

349. Aylmer, John. AN HARBOROWE FOR FAITHFULL AND TREWE SUBJECTS AGAYNST THE LATE BLOWNE BLASTE CONCERNING THE GOVERNMENT OF WEMEN. London, 1559.

> An answer to Knox (previous item).

350. Machiavelli, Niccolo. THE ARTE OF WARRE, tr. Peter Whitehorne. 2 pts. London, 1560-62.

> Other editions in 1574 and 1588.

351. Jewel, John. AN APOLOGIE, OR AUNSWER IN DEFENCE OF THE CHURCH OF ENGLAND, tr. Ann, Lady Bacon. London, 1562.

> The original Latin text published the same year; both texts kept in print throughout the sixteenth and seventeenth centuries; see also 58.

    A. _____. AN APOLOGY OF THE CHURCH OF ENGLAND, tr. Lady Ann Bacon, ed. J. E. Booty. Cornell University Press: Folger Documents, 1963.

352. _____. A DEFENCE OF THE APOLOGIE OF THE CHURCHE OF ENGLANDE. London, 1567.

> Other editions in 1570, 1571.

    a. Booty, John E. JOHN JEWEL AS APOLOGIST OF THE CHURCH OF ENGLAND. London, 1963.

353. Bullein, William. A DIALOGUE. . .AGAINST THE FEVER PESTILENCE. London, 1564.

> A popular medication of social comment composed of realistic observations, anecdotes, and satire; reprinted in 1573 and 1578.

A. _____ . A DIALOGUE AGAINST THE FEVER PESTILENCE, ed. M. W. and A. H. Bullen. EETS ES 52. London, 1888.

a. Mitchell, William S. "William Bullein, Elizabethan Physician and Author," MEDICAL HISTORY, 3 (1959), 187-200.

354. Awdeley, John. THE FRATERNITIE OF VACABONDES. London, 1565.

A realistic record of the language of London streets and forerunner of the "character;" another edition in 1575; see VI.1.

A. _____ . THE FRATERNITYE OF VACABONDES et al., ed. Edward Viles and F. J. Furnivall. EETS ES 9. London, 1869.

355. Harman, Thomas. A CAVEAT OR WARENING FOR COMMEN CURSETORS. London, 1567.

A blunt and disparaging look at the down-and-out; in VI.1.

A. Harman, Thomas. A CAVEAT. . .FOR COMMEN CURSETORS et al., ed. Edward Viles and F. J. Furnivall. EETS ES 9. London, 1869.

356. Fortescue, Sir John. A LEARNED COMMENDATION OF THE POLITIQUE LAWES OF ENGLAND, tr. Richard Mulcaster. London, 1567.

A translation of Fortescue's legal classic, DE LAUDIBUS LEGUM ANGLIAE; other editions in 1583, 1599, and 1616; see also 336.

357. Rastell, John. THE EXPOSICIONS OF THE TERMES OF THE LAWES WITH DIVERS RULES. London, 1567.

A legal vade mecum kept continuously in print until well into the seventeenth century.

358. Cartwright, Thomas. A SECOND ADMONITION TO THE PARLIAMENT. London, 1572.

An important document in the development of Presbyterianism in Britain, by a troublesome controversialist at Cambridge.

A. _____ . CARTWRIGHTIANA, ed. Albert Peel and L. H. Carlson. London: Elizabethan Nonconformist Texts, 1951.

a. Pearson, Andrew F. S. THOMAS CARTWRIGHT AND ELIZABETHAN PURITANISM, 1535-1603. Cambridge, 1925.

b. McGinn, Donald J. THE ADMONITION CONTROVERSY. Rutgers University Press, 1949.

359. Hake, Edward. A TOUCHSTONE FOR THIS TIME PRESENT. London, 1574.

A moralistic expose of contemporary abuses, especially in the Church.

360. Scot, Reginald. A PERFITE PLATFORME OF A HOPPE GARDEN. London, 1574.

Other editions in 1576 and 1578.

361. _____. THE DISCOVERIE OF WITCHCRAFT. London, 1584.

A rational and humane mind in defense of those persecuted as witches.

A. _____. THE DISCOVERIE OF WITCHCRAFT, ed. Rev. Montague Summers. London, 1930.

B. _____. THE DISCOVERIE OF WITCHCRAFT, ed. Hugh R. Williamson. University of Southern Illinois Press, 1965.

362. Turberville, George. THE BOOKE OF FAULCONRIE OR HAUKING. London, 1575.

A dignified account of an aristocratic sport; enlarged in 1611.

363. _____. THE NOBLE ARTE OF VENERIE OR HUNTING. London, 1575.

Revised in 1611.

A. Turberville, George. BOOKE OF HUNTING, 1576. Oxford: Tudor and Stuart Library, 1908.

364. Gascoigne, George. THE SPOYLE OF ANTWERPE. London, 1577(?).

A soldier's eye-witness account of the sacking of Antwerp by the Spaniards in November 1576; see also 544.

365. Northbrooke, John. A TREATISE WHEREIN DICING, DANCING, VAIN PLAYS OR INTERLUDES, WITH OTHER IDLE PASTIMES. . .ARE REPROVED. London, ca. 1577.

The earliest of the Puritanical protests against the theatre; reprinted 1579. See also 56-57.

A.   . A TREATISE AGAINST DICING, DANCING, PLAYS, AND INTERLUDES, ed. John P. Collier. London: Shakespeare Society, 1843.

366. Gosson, Stephen. THE SCHOOLE OF ABUSE. London, 1579.

A moralistic attack on the arts, especially the theatre, which produced a storm of controversy and the flotsam of Sidney's DEFENCE OF POESIE (636); another edition in 1587; in IX.E (selections); see also 632.

A.   . THE SCHOOLE OF ABUSE, ed. Edward Arber. London: English Reprints, 1869.

a. Ringler, William A., Jr. "The First Phase of the Elizabethan Attack on the Stage, 1558-1579," HLQ, 5 (1941-42), 391-418.

b. Kinney, Arthur F. "Stephen Gosson's Art of Argumentation in THE SCHOOLE OF ABUSE," SEL, 7 (1967), 41-54.

367. Gosson, Stephen. THE EPHEMERIDES OF PHIALO. London, 1579.

Continuation of SCHOOLE OF ABUSE; another edition in 1586.

368.   . PLAYES CONFUTED IN FIVE ACTIONS. London, 1582.

369.   . QUIPPES FOR UPSTART NEWFANGLED GENTLEWOMEN. London, 1595.

An invective against the foibles of women, especially foreign fashions.

A.   . PLEASANT QUIPPES FOR UPSTART NEWFANGLED GENTLEWOMEN, ed. Edwin J. Howard. Oxford, Ohio, 1942.

a. Ringler, William A., Jr. STEPHEN GOSSON: A BIOGRAPHICAL AND CRITICAL STUDY. Princeton University Press, 1942.

370. Munday, Anthony. THE ENGLISH ROMAYNE LYFE. London, 1582.

Munday's first-hand account of life at the English College in Rome; see also 552.

A.   . THE ENGLISH ROMAYNE LYFE, ed. G. B. Harrison. London: Bodley Head Quartos, 1925.

371. Smith, Sir Thomas. DE REPUBLICA ANGLORUM. THE MANER OF

GOVERNEMENT. . .OF ENGLAND. London, 1583.

> A description of the constitution and government of England; kept in print until the end of the seventeenth century.

A. _____. DE REPUBLICA ANGLORUM; A DISCOURSE ON THE COMMONWEALTH OF ENGLAND, ed. Leonard Alston and F. W. Maitland. Cambridge University Press, 1906.

a. Dewar, Mary. SIR THOMAS SMITH: A TUDOR INTELLECTUAL IN OFFICE. London, 1964.

372. Stubbes, Philip. THE ANATOMIE OF ABUSES. London, 1583.

> Among much social commentary, a continuation of the controversy about the immorality of stage plays; see also 73.

A. _____. ANATOMY OF THE ABUSES IN ENGLAND, ed. F. J. Furnivall. 3 vols. London: New Shakespeare Society, 1877-82.

a. Pearson, Terry P. "The Composition and Development of Philip Stubbes's 'Anatomie of Abuses'," MLR, 56 (1961), 321-32.

373. Harvey, Richard. AN ASTROLOGICALL DISCOURSE UPON THE GREAT AND NOTABLE CONJUNCTION OF THE TWO SUPERIOUR PLANETS, SATURNE & JUPITER. London, 1583.

374. Lodge, Thomas. AN ALARUM AGAINST USURERS. London, 1584.

> An expose of chicanery; see also 574-578.

375. Whetstone, George. A MIROUR FOR MAGESTRATES OF CYTIES. . . . A TOUCHSTONE FOR THE TIME. London, 1584.

> Continues castigation of the theatre, as well as other urban evils.

376. _____. THE ENGLISH MYRROR. London, 1586.

377. Rankins, William. THE MIRROUR OF MONSTERS. London, 1587.

> The vices of play-going again exposed.

378. Gifford, George. A DISCOURSE OF THE SUBTILL PRACTISES OF DEVILLES. London, 1587.

379. _____. A DIALOGUE CONCERNING WITCHES AND WITCHCRAFTES.

London, 1593.

A sober look at a sordid subject in the heyday of witch-hunting.

A. _____. A DIALOGUE CONCERNING WITCHES AND WITCH-CRAFTES, ed. Beatrice White. Oxford: Shakespeare Association, 1931.

380. Mascall, Leonard. THE FIRST BOOKE OF CATTELL. London, 1587.

An oft-reprinted manual of animal husbandry.

381. Udall, John. THE STATE OF THE CHURCH OF ENGLANDE. London, 1588.

382. Lyly, John. PAPPE WITH AN HATCHET. London, 1589.

A professional writer hired to argue for the bishops in the Martin-Marprelate controversy; attributed to Lyly; see also 550-551.

A. Pierce, William, ed. THE MARPRELATE TRACTS, 1588, 1589. London, 1911.

a. Wilson, J. Dover. "The Marprelate Controversy," in THE CAMBRIDGE HISTORY OF ENGLISH LITERATURE, ed. A. W. Ward and A. R. Waller. 15 vols. Cambridge University Press, 1907-27. III, 374-98.

b. Pierce, William. AN HISTORICAL INTRODUCTION TO THE MARPRELATE TRACTS. London, 1908.

c. McGinn, Donald J. JOHN PENRY AND THE MARPRELATE CONTROVERSY. Rutgers University Press, 1966.

d. Anselment, Raymond A. "Rhetoric and the Dramatic Satire of Martin Marprelate," SEL, 10 (1970), 103-19.

383. Nashe, Thomas. AN ALMOND FOR A PARRAT. London, ca. 1589.

A reply to Martin Marprelate; attributed to Nashe; see also 382, 391-396, 584.

384. _____. THE ANATOMIE OF ABSURDITIE. London, 1589.

Witty potshots at every ridiculous thing in sight, including Philip Stubbes.

A. _____. THE ANATOMIE OF ABSURDITIE, ed. John P. Collier. London, 1866.

a. Allen, Don C. "The Anatomie of Absurditie: A Study in Literary Apprenticeship," SP, 32 (1935), 170-76.

385. Cooper, Thomas. AN ADMONITION TO THE PEOPLE OF ENGLAND. London, 1589.

An anti-Martin-Marprelate tract by the learned lexicographer and Bishop of Lincoln.

386. Harvey, Richard. PLAINE PERCEVALL THE PEACE-MAKER OF ENGLAND. SWEETLY INDEVORING. . .TO BOTCH UP A RECONCILIATION BETWEEN MAR-TON AND MAR-TOTHER. London, 1590.

A Harvey contribution to the Martin Marprelate controversy which incidentally attacks Greene and Nashe, and therefore drew their fire on the Harvey brothers.

A. _____. PLAINE PERCEVALL, THE PEACE-MAKER OF ENGLAND. London, 1860.

387. Harvey, Gabriel. FOURE LETTERS, AND CERTAINE SONNETS. London, 1592.

An attack on those who had attacked Martin Marprelate, and especially Greene.

A. _____. FOURE LETTERS AND CERTAINE SONNETS, ed. G. B. Harrison. London: Bodley Head Quartos, 1922.

388. _____. PIERCES SUPEREROGATION, OR A NEW PRAYSE OF THE OLD ASSE. London, 1593.

Harvey's bombastic (though ineffectual) reply to Nashe's STRANGE NEWS (392), which had rendered him apoplectic with rage.

389. _____. A NEW LETTER OF NOTABLE CONTENTS. London, 1593.

Harvey's continuation of the quarrel with Nashe, with anger as the insuperable dominant passion.

390. _____. THE TRIMMING OF THOMAS NASHE GENTLEMAN. London, 1597.

An impotent retort, showing Harvey to be exhausted from uncontrolled emotion.

A. _____. THE WORKS, ed. Rev. A. B. Grosart. 3 vols. London, 1884–85.

    a. Sanders, Chauncey. ROBERT GREENE AND THE HARVEYS. Indiana University Press, 1931.

    b. Wilson, Harold S. "The Humanism of Gabriel Harvey," in J. Q. ADAMS MEMORIAL STUDIES, ed. J. G. McManaway et al. Washington, D.C., 1948, pp. 707–21.

391. Nashe, Thomas. PIERCE PENILESSE, HIS SUPPLICATION TO THE DIVELL. London, 1592.

    An energetic satire against the current ways of practising the seven deadly sins, tempered by an apologia for the theatre; the opening diatribe in Nashe's quarrel with Richard and Gabriel Harvey (see 386–390); in VI.Q; see also 383–384, 584.

    a. McGinn, Donald J. "The Allegory of the 'Beare' and the 'Foxe' in Nashe's PIERCE PENILESSE," PMLA, 61 (1946), 431–53.

    b. Snortum, Niel K. "The Title of Nash's PIERCE PENNILESS," MLN, 72 (1957), 170–73.

    c. Petti, Anthony G. "Political Satire in PIERCE PENILESSE HIS SUPLICATION TO THE DIVELL," NEOPHIL, 45 (1961), 139–50.

392. Nashe, Thomas. STRANGE NEWES, OF THE INTERCEPTING CERTAINE LETTERS AND A CONVOY OF VERSES. London, 1592.

    A continuation of the Nashe-Harvey quarrel that defends Greene and gives Nashe an opportunity to demolish Gabriel Harvey by means of incomparable invective.

393. _____. HAVE WITH YOU TO SAFFRON-WALDEN. London, 1596.

    The final blast in the Nashe-Harvey quarrel, with Nashe at the top of his prose form.

    a. Perkins, David. "Issues and Motivations in the Nashe-Harvey Quarrel," PQ, 39 (1960), 224–33.

394. Nashe, Thomas. CHRISTS TEARES OVER JERUSALEM. London, 1593.

    A thick-tongued warning to London that God punishes the wicked, in the tradition of Jeremiah's lamentations; reprinted 1594 and 1613.

395. _____. THE TERRORS OF THE NIGHT. London, 1594.

> A university wit's view of the occult with an almost
> Lucretian disparagement of superstition.

a. Harlow, C. G. "Thomas Nashe, Robert Cotton the Antiquary,
and THE TERRORS OF THE NIGHT," RES, 12 (1961), 7-23.

396. Nashe, Thomas. LENTEN STUFFE. London, 1599.

> A mock-encomium of red herring in the witty tradition
> of Erasmus' PRAISE OF FOLLY.

A. _____. WORKS, ed. R. B. McKerrow, rev. F. P. Wilson.
5 vols. Oxford, 1958.

B. _____. SELECTED WRITINGS, ed. Stanley Wells. Harvard
University Press, 1965.

i. Tannenbaum, Samuel A. THOMAS NASHE, A CONCISE
BIBLIOGRAPHY. New York, 1941.

ii. Johnson, Robert C. ELIZABETHAN BIBLIOGRAPHIES SUPPLE-
MENTS, V: THOMAS NASHE et al. London, 1968.

a. McGinn, Donald J. "Nashe's Share in the Marprelate Controversy," PMLA, 59 (1944), 952-84.

b. Summersgill, Travis L. "The Influence of the Marprelate Controversy upon the Style of Thomas Nashe," SP, 48 (1951), 145-
60.

c. Miller, Edwin H. "The relationship of Robert Greene and
Thomas Nashe (1588-1592)," PQ, 33 (1954), 353-67.

d. Hibbard, George R. THOMAS NASHE: A CRITICAL INTRO-
DUCTION. Harvard University Press, 1962.

e. Harlow, C. G. "Nashe's Visit to the Isle of Wight and His
Publications of 1592-4," RES, 14 (1963), 225-42.

397. Greene, Robert. A NOTABLE DISCOVERY OF COOSENAGE. London,
1591. THE SECOND PART OF CONNY-CATCHING. London, 1591.
THE THIRD AND LAST PART OF CONNY-CATCHING. London, 1592.

> A vital expose from a wry observer of London life; in
> VI.I; the LAST PART in VI.Q; see also 390.a, 396.c,
> 478-480, 561-573.

A. _____ . A NOTABLE DISCOVERY OF COOSNAGE, 1591. THE SECOND PART OF CONNY-CATCHING, 1592, ed. G. B. Harrison. London: Bodley Head Quartos, 1923.

B. _____ . THE THIRDE & LAST PART OF CONNY-CATCHING . . . . .A DISPUTATION BETWEENE A HEE CONNY-CATCHER AND A SHEE CONNY-CATCHER, ed. G. B. Harrison. London: Bodley Head Quartos, 1923.

a. Johnson, Francis R. "The Editions of Robert Greene's Three Parts of 'Conny-Catching': A Bibliographical Analysis," LIBRARY, 5th series, 9 (1954), 17-24.

398. Anon. THE DEFENCE OF CONNY CATCHING. London, 1592.

Purportedly a refutation of Greene's cony-catching pamphlets, though probably the work of Greene himself, at least in part; in 400.A.

a. Shapiro, I. A. "An Unsuspected Earlier Edition of the Defence of Conny-Catching," LIBRARY, 5th series, 18 (1963), 88-112.

399. Greene, Robert. A DISPUTATION, BETWEEN A HEE CONNY-CATCHER, AND A SHEE CONNY-CATCHER. London, 1592.

A cynical dialogue between Laurence and Nan, two rascals who reveal the philosophy and methodology of roguery; other editions in 1615, 1617, 1621, and 1637. See VI.I, 397.B.

400. _____ . THE BLACKE BOOKES MESSENGER. London, 1592.

A full case-history of a particular criminal named Ned Browne; in VI.I.

A. _____ . THE BLACKE BOOKES MESSENGER, 1592, AND THE DEFENCE OF CONNY-CATCHING, 1592, ed. G. B. Harrison. London: Bodley Head Quartos, 1924.

401. _____ . A QUIP FOR AN UPSTART COURTIER. London, 1592.

A disparagement of new manners in preference for the old; three editions in 1592, and others in 1606, 1620, 1622, and 1635.

a. Miller, Edwin H. "Deletions in Robert Greene's A QUIP FOR AN UPSTART COURTIER (1592)," HLQ, 15 (1951-52), 277-82.

b. _____ . "The Sources of Robert Greene's 'A Quip for an Upstart Courtier' (1592)," N&Q, 198 (1953), 148-52, 187-91.

c. _____ . "The Editions of Robert Greene's A QUIP FOR AN UPSTART COURTIER (1592)," SB, 6 (1954), 107-16.

d. Parker, R. B. "Alterations in the First Edition of Greene's A QUIP FOR AN UPSTART COURTIER (1592)," HLQ, 23 (1959-60), 181-86.

e. Shapiro, I. A. "The First Edition of Greene's QUIP FOR AN UPSTART COURTIER," SB, 14 (1961), 212-18.

402. Rich, Barnabe. GREENES NEWES BOTH FROM HEAVEN AND HELL. London, 1593.

An amusing report from the wandering ghost of Robert Greene; see also 487, 554-556.

A. _____ . GREENES NEWES BOTH FROM HEAVEN AND HELL . . .AND GREENES FUNERALLES, ed. R. B. McKerrow. Stratford-upon-Avon, 1911.

403. Chettle, Henry. KIND-HARTS DREAME. London, 1593.

A topical narrative, interesting largely as an apologia for Greene, which touches upon Shakespeare; see also 592.

A. _____ . KIND-HARTES DREAME 1592, and William Kemp, NINE DAIES WONDER 1600, ed. G. B. Harrison. London: Bodley Head Quartos, 1923.

a. Jenkins, Harold. THE LIFE AND WORK OF HENRY CHETTLE. London, 1934.

b. Thomas, Sidney. "The Printing of GREENES GROATSWORTH OF WITTE and KIND-HARTS DREAME," SB, 19 (1966), 196-97.

404. Markham, Gervase. A DISCOURSE OF HORSMANSHIPPE. London, 1593.

Reprinted 1595, 1597, 1599, 1606; see also 607.

405. Hooker, Richard. OF THE LAWES OF ECCLESIASTICALL POLITIE. 8 pts. London, 1594-1662.

The semi-official apologia for the Anglican establishment, which uses the argument of a divinely-sanctioned natural order to steer a safe course between the Scylla of papistry and the Charybdis of Calvinism. The history of this book is extremely complicated, and the last part was not published until 1662.

A. _____. THE WORKS, ed. Rev. John Keble. 7th ed. 3 vols. Oxford University Press, 1888.

B. _____. HOOKER'S ECCLESIASTICAL POLITY, BOOK VIII, ed. Raymond A. Houk. Columbia University Press, 1931.

i. Hill, W. Speed. RICHARD HOOKER: A DESCRIPTIVE BIBLI-OGRAPHY OF THE EARLY EDITIONS: 1593-1724. Case Western Reserve University Press, 1970.

a. Walton, Izaak. LIFE OF DR. RICHARD HOOKER. London, 1665.

See also 515.A.

b. Foakes-Jackson, Rev. F. J. "Of the Laws of Ecclesiastical Polity," in THE CAMBRIDGE HISTORY OF ENGLISH LITERA-TURE, ed. A. W. Ward and A. R. Waller. 15 vols. Cambridge University Press, 1907-27. III, 399-417.

c. Boughner, Daniel C. "Notes on Hooker's Prose," RES, 15 (1939), 194-200.

d. Sisson, Charles J. THE JUDICIOUS MARRIAGE OF MR. HOOKER AND THE BIRTH OF THE LAWS OF ECCLESIASTICAL POLITY. Cambridge University Press, 1940.

e. Davies, Ebenezer T. THE POLITICAL IDEAS OF RICHARD HOOKER. London, 1946.

f. Shirley, F. John. RICHARD HOOKER AND CONTEMPORARY POLITICAL IDEAS. London, 1949.

g. Munz, Peter. THE PLACE OF HOOKER IN THE HISTORY OF THOUGHT. London, 1952.

h. Stueber, Sister M. Stephanie. "The Balanced Diction of Hooker's POLITY," PMLA, 71 (1956), 808-26.

i. McGrade, Arthur S. "The Coherence of Hooker's Polity: The Books on Power," JHI, 24 (1963), 163-82.

j. Marshall, John S. HOOKER AND THE ANGLICAN TRADITION: AN HISTORICAL AND THEOLOGICAL STUDY OF HOOKER'S

'ECCLESIASTICAL POLITY'. University of the South Press, 1963.

k. Grislis, Egil. "Richard Hooker's Image of Man," RenP 1963 (Durham, North Carolina), 1964, pp. 73-84.

l. Hill, W. Speed. "The Authority of Hooker's Style," SP, 67 (1970), 328-38.

m. _____. "Doctrine and Polity in Hooker's LAWS," ELR, 2 (1972), 173-93.

406. Harington, Sir John. THE METAMORPHOSIS OF AJAX. London, 1596.

A mock encomium of the water-closet in a Rabelaisian vein, by a godson of Queen Elizabeth.

A. _____. A NEW DISCOURSE OF A STALE SUBJECT, CALLED THE METAMORPHOSIS OF AJAX, ed. Elizabeth S. Donno. London, 1962.

407. James I. DAEMONOLOGIE. Edinburgh, 1597.

A learned critique of witchcraft; reprinted in 1603.

A. _____. DAEMONOLOGIE et al., ed. G. B. Harrison. London: Bodley Head Quartos, 1924.

408. Stow, John. A SURVAY OF LONDON. London, 1598.

A minute description of Elizabeth's metropolis; augmented by Stow in 1603, by Anthony Munday in 1618, and by Henry Dyson in 1633.

A. _____. A SURVEY OF LONDON, ed. Ernest Rhys. London: Everyman's, 1906.

B. _____. A SURVEY OF LONDON, ed. Charles L. Kingsford. 2 vols. Oxford, 1908.

The text of 1603 with an account of Stow and a bibliography.

409. Floyd, Thomas. THE PICTURE OF A PERFIT COMMON WEALTH. London, 1600.

An academic study of the relation between rulers and subjects.

410. Gentillet, Innocent. A DISCOURSE UPON THE MEANES OF WEL GOV-

ERNING. . .AGAINST NICHOLAS MACCHIAVELL, tr. Simon Patericke. London, 1602.

Another edition in 1608.

411. Breton, Nicholas. A MERRIE DIALOGUE BETWIXT THE TAKER AND MIS-TAKER. London, 1603.

A sentimental reprise of Greene's underworld characters; reprinted in 1635 as A MAD WORLD MY MASTERS; see also 494-495, 602-606.

412. _____. A DIALOGUE FULL OF PITHE AND PLEASURE: BETWENE THREE PHYLOSOPHERS. London, 1603.

a. Monroe, Nellie E. NICHOLAS BRETON AS A PAMPHLETEER. Philadelphia, 1929.

413. Crosse, Henry. VERTUES COMMON-WEALTH. London, 1603.

A moralistic view of contemporary manners; another edition in 1605.

A. Crosse, Henry. VERTUES COMMON-WEALTH, ed. Rev. A. B. Grosart. Manchester, 1878.

414. Dekker, Thomas. THE WONDERFULL YEARE. London, 1603.

A graphic description of London in the grip of the plague; in VI.Q.

A. _____. THE WONDERFULL YEARE 1603, ed. G. B. Harrison. London: Bodley Head Quartos, 1924.

B. _____. THE PLAGUE PAMPHLETS, ed. F. P. Wilson. Ox-ford, 1925.

a. Camden, Carroll, Jr. "The Wonderful Yeere," in STUDIES IN HONOR OF DEWITT T. STARNES, ed. T. P. Harrison et al. University of Texas Press, 1967, pp. 163-79.

415. Dekker, Thomas. NEWES FROM HELL, BROUGHT BY THE DIVELLS CAR-RIER. London, 1606.

An attempt to cash in on Nashe's popularity (see 391); revised in 1607 as A KNIGHTS CONJURING.

416. _____. THE SEVEN DEADLY SINNES OF LONDON. London, 1606.

Dekker again following the footsteps of Nashe; see
384, 394.

A. _____. THE SEVEN DEADLY SINS OF LONDON, ed. Edward
Arber. London: English Scholar's Library, 1879.

B. _____. THE SEVEN DEADLY SINNES OF LONDON, ed. H.
F. B. Brett-Smith. Oxford: Percy Reprints, 1922.

417. _____. THE BELMAN OF LONDON. London, 1608.

An expose of London's low-life; see also 421.

418. _____. LANTHORNE AND CANDLE-LIGHT. London, 1608.

Another fond look at skulduggery, continuing THE BELMAN
OF LONDON and romanticizing roguery; other editions in
1609, 1616, 1620, and 1630; in VI.I.

419. _____. THE GULS HORNE-BOOKE. London, 1609.

An ironic courtesy book for young gallants in London
with the intent of satirizing them.

A. _____. THE GULL'S HORNBOOK, ed. R. B. McKerrow.
London, 1904.

B. _____. THE NON-DRAMATIC WORKS, ed. Rev. A. B. Grosart.
5 vols. London: Huth Library, 1884-86.

C. _____. THE WONDERFUL YEAR. . .AND SELECTED WRIT-
INGS, ed. E. D. Pendry. London, 1967.

i. Tannenbaum, Samuel A. THOMAS DEKKER, A CONCISE
BIBLIOGRAPHY. New York, 1939. SUPPLEMENT. New
York, 1945.

ii. Donovan, Dennis G. ELIZABETHAN BIBLIOGRAPHIES SUPPLE-
MENTS, II: THOMAS DEKKER et al. London, 1967.

a. Gregg, Kate L. THOMAS DEKKER: A STUDY IN ECONOMIC
AND SOCIAL BACKGROUNDS. University of Washington Press,
1924.

b. Shaw, Philip. "The Position of Thomas Dekker in Jacobean
Prison Literature," PMLA, 62 (1947), 366-91.

c. Jones-Davies, Marie Therese. UN PEINTRE DE LA VIE LON-
DONIENNE, THOMAS DEKKER. Paris, 1958.

d. Price, George R. THOMAS DEKKER. New York: Twayne,
1969.

420. Rowlands, Samuel. GREENES GHOST HAUNTING CONIE-CATCHERS.
London, 1602.

Anecdotes from London lowlife in the tradition of Robert
Greene.

421. _____. MARTIN MARK-ALL, BEADLE OF BRIDEWELL. London, 1610.

A response to Dekker's BELMAN OF LONDON (417).

A. _____. THE COMPLETE WORKS, ed. Sir Edmund Gosse.
3 vols. Glasgow: Hunterian Club, 1880.

422. Bodin, Jean. THE SIX BOOKES OF A COMMONWEALE, tr. Richard
Knolles. London, 1606.

A classic from the famous French jurist.

A. _____. THE SIX BOOKES OF A COMMONWEALE, tr. Richard
Knolles, ed. Kenneth D. McRae. Harvard University Press, 1962.

a. Franklin, Julian H. JEAN BODIN AND THE SIXTEENTH-
CENTURY REVOLUTION IN THE METHODOLOGY OF LAW
AND HISTORY. Columbia University Press, 1963.

423. Perkins, William. A DISCOURSE OF THE DAMNED ART OF WITCH-
CRAFT. Cambridge, 1608.

424. Donne, John. PSEUDO-MARTYR. London, 1610.

An argument against the pseudo-martyrdom of the Catholic
who refuses to take the oath of allegiance; see also 89-
91.

425. _____. IGNATIUS HIS CONCLAVE. London, 1611.

A witty and erudite satire against the Jesuits which sets
Loyola in debate as the champion of Hell; first published
in Latin the same year.

A. _____. IGNATIUS HIS CONCLAVE, ed. C. M. Coffin.
Columbia University Press, 1941.

B. _____. IGNATIUS HIS CONCLAVE: AN EDITION OF THE LATIN AND ENGLISH TEXTS, ed. T. S. Healy, S.J. Oxford, 1969.

426. Heywood, Thomas. AN APOLOGY FOR ACTORS. London, 1612.

The last (and best) word in the controversy over the immorality of the stage begun by Gosson (see 366); in IX.E (selections).

A. _____. AN APOLOGY FOR ACTORS, ed. R. H. Perkinson. New York: Scholars' Facsimiles, 1941.

i. Tannenbaum, Samuel A. THOMAS HEYWOOD: A CONCISE BIBLIOGRAPHY. New York, 1939.

ii. Donovan, Dennis G. ELIZABETHAN BIBLIOGRAPHIES SUPPLE-MENTS, II: THOMAS HEYWOOD et al. London, 1967.

a. Boas, Frederick S. THOMAS HEYWOOD. London, 1950.

427. Selden, John. TITLES OF HONOR. London, 1614.

A comprehensive examination of the source of govern-mental power throughout the ages by one of the most learned men of the time; another edition in 1631.

428. Cotta, John. THE TRIALL OF WITCH-CRAFT SHEWING THE TRUE METH-ODE OF THE DISCOVERY. London, 1616.

A learned examination of the belief in witchcraft and of the methods for identifying witches.

429. Mynshul, Geffray. CERTAINE CHARACTERS AND ESSAYES OF PRISON AND PRISONERS. London, 1618.

The efforts of a young lawyer to pass the time while in prison for debt.

430. Mun, Thomas. A DISCOURSE OF TRADE UNTO THE EAST INDIES. London, 1621.

431. Reynolds, John. THE TRIUMPHS OF GODS REVENEGE, AGAINST THE CRYING AND EXECRABLE SINNE OF MURTHER. 3 vols. London, 1621-24.

Middle-class morality titillating itself with an enormous collection of bloody stories; kept in print throughout the seventeenth century, and after 1657 illustrated with cop-per plates.

432. Taylor, John (the Water-poet). THE UNNATUREL FATHER: OR A CRUEL MURTHER COMMITTED BY ONE JOHN ROWSE. London, 1621.

> See also 258-260.

433. _____. A FAMOUS FIGHT AT SEA. London, 1627.

434. _____. THE GREAT EATER OF KENT, OR PART OF THE EXPLOITS OF NICHOLAS WOOD. London, 1630.

435. _____. THE CARRIERS COSMOGRAPHIE. OR A BRIEFE RELATION OF THE INNES IN AND NEERE LONDON. London, 1637.

> A. _____. WORKS, ed. Charles Hindley. 2 vols. London, 1872.

436. Powell, Thomas. TOM OF ALL TRADES. OR THE PLAINE PATH-WAY TO PREFERMENT. London, 1631.

> A wise look at the young man's opportunities among the professions.

> A. _____. TOM OF ALL TRADES, ed. F. J. Furnivall. London: New Shakespeare Society, 1876.

437. Barclay, John. THE MIRROUR OF MINDES, tr. Thomas May. London, 1631.

> Observations on the character of the major European nations; first published in Latin, 1614; reprinted in English, 1633.

438. Lupton, Donald. LONDON AND THE COUNTREY CARBONADOED AND QUARTRED INTO SEVERALL CHARACTERS. London, 1632.

> A delightful account of the sights in and around London.

439. Prynne, William. HISTRIO-MASTIX: THE PLAYERS SCOURGE. London, 1633.

> Disapproval of the theatre revived in a scathing attack.

440. Machiavelli, Niccolo. PRINCE et al., tr. Edward Dacres. London, 1640.

> The first English rendering of THE PRINCE, though Machiavelli was already widely known in England.

> A. _____. PRINCE, tr. Edward Dacres, ed. Henry Cust. London:

Tudor Translations, 1905.

B. _____ . THE PRINCE, tr. Edward Dacres, ed. W. E. C. Baynes. London, 1929.

a. Raab, Felix. THE ENGLISH FACE OF MACHIAVELLI: A CHANGING INTERPRETATION, 1500-1700. London, 1964.

441. Howell, James. DENDROLOGIA. DODONA'S GROVE. London, 1640.

An international report on the times in the form of easily penetrated allegory; second part in 1650; see also 270, 470.

442. Hartlib, Samuel. A DESCRIPTION OF THE FAMOUS KINGDOME OF MACARIA. London, 1641.

In the tradition of More's UTOPIA.

A. _____ . A DESCRIPTION OF THE FAMOUS KINGDOME OF MACARIA, in Charles Webster, ed. SAMUEL HARTLIB AND THE ADVANCEMENT OF LEARNING. Cambridge University Press, 1970.

443. Milton, John. OF REFORMATION TOUCHING CHURCH-DISCIPLINE IN ENGLAND. London, 1641.

Milton's entry into controversy, of course on behalf of the Puritan cause.

a. Duvall, Robert F. "Time, Place, Persons: The Background for Milton's OF REFORMATION," SEL, 7 (1967), 107-18.

444. Milton, John. OF PRELATICALL EPISCOPACY. London, 1641.

An argument against the conservative assumption that episcopal authority could be traced back to the Apostles.

445. _____ . ANIMADVERSIONS UPON THE REMONSTRANTS DEFENCE AGAINST SMECTYMNUUS. London, 1641.

An angry and heavy-handed attack against the conservative position expounded by Bishop Joseph Hall.

446. _____ . THE REASON OF CHURCH-GOVERNMENT URG'D AGAINST PRELATY. London, 1642.

The strongest and fullest argument for presbyterianism rather than episcopacy in church organization, with an important passage of autobiographical revelation; see also l.ss.

   a. Kranidas, Thomas. " 'Decorum' and the Style of Milton's Antiprelatical Tracts," SP, 62 (1965), 176-87.

447. Milton, John. AN APOLOGY AGAINST A PAMPHLET CALL'D A MODEST CONFUTATION OF THE ANIMADVERSIONS UPON THE REMONSTRANT AGAINST SMECTYMNUUS. London, 1642.

   Largely a defence against the personal attacks by Bishop Joseph Hall and his son.

448. _____. THE DOCTRINE AND DISCIPLINE OF DIVORCE. London, 1643.

   A remarkably modern document in favor of divorce that argues on humane and reasonable grounds, though none-theless with overtones of special pleading.

   a. Svendsen, Kester. "Science and Structure in Milton's DOCTRINE OF DIVORCE," PMLA, 67 (1952), 435-45.

449. Milton, John. AREOPAGITICA. A SPEECH FOR THE LIBERTY OF UNLICENC'D PRINTING. London, 1644.

   The enduring plea for freedom of thought, and specifically for freedom of the press, written with erudition and passion in the form of a classical oration.

   a. Kendall, Willmoore. "How to Read Milton's AREOPAGITICA," JOURNAL OF POLITICS, 22 (1960), 439-73.

   b. Evans, John X. "Imagery as Argument in Milton's AREOPAGITICA," TSLL, 8 (1966), 189-205.

   c. Wittreich, Joseph A., Jr. "Milton's AREOPAGITICA: Its Isocratic and Ironic Contexts," MiltonS, 4 (1972), 101-15.

450. Milton, John. TETRACHORDON. London, 1645.

   An examination of those "four places" in Scripture which support an argument in favor of divorce.

451. _____. COLASTERION. London, 1645.

   A methodical refutation of his opponents on the divorce issue, which is not nearly so exciting as the positive arguments for divorce.

452. _____. THE TENURE OF KINGS AND MAGISTRATES. London, 1649.

A rational argument that, because men are created free, their submission to a ruler is a voluntary contract which may be terminated; specifically referring, of course, to the execution of Charles I.

a. Hughes, Merritt Y. "Milton's Treatment of Reformation History in THE TENURE OF KINGS AND MAGISTRATES," in Richard F. Jones et al., THE SEVENTEENTH CENTURY: STUDIES IN THE HISTORY OF ENGLISH THOUGHT AND LITERATURE FROM BACON TO POPE. Stanford University Press, 1951, pp. 247-63.

b. Shawcross, John T. "Milton's 'Tenure of Kings and Magistrates': Date of Composition, Editions, and Issues," PBSA, 60 (1966), 1-8.

453. Milton, John. EIKONOKLASTES. London, 1649.

A painstaking refutation of the EIKON BASILIKE ("the portrait of the king"), a fabricated autobiography of Charles I distributed by the royalists as propaganda for their cause; see also 462.

A. _____. PROSE SELECTIONS, ed. Merritt Y. Hughes. New York, 1947.

B. _____. COMPLETE PROSE WORKS, ed. Don M. Wolfe et al. 5 vols. Yale University Press, 1953-71.

C. _____. THE PROSE, ed. J. Max Patrick. Garden City, New York: Anchor, 1967.

a. Thompson, Elbert N. S. "Milton's Prose Style," PQ, 14 (1935), 1-15.

b. Wolfe, Don M. MILTON IN THE PURITAN REVOLUTION. London, 1941. Revised, 1963.

c. Barker, Arthur E. MILTON AND THE PURITAN DILEMMA, 1641-1660. University of Toronto Press, 1942.

d. Kranidas, Thomas. THE FIERCE EQUATION: A STUDY OF MILTON'S DECORUM. The Hague, 1965.

e. Hamilton, K. G. "The Sturcture of Milton's Prose," in LANGUAGE AND STYLE IN MILTON, ed. Ronald D. Emma and John T. Shawcross, New York, 1967, pp. 304-32.

f. Major, John M. "Milton's View of Rhetoric," SP, 64 (1967),
685-711.

g. Shawcross, John T. and Michael Lieb, eds. ACHIEVEMENTS
OF THE LEFT HAND: ESSAYS ON MILTON'S PROSE WORKS.
University of Massachusetts Press, 1973.

454. Goodwin, John. ANTI-CAVALIERISME. London, 1642.

An argument in favor of the Civil War by a popular
republican preacher.

455. _____. THEOMAXIA. London, 1644.

Sermons in the rebels' cause, strongly advocating civil
and religious freedom.

456. Williams, Roger. THE BLOUDY TENENT, OF PERSECUTION, FOR CAUSE
OF CONSCIENCE. London, 1644.

A vigorous argument for religious freedom and the separa-
tion of church and state, by the founder of Rhode Island.

A. _____. COMPLETE WRITINGS, ed. Perry Miller. 7 vols.
New York, 1963.

457. Cary, Lucius, Viscount Falkland. OF THE INFALLIBILITIE OF THE CHURCH
OF ROME. Oxford, 1645.

A poignant statement by a heroic royalist.

a. Weber, Kurt. LUCIUS CARY, SECOND VISCOUNT FALKLAND.
Columbia University Press, 1940.

458. Lilly, William. THE STARRY MESSENGER; OR, AN INTERPRETATION OF
THAT STRANGE APPARITION OF THREE SUNS SEENE IN LONDON, 19.
NOVEMB. 1644. London, 1645.

459. _____. A COLLECTION OF ANCIENT AND MODERNE PROPHESIES
CONCERNING THESE PRESENT TIMES. London, 1645.

460. _____. MONARCHY OR NO MONARCHY IN ENGLAND. London,
1651.

An astrologer in the service of the parliamentary forces;
see also 329.

461. Edwards, Thomas. GANGRAENA. London, 1646.
A virulent and outrageous attack on any who deviated

from strict puritanism; followed immediately by a host of
rebuttals and two sequels.

462. Charles I. EIKON BASILIKE. THE POURTRAICTURE OF HIS SACRED
MAJESTIE. London, 1648.

A spurious autobiography of the martyred king fabricated
probably by John Gauden to discredit the anti-royalists.

A. _____. EIKON BASILIKE, ed. Philip A. Knachel. Cornell
University Press: Folger Documents, 1966.

463. Hobbes, Thomas. HUMANE NATURE. London, 1650.

Written in 1640, and already espousing the Hobbesian
doctrine of politics based upon psychology; another
edition in 1651.

464. _____. LEVIATHAN. OR, THE MATTER, FORME, & POWER OF A
COMMON-WEALTH, ECCLESIASTICALL AND CIVILL. London, 1651.

A classic in political science which with iron-clad logic
proposes a society based on the premise that life is nasty,
brutish, and short.

A. _____. LEVIATHAN, ed. A. R. Waller. Cambridge University Press, 1904.

B. _____. LEVIATHAN, ed. A. D. Lindsay. London: Everyman's,
1914.

C. _____. LEVIATHAN, ed. Michael Oakeshott. Oxford, 1947.

a. Collingwood, Robin G. THE NEW LEVIATHAN. Oxford, 1942.

b. Engel, S. Morris. "Hobbes's 'Table of Absurdities'," PhR, 70
(1961), 533-43.

c. Mintz, Samuel I. THE HUNTING OF LEVIATHAN. Cambridge University Press, 1962.

d. Hood, Francis C. THE DIVINE POLITICS OF THOMAS HOBBES:
AN INTERPRETATION OF LEVIATHAN. Oxford, 1964.

e. Steadman, John M. "LEVIATHAN and Renaissance Etymology,"
JHI, 28 (1967), 575-76.

f. McNeilly, Frederick S. THE ANATOMY OF LEVIATHAN.
    London, 1968.

g. Gauthier, David P. THE LOGIC OF LEVIATHAN: THE MORAL
    AND POLITICAL THEORY OF THOMAS HOBBES. Oxford, 1969.

465. Hobbes, Thomas. OF LIBERTIE AND NECESSITIE. London, 1654.

    Another controversial document confounding politics,
    religion, and philosophy.

A. _____. OF LIBERTY AND NECESSITY, ed. Baron Cay von
    Brockdorff. Kiel, 1938.

B. _____. THE ENGLISH WORKS, ed. Sir William Molesworth.
    11 vols. London, 1839-45.

i. Macdonald, Hugh, and Mary Hargreaves. THOMAS HOBBES:
    A BIBLIOGRAPHY. London, 1952.

a. Sorley, W. R. "Hobbes and Contemporary Philosophy," in
    THE CAMBRIDGE HISTORY OF ENGLISH LITERATURE, ed.
    A. W. Ward and A. R. Waller. 15 vols. Cambridge Uni-
    versity Press, 1907-27. VII,276-303.

466. Ross, Alexander. LEVIATHAN DRAWN OUT WITH A HOOK. London,
    1653.

    Against Hobbes; see also 644.

467. Harrington, James. THE COMMONWEALTH OF OCEANA. London,
    1656.

    A fantasy which by intention is a critique of Hobbes.

A. _____. OCEANA, ed. S. B. Liljegren. Heidelberg, 1924.

468. _____. POLITICAL DISCOURSES. London, 1660.

    The political theories of a learned and intelligent re-
    publican.

a. Russell-Smith, Hugh F. HARRINGTON AND HIS OCEANA.
    Cambridge University Press, 1914.

b. Blitzer, Charles. AN IMMORTAL COMMONWEALTH: THE
    POLITICAL THOUGHT OF JAMES HARRINGTON. Yale Uni-
    versity Press, 1960.

469. Whitlock, Richard. ZOOTOMIA, OR OBSERVATIONS ON THE PRESENT MANNERS OF THE ENGLISH. London, 1654.

470. Howell, James. LONDINOPOLIS. London, 1657.

    A pleasant and complete tour of London and Westminster; see also 270, 441.

VII. ESSAYS

VII. Essays

The essay is a personal statement about a limited topic. As a distinct genre in England it began in 1597 when Francis Bacon published a slim volume modelled on the essays of Montaigne. Before that time, however, various authors had recorded their ruminations on personal experience in a form which precursed the essay.

Early in the seventeenth century a specialized sort of essay, the "character," came into vogue. This is a witty and often facetious sketch of a person representing a type or group rather than an individual.

See also entries 31, 74, 91, 164, 324, 353, 354, 429, 462, 463-65, 709, 712, 714, 725, 730, 747, 754, 762.

A. Murphy, Gwendolen, ed. A CABINET OF CHARACTERS. London, 1925.

B. Withington, Robert, ed. ESSAYS AND CHARACTERS: MONTAIGNE TO GOLDSMITH. New York, 1933.

i. Murphy, Gwendolen. A BIBLIOGRAPHY OF ENGLISH CHARACTER-BOOKS 1608-1700. Oxford University Press, 1925.

a. MacDonald, Wilbert L. BEGINNINGS OF THE ENGLISH ESSAY. University of Toronto Press, 1914.

b. Walker, Hugh. THE ENGLISH ESSAY AND ESSAYISTS. London, 1915.

c. Thompson, Elbert N. S. STYLE OF THE ENGLISH ESSAY. University of Iowa Press, 1925.

d. _____. THE SEVENTEENTH-CENTURY ENGLISH ESSAY. University of Iowa Press, 1926.

e. Bush, Douglas. "Essays and Characters," in ENGLISH LITERA-
TURE IN THE EARLIER SEVENTEENTH CENTURY 1600-1660.
Oxford, 1945, pp. 181-208.

f. Clausen, Wendell. "The Beginnings of English Character-Writ-
ing in the Early Seventeenth Century," PQ, 25 (1946), 32-45.

g. Boyce, Benjamin. THE THEOPHRASTAN CHARACTER IN EN-
GLAND TO 1642. Harvard University Press, 1947.

h. _____. THE POLEMIC CHARACTER 1640-1661. University
of Nebraska Press, 1955.

471. Hilton, Walter. OF ANGEL'S SONG ca. 1380.

A first-hand account of mystical ecstasy; in I.P; see
also 18.

A. _____. MINOR WORKS, tr. D. Jones. London, 1929.

472. Julian of Norwich. REVELATIONS OF DIVINE LOVE. ca. 1390.

An autobiographical account of sixteen visitations re-
counted upon sober reflection.

A. _____. REVELATIONS OF DIVINE LOVE, ed. Sister A. M.
Reynolds. London, 1957.

B. _____. REVELATION OF DIVINE LOVE, ed. Grace Warreck.
London, 1952.

a. Chambers, P. F. JULIANA OF NORWICH: AN INTRODUC-
TORY APPRECIATION AND AN INTERPRETATIVE ANTHOLOGY.
London, 1955.

b. Wilson, R. M. "Three Middle English Mystics," E&S, 9 (1956),
87-112.

Richard Rolle, Julian of Norwich, Margery Kempe.

c. Molinari, Paul. JULIAN OF NORWICH. London, 1958.

d. Stone, Robert K. MIDDLE ENGLISH PROSE STYLE: MARGERY
KEMPE AND JULIAN OF NORWICH. The Hague, 1970.

473. Kempe, Margery. A TREATISE OF CONTEMPLATION. ca. 1440.

An autobiographical statement by a far from reticent

mystic who believed in possession; printed by Wynken de
Worde in 1501; see also 472.b, 472.d.

A. _____. THE BOOK OF MARGERY KEMPE, ed. Sanford B.
Meech and Hope E. Allen. EETS OS 212. London, 1940.

B. _____. THE BOOK OF MARGERY KEMPE, tr. W. Butler-
Bowdon. Oxford: World's Classics, 1936.

a. Cholmeley, Katharine. MARGERY KEMPE, GENIUS AND
MYSTIC. London, 1947.

b. Collis, Louise. MEMOIRS OF A MEDIEVAL WOMAN: THE
LIFE AND TIMES OF MARGERY KEMPE. New York, 1964.

474. More, Sir Thomas. THE APOLOGYE OF SYR THOMAS MORE. London,
1533.

More's apologia pro vita sua in a mellow mood; see also
339-342.

A. _____. THE APOLOGYE OF SYR THOMAS MORE, KNYGHT,
ed. Arthur I. Taft. EETS OS 180. London, 1930.

475. _____. A DIALOGE OF COMFORT AGAINST TRIBULACION. London,
1553.

A devotional exercise written in 1534-35 while in prison
awaiting execution.

A. _____. A DIALOGUE OF COMFORT, ed. Monica Stevens.
London, 1951.

B. _____. A DIALOGUE OF COMFORT AGAINST TRIBULATION,
ed. Leland Miles. Indiana University Press, 1965.

a. Miles, Leland. "The DIALOGUE OF COMFORT and More's
Execution: Some Comments on Literary Purpose," MLR, 61
(1966), 556-60.

b. _____. "The Literary Artistry of Thomas More: The DIALOGUE
OF COMFORT," SEL, 6 (1966), 7-33.

c. Martz, Louis L. "The Design of More's DIALOGUE OF COM-
FORT," MOREANA, 15-16 (1967), 331-46.

476. More, Sir Thomas. THE WORKES OF SIR THOMAS MORE. . .WRYTTEN

BY HIM IN THE ENGLYSH TONGE, ed. William Rastell. London, 1557.

A. _____. SELECTIONS FROM HIS ENGLISH WORKS, ed. P. S. and H. M. Allen. Oxford, 1924.

B. _____. THE ENGLISH WORKS, ed. W. E. Campbell and A. W. Reed. 2 vols. London, 1927-31.

a. Marc'hadour, Germain. "More's English Works: Towards a Census and an Anatomy," MOREANA, 13 (1967), 69-78.

477. Heron, Haly. THE KAYES OF COUNSAILE. London, 1579.

A. _____. THE KAYES OF COUNSAILE: A NEW DISCOURSE OF MORALL PHILOSOPHIE, ed. Virgil B. Heltzel. Liverpool, 1954.

a. Heltzel, Virgil B. "Haly Heron: Elizabethan Essayist and Euphuist," HLQ, 16 (1952-53), 1-21.

478. Greene, Robert. GREENES GROATSWORTH OF WITTE, BOUGHT WITH A MILLION OF REPENTANCE. London, 1592.

A grim personal statement that hovers between fiction and deathbed confession; other editions in 1596, 1617, 1621, 1629, 1637; see also 397-401, 403.b, 561-573.

479. _____. THE REPENTANCE OF ROBERT GREENE. London, 1592.

The final confession of Greene written more in despair than repentance.

A. _____. GROATS-WORTH OF WITTE. . .AND THE REPENTANCE OF ROBERT GREENE, ed. G. B. Harrison. London: Bodley Head Quartos, 1923.

a. Jenkins, Harold. "On the Authenticity of Greene's GROATS-WORTH OF WIT and THE REPENTANCE OF ROBERT GREENE," RES, 11 (1935), 28-41.

480. Greene, Robert. GREENES VISION. London, 1592.

A dream-allegory featuring Chaucer and Gower, purportedly composed on Greene's deathbed.

481. Ashley, Robert. OF HONOUR [1596], ed. Virgil B. Heltzel. Huntington Library, 1947.

Printed from manuscript.

a. Heltzel, Virgil B. "Robert Ashley: Elizabethan Man of Letters," HLQ, 10 (1946-47), 349-63.

482. Bacon, Francis. ESSAYES. London, 1597.

A sharp and well-informed mind reflecting upon man and his multitudinous experiences. The first edition contained ten essays; augmented to thirty-eight in 1612, and fifty-eight in 1625; see also l.s, l.ss, 172, 315-316.

A. _____. THE WORKS, ed. James Spedding, Robert L. Ellis, and Douglas D. Heath. 14 vols. London, 1857-74.

B. _____. ESSAYS, ed. Geoffrey Grigson. Oxford University Press: World's Classics, 1937.

The 1625 text, with the 1597 text in an appendix.

C. _____. SELECTED WRITINGS, ed. H. G. Dick. New York: Modern Library, 1955.

i. Gibson, R. W. FRANCIS BACON: A BIBLIOGRAPHY OF HIS WORKS AND OF BACONIANA TO THE YEAR 1750. Oxford, 1950.

a. Crane, R. S. "The Relation of Bacon's ESSAYS to His Programme for the Advancement of Learning," in SCHELLING ANNIVERSARY PAPERS. New York, 1923, pp. 87-105.

b. Zeitlin, Jacob. "The Development of Bacon's ESSAYS--with Special Reference to the Question of Montaigne's Influence Upon Them," JEGP, 27 (1928), 496-519.

c. Green, Adwin W. SIR FRANCIS BACON: HIS LIFE AND WORKS. Denver, 1952.

d. Patrick, J. Max. FRANCIS BACON. London, 1961.

e. Whittaker, Virgil K. FRANCIS BACON'S INTELLECTUAL MILIEU. Los Angeles: Clark Library, 1962.

f. Green, A. Wigfall. SIR FRANCIS BACON. New York: Twayne, 1966.

g. Wallace, Karl R. FRANCIS BACON ON THE NATURE OF

MAN. University of Illinois Press, 1967.

h. Rossi, Paolo. FRANCIS BACON: FROM MAGIC TO SCIENCE, tr. Sacha Rabinovitch. London, 1968.

i. Vickers, Brian. FRANCIS BACON AND RENAISSANCE PROSE. Cambridge University Press, 1968.

483. Cornwallis, Sir William. ESSAYES. 2 pts. London, 1600-01.

Reflective and moralistic exercises in Stoicism; augmented in 1610 and 1632.

A. _____. ESSAYES, ed. D. C. Allen. Johns Hopkins Press, 1946.

484. _____. ESSAYES, OR RATHER, ENCOMIONS, PRAYSES OF SADNESSE. London, 1616.

485. _____. ESSAYES OF CERTAINE PARADOXES. London, 1616.

486. Johnson, Robert. ESSAIES, OR RATHER IMPERFECT OFFERS. London, 1601.

Sixteen cool essays of interest to the gentleman; other editions in 1607, 1613, 1638; see also 235.

A. _____. ESSAIES, ed. Robert H. Bowers. Gainesville, Florida: Scholars' Facsimiles, 1955.

487. Rich, Barnabe. FAULTES FAULTS AND NOTHING ELSE BUT FAULTES. London, 1606.

A medley of satiric ruminations and a forerunner of the "character"; see also 402, 554-556.

A. _____. FAULTES FAULTS AND NOTHING ELSE BUT FAULTES, ed. Melvin H. Wolf. Gainesville, Florida: Scholars' Facsimiles; 1965.

488. Cuffe, Henry. THE DIFFERENCES OF THE AGES OF MANS LIFE. London, 1607.

A long and learned essay on the four ages of man set in a sweeping context of time and the deity; other editions in 1633 and 1640.

489. Hall, Joseph. CHARACTERS OF VERTUES AND VICES. London, 1608.

The first formal collection of that specialized essay, the
Theophrastan "character"; see also 80-83, 612.

A. _____. HEAVEN UPON EARTH AND CHARACTERS OF VER-
TUES AND VICES, ed. Rudolf Kirk. Rutgers University Press,
1948.

490. Tuvill, Daniel. ESSAIES POLITICKE, AND MORALL. London, 1608.

491. _____. ESSAYES, MORALL AND THEOLOGICALL. London, 1609.

A. _____. ESSAYS POLITIC AND MORAL, AND ESSAYS MORAL
AND THEOLOGICAL, ed. John L. Lievsay. University of Virginia Press: Folger Documents, 1971.

a. Lievsay, John L. "Tuvill's Advancement of Bacon's Learning,"
HLQ, 9 (1945-46), 11-31.

492. Donne, John. BIATHANATOS. London, 1644.

A casuistical defence of suicide, written ca. 1608; see
also 89-91, 424-425.

A. _____. BIATHANATOS, ed. J. W. Hebel. New York:
Facsimile Text Society, 1930.

493. Overbury, Sir Thomas. CHARACTERS, appended to A WIFE, NOW THE
WIDDOW OF SIR THOMAS OVERBURYE. London, 1614.

The most popular of the books of characters; oft-reprinted
and augmented.

A. _____. THE MISCELLANEOUS WORKS IN PROSE AND
VERSE, ed. Edward F. Rimbault. London, 1890.

B. _____. THE OVERBURIAN CHARACTERS, ed. W. J. Paylor.
Oxford: Percy Reprints, 1936.

C. _____. THE "CONCEITED NEWES" OF SIR THOMAS OVER-
BURY AND HIS FRIENDS, ed. James E. Savage. Gainesville,
Florida: Scholars' Facsimiles, 1968.

a. White, Beatrice. CAST OF RAVENS: THE STRANGE CASE
OF SIR THOMAS OVERBURY. London, 1965.

494. Breton, Nicholas. CHARACTERS UPON ESSAIES MORALL, AND DIVINE.
London, 1615.

Sixteen characters; see also 411–412, 602–606.

495. _____. FANTASTICKS. London, 1626.

Engaging essays on simple subjects, showing a delight in observation and unsophisticated musing.

496. Stephens, John. SATYRICAL ESSAYES, CHARACTERS AND OTHERS. London, 1615.

A collection of characters.

497. Drummond, William. A MIDNIGHTS TRANCE: WHERIN IS DISCOURSED OF DEATH, THE NATURE OF SOULES, AND ESTATE OF IMMORTALITIE. London, 1619.

A. _____. A MIDNIGHTS TRANCE, ed. Robert Ellrodt. Oxford: Luttrell Society, 1951.

498. Brathwaite, Richard. ESSAIES UPON THE FIVE SENSES. London, 1620.

An essay upon each of the five senses plus miscellanea, all with a moral cast; another edition in 1635; see also 625–626, 677–678.

499. _____. WHIMZIES: OR, A NEW CAST OF CHARACTERS. London, 1631.

500. Mason, William. A HANDFUL OF ESSAIES. OR IMPERFECT OFFERS. London, 1621.

501. Felltham, Owen. RESOLVES DIVINE, MORALL, POLITICALL. London, ca. 1623.

A hundred wide-ranging essays, augmented to two hundred in the second edition (1628); oft-reprinted.

A. _____. RESOLVES DIVINE, MORALL AND POLITICALL, ed. O. Smeaton. London: Temple Classics, 1904.

a. Robertson, Jean. "The Use Made of Owen Felltham's 'Resolves': A Study in Plagiarism," MLR, 39 (1944), 108-15.

b. McCrea, Hazlett. " 'New France and Various Composition': Development in the Form of Owen Felltham's RESOLVES," MP, 51 (1953-54), 93-101.

502. Earle, John. MICRO-COSMOGRAPHIE. London, 1628.

Perhaps the most interesting of the books of characters, especially for those drawn from college life; enlarged in 1629 and frequently thereafter to 1669.

A. _____ . MICRO-COSMOGRAPHIE, ed. Edward Arber. London: English Reprints, 1868.

B. _____ . THE AUTOGRAPH MANUSCRIPT OF MICROCOSMO-GRAPHIE. Leeds: Scolar Press Facsimile, 1966.

503. Saltonstall, Wye. PICTURAE LOQUENTES. OR PICTURES DRAWNE FORTH IN CHARACTERS. London, 1631.

A collection of characters; another edition in 1635.

A. _____ . PICTURAE LOQUENTES, ed. C. H. Wilkinson. Oxford: Luttrell Society, 1946.

504. Lenton, Francis. CHARACTERISMI OR LENTONS LEASURES. London, 1631.

A full set of forty-one characters.

505. Peacham, Henry. THE TRUTH OF OUR TIMES. REVEALED OUT OF ONE MANS EXPERIENCE BY WAY OF ESSAY. London, 1638.

A collection of essays.

A. _____ . THE TRUTH OF OUR TIMES, ed. R. R. Cawley. Columbia University Press: Facsimile Text Society, 1942.

506. _____ . THE ART OF LIVING IN LONDON. London, 1642.

A brief treatise giving advice on city life.

A. _____ . THE COMPLETE GENTLEMAN, THE TRUTH OF OUR TIMES, AND THE ART OF LIVING IN LONDON, ed. Virgil B. Heltzel. Cornell University Press: Folger Documents, 1962.

507. Fuller, Thomas. THE HOLY STATE. THE PROPHANE STATE. Cambridge, 1642.

A miscellany for moral instruction comprising characters, thumbnail biographies, and capsule essays; see also 102, 177-80, 273.

A. _____ . THE HOLY STATE AND THE PROFANE STATE, ed. Maximilian G. Walten. Columbia University Press, 1938.

a. Houghton, Walter E., Jr. THE FORMATION OF THOMAS FULLER'S HOLY AND PROFANE STATES. Harvard University Press, 1938.

508. Fuller, Thomas. GOOD THOUGHTS IN BAD TIMES, CONSISTING OF PERSONALL MEDITATIONS, SCRIPTURE OBSERVATIONS, HISTORICALL APPLICATIONS. Exeter, 1645. GOOD THOUGHTS IN WORSE TIMES. London, 1647. MIXT CONTEMPLATIONS IN BETTER TIMES. London, 1660.

Personal reflections of a moral man during the Civil War and the Commonwealth; at least ten editions of GOOD THOUGHTS IN BAD TIMES by 1680.

A. _____. THOUGHTS AND CONTEMPLATIONS: GOOD THOUGHTS IN BAD TIMES, MIXT CONTEMPLATIONS IN BETTER TIMES, ed. James O. Wood. London, 1964.

509. Browne, Sir Thomas. RELIGIO MEDICI. London, 1643.

"The religion of a doctor," an honest and searching self-examination by a Christian who stood at the bifurcation between religion and science; written 1634, with an unauthorized edition in 1642; see also I.dd, I.ss, 326.

A. _____. RELIGIO MEDICI, ed. Jean-Jacques Denonain. Cambridge University Press, 1955.

a. Huntley, Frank L. "The Publication and Immediate Reception of RELIGIO MEDICI," LIBRARY QUARTERLY, 25 (1955), 203-18.

510. Digby, Sir Kenelm. OBSERVATIONS UPON RELIGIO MEDICI. London, 1643.

Reprinted in 1644, and after 1659 regularly printed with Browne's RELIGIO MEDICI (509).

A. Browne, Sir Thomas. BROWNE'S RELIGIO MEDICI AND DIGBY'S OBSERVATIONS. Oxford University Press: Tudor and Stuart Library, 1909.

511. _____. HYDRIOTAPHIA, URNE-BURIALL, OR, A DISCOURSE OF THE SEPULCHRALL URNES LATELY FOUND IN NORFOLK. TOGETHER WITH THE GARDEN OF CYRUS, OR THE QUINCUNCIALL LOZENGE. London, 1658.

HYDRIOTAPHIA, a report on ancient cinerary urns recently found in Norfolk, which (like Milton's LYCIDAS) serves as a vehicle for the author's thoughts on time,

mutability, and death; GARDEN OF CYRUS, a discursive
treatise on the omnipresence in nature of the quincunx
(five points arranged as on a die), showing the reluctance
of even the most inquiring mind to forego the old science.

A. _____. THE WORKS, ed. Geoffrey Keynes. 6 vols. London, 1928-31. Rev. ed. 4 vols. University of Chicago Press, 1964.

B. _____. URNE BURIALL AND THE GARDEN OF CYRUS, ed. John Carter. Cambridge University Press, 1958.

C. _____. RELIGIO MEDICI, AND OTHER WORKS, ed. L. C. Martin. Oxford, 1964.

    Contains also HYDRIOTAPHIA and GARDEN OF CYRUS.

D. _____. THE PROSE, ed. Norman Endicott. New York University Press: Stuart Editions, 1968.

i. Keynes, Geoffrey L. A BIBLIOGRAPHY OF SIR THOMAS BROWNE. 2nd ed. Oxford, 1968.

ii. Donovan, Dennis G. ELIZABETHAN BIBLIOGRAPHIES SUPPLEMENTS, X: SIR THOMAS BROWNE AND ROBERT BURTON. London, 1968.

iii. _____. "Recent Studies in Browne," ELR, 2 (1972), 271-79.

a. Heideman, Margaret A. "HYDRIOTAPHIA and THE GARDEN OF CYRUS: A Paradox and a Cosmic Vision," UTQ, 19 (1949-50), 235-46.

b. Warren, Austin. "The Style of Sir Thomas Browne," KR, 13 (1951), 674-87.

c. Huntley, Frank L. "Sir Thomas Browne: The Relationship of URN BURIAL and THE GARDEN OF CYRUS," SP, 53 (1956), 204-19.

d. Moloney, Michael F. "Metre and CURSUS in Sir Thomas Browne's Prose," JEGP, 58 (1959), 60-67.

e. Bennett, Joan. SIR THOMAS BROWNE. Cambridge University Press, 1962.

f. Huntley, Frank L. SIR THOMAS BROWNE: A BIOGRAPHICAL
AND CRITICAL STUDY. University of Michigan Press, 1962.

g. Williamson, George. "The Purple of URN BURIAL," MP, 62
(1964-65), 110-17.

h. Mackenzie, Norman. "Sir Thomas Browne as a Man of Learning:
A Discussion of URN BURIAL and THE GARDEN OF CYRUS,"
ESA, 10 (1967), 67-86.

i. _____. "The Concept of Baroque and Its Relation to Sir Thomas
Browne's RELIGIO MEDICI and URN BURIAL," ESA, 10 (1967),
147-66.

j. Nathanson, Leonard. THE STRATEGY OF TRUTH: A STUDY
OF SIR THOMAS BROWNE. University of Chicago Press, 1967.

512. Howell, James. EPISTOLAE HO-ELIANAE. London, 1645.

A collection of worldly and witty essays in the form of
epistles, successively augmented to 1655, and six editions by 1688.

A. _____. FAMILIAR LETTERS OR EPISTOLAE HO-ELIANAE.
3 vols. London: Temple Classics, 1903.

B. _____. EPISTOLAE HO-ELIANAE, ed. Joseph Jacobs. London, 1892.

a. Vann, William H. NOTES ON THE WRITINGS OF JAMES
HOWELL. Baylor University Press, 1924.

513. Hall, John. HORAE VACIVAE, OR, ESSAYS. London, 1646.

514. Raleigh, Sir Walter. JUDICIOUS AND SELECT ESSAYES AND OBSERVA-
TIONS. London, 1650.

Of course, written much earlier; another edition in 1667;
see also 169, 229-230, 679.

515. Walton, Izaak. THE COMPLEAT ANGLER, OR THE CONTEMPLATIVE
MANS RECREATION. London, 1653.

A much loved statement of Walton's joie de vivre made
in a casual style with a wealth of anecdotal details;
often revised and augmented by Walton.

A. _____. THE COMPLEAT ANGLER, THE LIVES OF DONNE,

WOTTON, HOOKER, HERBERT, & SANDERSON, ed. Geoffrey L. Keynes. London, 1929.

B. _____. THE COMPLEAT ANGLER, ed. John Buchan. Oxford University Press: World's Classics, 1935.

C. _____. THE COMPLETE ANGLER. London: Everyman's, 1953.

i. Donovan, Dennis G. "Recent Studies in Burton and Walton," ELR, 1 (1971), 294-303.

a. Oliver, H. J. "Izaak Walton's Prose Style," RES, 21 (1945), 280-88.

b. _____. "The Composition and Revisions of THE COMPLEAT ANGLER," MLR, 42 (1947), 295-313.

c. Cooper, John R. THE ART OF THE COMPLEAT ANGLER. Duke University Press, 1968.

516. Culpeper, Sir Thomas. MORALL DISCOURSES AND ESSAYES UPON SEVERALL SELECT SUBJECTS. London, 1655.

517. Flecknoe, Richard. ENIGMATICALL CHARACTERS. London, 1658.

A large collection of characters from the poet whom Dryden immortalized; two more editions by 1669.

518. Osborne, Francis. A MISCELLANY OF SUNDRY ESSAYES, LETTERS AND CHARACTERS, PARADOXES, AND PROBLEMATICALL DISCOURSES. London, 1659.

See also 682.

519. Smith, John. SELECT DISCOURSES, ed. John Worthington. London, 1660.

Ten lectures by the most provocative of the Cambridge Platonists.

VIII.   NARRATIVE FICTION

VIII. Narrative Fiction

The antecedents of prose narrative in our period were biblical tales, classical legends, medieval romances, and jests, and the diversity of narrative fiction reflects this variety. Much of the work is openly imitative, and even the best has the dual aim of instructing as well as pleasing. Reading as pure recreation did not arrive until well into the seventeenth century.

See also entries 23, 170; IV: r, 200, 315; VI: I, VI.R, VI.b, 342, 353, 354, 397-401, 402, 403, 411-12, 414-19, 420, 431, 441, 442, 467, 478-80, 487, 646, 693, 694, 695, 698, 699, 700, 702, 703, 704, 705, 710, 714, 717, 718, 721, 722, 725, 735, 738, 740-41, 750, 764.

A. Thoms, William J., ed. EARLY ENGLISH PROSE ROMANCES. 2nd ed. 3 vols. London, 1858.

B. Hazlitt, William C., ed. SHAKESPEARE JEST-BOOKS. 3 vols. London, 1864.

C. _____., ed. SHAKESPEARE'S LIBRARY. 2nd ed. 6 vols. London, 1875.

D. Ashton, John, ed. ROMANCES OF CHIVALRY. New York, 1887.

E. Morley, Henry, ed. EARLY PROSE ROMANCES. London, 1889.

   Based on Thoms (VIII: A).

F. Saintsbury, George, ed. SHORTER NOVELS: ELIZABETHAN AND JACOBEAN. London: Everyman's, 1929.

   Contains Deloney, JACK OF NEWBERIE; Deloney, THOMAS OF READING; Nashe, UNFORTUNATE TRAVELLER; Greene, GWYDONIUS.

G. O'Brien, Edward J., ed. ELIZABETHAN TALES. London, 1937.

> Twenty-five tales from Painter, Pettie, Rich, Whetstone, Greene, etc.

H. Ashley, Robert, and E. M. Moseley, eds. ELIZABETHAN FICTION. New York: Rinehart Editions, 1953.

> Contains Gascoigne, MASTER F. J.; Lyly, EUPHUES; Sidney, ARCADIA (excerpt); Nashe, UNFORTUNATE TRAVELLER; Deloney, JACK OF NEWBURY.

I. Winny, James, ed. THE DESCENT OF EUPHUES. Cambridge University Press, 1957.

> Contains Lyly, EUPHUES; Greene, PANDOSTO; Chettle, PIERS PLAINNESS.

J. Zall, Paul M., ed. A HUNDRED MERRY TALES AND OTHER ENGLISH JESTBOOKS OF THE FIFTEENTH AND SIXTEENTH CENTURIES. University of Nebraska Press, 1963.

K. Mish, Charles C., ed. SHORT FICTION OF THE SEVENTEENTH CENTURY. Garden City, New York: Anchor: 1963.

> Contains Godwin, MAN IN THE MOON, et al.

L. Lawlis, Merritt E., ed. ELIZABETHAN PROSE FICTION. New York, 1967.

> Contains Gascoigne, MASTER F. J.; Lyly, EUPHUES; Greene, PANDOSTO; Lodge, ROSALIND; Nashe, UN-FORTUNATE TRAVELLER; Deloney, THOMAS OF READ-ING; et al.

i. Esdaile, Arundell. A LIST OF ENGLISH TALES AND PROSE ROMANCES PRINTED BEFORE 1740. London: Bibliographical Society, 1912.

ii. O'Dell, Sterg. A CHRONOLOGICAL LIST OF PROSE FICTION IN ENGLISH PRINTED IN ENGLAND AND OTHER COUNTRIES, 1475-1640. M. I. T. Press, 1954.

iii. Mish, Charles C. ENGLISH PROSE FICTION, 1600-1700: A CHRONOLOGICAL CHECKLIST. 2nd ed. 3 vols. Charlottes-ville, Virginia: Bibliographical Society, 1967.

iv. Bonheim, Helmut. THE ENGLISH NOVEL BEFORE RICHARDSON: A CHECKLIST OF TEXTS AND CRITICISM TO 1970. Metuchen,

New Jersey, 1971.

a. Raleigh, Sir Walter A. THE ENGLISH NOVEL. London, 1894.

    A history of the novel to Sir Walter Scott.

b. Saintsbury, George. THE FLOURISHING OF ROMANCE AND
    THE RISE OF ALLEGORY. Edinburgh, 1897.

c. Underhill, John G. SPANISH LITERATURE IN THE ENGLAND
    OF THE TUDORS. New York, 1899.

d. Chandler, Frank W. ROMANCES OF ROGUERY. Columbia
    University Press, 1899.

    A study of the picaresque tradition in Spain and
    elsewhere.

e. Jusserand, J. J. THE ENGLISH NOVEL IN THE TIME OF
    SHAKESPEARE. 4th ed. London, 1901.

f. Atkins, J. W. H. "Elizabethan Prose Fiction," in THE CAM-
    BRIDGE HISTORY OF ENGLISH LITERATURE, ed. A. W. Ward
    and A. R. Waller. 15 vols. Cambridge University Press, 1907-
    27. III, 339-73.

g. Mosher, Joseph A. THE EXEMPLUM IN THE EARLY RELIGIOUS
    AND DIDACTIC LITERATURE OF ENGLAND. Columbia Uni-
    versity Press, 1911.

h. Morgan, Charlotte E. THE RISE OF THE NOVEL OF MANNERS:
    A STUDY OF ENGLISH PROSE FICTION BETWEEN 1600 and
    1740. Columbia University Press, 1911.

i. Wolff, Samuel L. THE GREEK ROMANCES IN ELIZABETHAN
    PROSE FICTION. Columbia University Press, 1912.

j. Crane, Ronald S. THE VOGUE OF MEDIEVAL CHIVALRIC
    ROMANCE DURING THE ENGLISH RENAISSANCE. Menosha,
    Wisconsin, 1919.

k. Baker, Ernest A. THE HISTORY OF THE ENGLISH NOVEL.
    10 vols. London, 1924-39. Vols. I-II.

l. Heidler, Joseph B. THE HISTORY, FROM 1700 TO 1800, OF
    ENGLISH CRITICISM OF PROSE FICTION. University of Illinois
    Press, 1928.

m. Lovett, Robert M., and Helen S. Hughes. THE HISTORY OF THE NOVEL IN ENGLAND. Boston, 1932.

n. Knights, L. C. "Elizabethan Prose," SCRUTINY, 2 (1934), 427-38.

o. Pruvost, Rene. MATTEO BANDELLO AND ELIZABETHAN FICTION. Paris, 1937.

p. Wilson, Frank P. "The English Jestbooks of the Sixteenth and Early Seventeenth Centuries," HLQ, 2 (1938-39), 121-58.

q. Wright, C. E. THE CULTIVATION OF SAGA IN ANGLO-SAXON ENGLAND. Edinburgh, 1939.

r. Parks, George B. "Before Euphues," in JOSEPH QUINCY ADAMS MEMORIAL STUDIES, ed. J. G. McManaway, et al. Washington, D. C., 1948, pp. 475-93.

s. Koller, Kathrine. "The Puritan Preacher's Contribution to Fiction," HLQ, II (1947-48), 321-40.

t. Mish, Charles C. "Best Sellers in Seventeenth-Century Fiction," PBSA, 47 (1953), 356-73.

u. Adams, Robert P. "Bold Bawdry and Open Manslaughter: The English New Humanist Attack on Medieval Romance," HLQ, 23 (1959-60), 33-48.

v. Boyce, Benjamin. "The Effect of the Restoration on Prose Fiction," TSL, 6 (1961), 77-83.

w. Jewkes, W. T. "The Literature of Travel and the Mode of Romance in the Renaissance," BNYPL, 67 (1963), 219-36.

x. Loomis, Roger S. THE DEVELOPMENT OF ARTHURIAN ROMANCE. London: Hutchinson University Library, 1963.

y. Schlauch, Margaret. ANTECEDENTS OF THE ENGLISH NOVEL, 1400-1600. Warsaw, 1963.

z. Teets, Bruce E. "Two Faces of Style in Renaissance Prose Fiction," in SWEET SMOKE OF RHETORIC, ed. Natalie G. Lawrence and J. A. Reynolds. University of Miami Press, 1964.

aa. Alter, Robert. ROGUE'S PROGRESS: STUDIES IN THE PICA-RESQUE NOVEL. Harvard University Press, 1964.

bb. Kahrl, Stanley, J. "Allegory in Practice: A Study of Narrative Styles in Medieval Exempla," MP, 63 (1965-66), 105-10.

cc. _____. "The Medieval Origins of the Sixteenth-Century English Jest-Books," SRen, 13 (1966), 166-83.

dd. Nelson, William. "The Boundaries of Fiction in the Renaissance: A Treaty Between Truth and Falsehood," ELH, 36 (1969), 30-58.

ee. Davis, Walter R. IDEAL AND ACT IN ELIZABETHAN FICTION. Princeton University Press, 1969.

520. Anon. APOLLONIUS OF TYRE, tr. anon. ca. 1000.

The legend of a classical hero which in this translation has a claim to be the first prose romance in English; see also 532, 585.

A. Anon. THE OLD ENGLISH APOLLONIUS OF TYRE, ed. Peter Goolden. Oxford University Press, 1958.

a. Chapman, C. O. "Beowulf and Apollonius of Tyre," MLN, 46 (1931), 439-43.

b. Goepp, P. H. "The Narrative Material in the 'Apollonius of Tyre'," ELH, 5 (1938), 150-72.

521. Leo. HISTORIA DE PRELIIS, tr. anon. ca. 1400.

An abridged translation of a Latin version of the ever-popular feats of Alexander the Great.

A. _____. THE PROSE LIFE OF ALEXANDER, tr. anon., ed. J. S. Westlake. EETS OS 143. London, 1913.

522. Joannes de Hildesheim. THE THREE KINGS OF COLOGNE, tr. anon. ca. 1400.

A legend of the three magi, whose relics rested in Cologne; first printed by Wynken de Worde in 1496, and reprinted in 1499, 1511, and 1526.

A. _____. THE THREE KINGS OF COLOGNE, tr. anon., ed.

Carl Horstmann. EETS ES 85. London, 1886.

523. Anon. DIVES ET PAUPER. 1405-10.

A homiletic, but lively, dialogue based upon the ten commandments; wrongly attributed to Henry Parker; printed by Richard Pynson in 1493 and by Thomas Berthelet in 1536.

a. Pfander, H. G. "Dives et Pauper," LIBRARY, 4th series, 14 (1933-34), 299-312.

b. Richardson, H. G. "Dives and Pauper," LIBRARY, 4th series, 15 (1934-35), 31-37.

524. Deguileville, Guillaume de. THE PYLGREMAGE OF THE SOWLE, tr. anon. ca. 1414.

A prose rendition of the popular dream-allegory describing man's journey through life from birth to death; printed by William Caxton in 1483.

A. _____. THE PILGRIMAGE OF THE LYF OF THE MANHODE, tr. anon., ed. William A. Wright. London: Roxburghe Club, 1869.

525. Etienne de Besancon. AN ALPHABET OF TALES, tr. anon. ca. 1420.

A translation of Etienne's ALPHABETUM NARRATIONUM, a collection of exempla useful to preachers arranged alphabetically according to subject matter.

A. _____. AN ALPHABET OF TALES, tr. anon., ed. Mary M. Banks. EETS OS 126-127. London, 1904-05.

a. Herbert. J. A. "The Authorship of the 'Alphabetum narrationum'," LIBRARY, 2nd series, 6 (1905), 94-101.

526. Anon. GESTA ROMANORUM, tr. anon. ca. 1450.

A collection of exemplary tales compiled in Latin probably in England ca. 1300 and rendered into English three times in the fifteenth century; early printed by Wynken de Worde.

A. Anon. THE EARLY ENGLISH VERSIONS OF THE GESTA ROMANORUM, tr. anon., ed. Sidney J. H. Herrtage. EETS ES 33. London, 1879.

a. Oesterley, Hermann. GESTA ROMANORUM. Berlin, 1872.

527. Anon. ROMAN DE MERLIN, tr. anon. ca. 1450.

A faithful prose rendering of a long French romance recounting King Arthur's early years.

A. Anon. MERLIN, OR THE EARLY HISTORY OF KING ARTHUR, tr. anon., ed. Henry B. Wheatley. EETS OS 10, 21, 36, 112. London, 1899.

528. Malory, Sir Thomas. MORTE D'ARTHUR. 1470.

An extensive redaction of Arthurian materials from French and English sources; printed by William Caxton in 1485, and reprinted 1498, 1529, 1557, ca. 1582, and 1634.

A. _____. LE MORTE DARTHUR, ed. William Caxton, ed. H. O. Sommer. 3 vols. London, 1889-91.

B. _____. THE WORKS, ed. Eugene Vinaver. 2nd ed. 3 vols. Oxford, 1967.

a. Vinaver, Eugene. MALORY. Oxford, 1929.

b. Baugh, A. C. "Documenting Sir Thomas Malory," SPECULUM, 8 (1933), 3-29.

c. Aurner, Nellie S. AN INTRODUCTION TO THE MORTE D'ARTHUR. New York, 1938.

d. Williams, Charles. "Malory and the Grail Legend," DUBLIN REVIEW, 1 (1944), 144-53.

e. Brewer, D. S. "Form in the MORTE DARTHUR," MAE, 21 (1952), 14-24.

f. Bradbrook, Muriel C. SIR THOMAS MALORY. London, 1958.

g. Davies, R. T. "Malory's 'Vertuose Love'," SP, 53 (1956), 459-69.

h. Loomis, Roger S., ed. ARTHURIAN LITERATURE IN THE MIDDLE AGES: A COLLABORATIVE HISTORY. Oxford, 1959.

i. Rumble, Thomas C. "Malory's 'Works' and Vinaver's Comments,"

JEGP, 59 (1960), 59-69.

j. Moorman, Charles. "Courtly Love in Malory," ELH, 27 (1960), 163-76.

k. _____. "Internal Chronology in Malory's MORTE DARTHUR," JEGP, 60 (1961), 240-249.

l. Bennett, Jack A. W., ed. ESSAYS ON MALORY. Oxford, 1963.

m. Lumiansky, Robert M., ed. MALORY'S ORIGINALITY: A CRITICAL STUDY OF LE MORTE DARTHUR. Johns Hopkins Press, 1964.

n. Moorman, Charles. THE BOOK OF KYNG ARTHUR: THE UNITY OF MALORY'S MORTE DARTHUR. University of Kentucky Press, 1965.

o. Matthews, William. THE ILL-FRAMED KNIGHT: A SKEPTICAL INQUIRY INTO THE IDENTITY OF SIR THOMAS MALORY. University of California Press, 1966.

p. Reiss, Edmund. SIR THOMAS MALORY. New York: Twayne, 1966.

q. Schueler, Donald, G. "The Tristram Section of Malory's MORTE DARTHUR," SP, 65 (1968), 51-66.

r. Field, P. J. C. "Description and Narration in Malory," SPECULUM, 43 (1968), 476-86.

s. _____. ROMANCE AND CHRONICLE: A STUDY OF MALORY'S PROSE STYLE. Indiana University Press, 1971.

529. Jean d'Arras. MELUSINE, tr. anon. ca. 1500.

A French aristocratic romance composed ca. 1390 which recounts the tragedy of a lamia.

A. _____. MELUSINE, tr. anon., ed. A. K. Donald. EETS ES 68. London, 1895.

530. Aubert, David. THE THREE KINGS' SONS, tr. anon. ca. 1500.

A French romance of a Christian king, his beautiful daughter, despicable infidels, and doughty knights; the original sometimes attributed to Aubert.

A. _____ . THE THREE KINGS' SONS, ed. F. J. Furnivall.
EETS ES 67. London, 1895.

531. Anon. VALENTINE AND ORSON, tr. Henry Watson. London: Wynken
de Worde, ca. 1503.

An English translation of a famous French romance of the
Charlemagne cycle composed between 1475-89, which in
turn was based upon a fourteenth century French poem;
several later editions.

A. Anon. VALENTINE AND ORSON, tr. Henry Watson, ed.
Arthur Dickson. EETS OS 204. London, 1937.

a. Dickson, Arthur. VALENTINE AND ORSON: A STUDY IN
LATE MEDIEVAL ROMANCE. Columbia University Press, 1929.

532. Anon. KYNGE APPOLYN OF THYRE, tr. Robert Copland. London:
Wynken de Worde, 1510.

See also 520.

A. Anon. KYNGE APPOLYN OF THYRE, tr. Robert Copland,
ed. E. W. Ashbee. London, 1870.

533. Anon. A C. MERY TALYS. London, ca. 1525.

The earliest book of jests that has survived; printed by
John Rastell.

A. Anon. A HUNDRED MERRY TALES, ed. W. C. Hazlitt. London, 1887.

B. Anon. A HUNDRED MERRY TALES, et al., ed. Paul M. Zall.
University of Nebraska Press, 1963.

534. Curtius Rufus, Quintus. THE ACTES OF THE GREATE ALEXANDER, tr.
John Brende. London, 1553.

535. B., A. MERIE TALES OF THE MAD MEN OF GOTAM. London, ca.
1565.

A collection in the jest-book tradition; attributed to
Andrew Boorde.

A. _____ . MERIE TALES OF THE MAD MEN OF GOTAM, ed.

Stanley J. Kahrl, and Richard Johnson, THE HISTORY OF TOM THUMBE, ed. Curt F. Buhler. Northwestern University Press: Renaissance English Text Society, 1965.

536. Apuleius. THE .XI. BOOKES OF THE GOLDEN ASSE, tr. William Adlington. London, 1566.

Other editions in 1571, 1582, 1596, and 1639; excerpts in XI; B.

A. _____. THE GOLDEN ASS, tr. William Adlington, ed. Charles Whibley. London: Tudor Translations, 1893.

B. _____. THE GOLDEN ASS, tr. William Adlington, ed. Sir Stephen Gaselee. London: Loeb Classical Library, 1915.

537. Boccaccio. PHILOCOPO, tr. Henry Grantham. London, 1566.

Other editions in 1567, 1571, and 1587.

538. Painter, William. THE PALACE OF PLEASURE. London, 1566.

A collection of sixty vivid tales that Painter selected from Livy, Aulus Gellius, Boccaccio, Bandello, and others; a second volume with thirty-four more tales appeared in 1567; other complete editions in 1569 and 1575.

A. _____. THE PALACE OF PLEASURE, ed. Joseph Jacobs. 3 vols. London, 1890. Reprinted New York: Dover Publications, 1966.

B. _____. THE PALACE OF PLEASURE, ed. Hamish Miles. 4 vols. London, 1929.

a. Bush, Douglas. "The Classical Tales in Painter's PALACE OF PLEASURE," JEGP, 23 (1924), 331-41.

b. Wright, Louis B. "William Painter and the Vogue of Chaucer as a Moral Teacher," MP, 31 (1933-34), 165-74.

c. Kimmelman, Elaine. "The Palace of Pleasure," BOSTON PUBLIC LIBRARY QUARTERLY, 2 (1950), 231-44.

d. Wright, Herbert G. "The Indebtedness of Painter's Translations from Boccaccio in THE PALACE OF PLEASURE to the French Version of Le Macon," MLR, 46 (1951), 431-35.

e. Buchert, Jean R. "Cinthio in THE PALACE OF PLEASURE: William Painter's Translations from GLI HECATOMMITHI," RenP 1969. Durham, North Carolina, 1970, pp. 1-8.

539. Anon. MERIE TALES. NEWLY IMPRINTED & MADE BY MASTER SKELTON POET LAUREAT. London, 1567.

Representative of the later jest-book tradition adulating certain folk-heroes, in this instance John Skelton.

540. Fenton, Geoffrey. CERTAINE TRAGICALL DISCOURSES. London, 1567.

Essentially a reworking of tales from Boaistuau and Belleforest, who in turn had cribbed them from Bandello; another edition in 1579.

A. _____. CERTAIN TRAGICAL DISCOURSES OF BANDELLO, ed. Robert L. Douglas. 2 vols. London: Tudor Translations, 1898.

a. Gottlieb, Stephen A. "Fenton's Novelle," RLC, 40 (1966), 121-28.

541. Heliodorus. AN AETHIOPIAN HISTORIE, tr. Thomas Underdowne. London, 1569.

One of the most popular classical romances; other editions of this translation in 1577, 1587, 1605, 1606, 1622, and 1627; excerpts in XI. B.

A. _____. AN AETHIOPIAN HISTORY, tr. Thomas Underdowne, ed. Charles Whibley. London: Tudor Translations, 1895.

542. Mexia, Pedro. THE FORESTE, tr. Thomas Fortescue. London, 1571.

A famous collection of trivia and anecdotes from Spain; another edition in 1576.

543. Guicciardini, Ludovico. THE GARDEN OF PLEASURE, tr. James Sanford. London, 1573.

Moral tales imported from Italy, told to instruct more than to please; another edition in 1576; see also 732-733.

544. Gascoigne, George. THE ADVENTURES OF MASTER F. J., in A HUNDRETH SUNDRIE FLOWRES. London, 1573.

A realistic story of amorous adventures in an Elizabethan manor house; extensively revised in 1575; in VIII.H, VIII.L.

A. ____. THE COMPLETE WORKS, ed. J. W. Cunliffe. 2 vols. Cambridge University Press, 1907-10.

i. Tannenbaum, Samuel A. GEORGE GASCOIGNE: A CONCISE BIBLIOGRAPHY. New York, 1942.

ii. Johnson, Robert C. ELIZABETHAN BIBLIOGRAPHIES SUPPLE-MENTS, IX: MINOR ELIZABETHANS [George Gascoigne et al.]. London, 1968.

a. Bradner, Leicester. "The First English Novel," PMLA, 45 (1930), 543-52.

b. Prouty, C. T. GEORGE GASCOIGNE: ELIZABETHAN COUR-TIER, SOLDIER, AND POET. Columbia University Press, 1942.

c. Adams, Robert P. "Gascoigne's MASTER F. J. as Original Fiction," PMLA, 73 (1958), 315-26.

d. Bradner, Leicester. "Point of View in George Gascoigne's Fiction," SSF, 3 (1965-66), 16-22.

e. Anderau, Alfred. GEORGE GASCOIGNE'S THE ADVENTURES OF MASTER F. J.: ANALYSE UND INTERPRETATION. Bern, 1966.

f. Smith, Charles W. "Structural and Thematic Unity in Gascoigne's THE ADVENTURES OF MASTER F. J.," PLL, 2 (1966), 99-108.

g. Lanham, Richard A. "Narrative Structure in Gascoigne's F. J.," SSF, 4 (1966-67), 42-50.

h. Johnson, Ronald C. "The Adventures of Master F. J.," in GEORGE GASCOIGNE. New York: Twayne, 1972, pp. 119-36.

545. Pettie, George. A PETITE PALLACE OF PETTIE HIS PLEASURE. London, 1576.

A pretty retelling of twelve old tales, mostly from Ovid; other editions ca. 1578, ca. 1580, 1608, and 1613; see also 551.b.

A. ____. A PETITE PALLACE OF PETTIE HIS PLEASURE, ed, Israel Gollancz. 2 vols. London: King's Classics, 1908.

B. _____. A PETITE PALLACE OF PETTIE HIS PLEASURE, ed. Herbert Hartman. Oxford University Press, 1938.

  a. Bush, Douglas. "The Petite Pallace of Pettie His Pleasure," JEGP, 27 (1928), 162-69.

546. Whetstone, George. THE ROCKE OF REGARD. London, 1576.

  In verse, though Part I contains the prose tale of "Rinaldo and Giletta."

  a. Prouty, Charles T. "Elizabethan Fiction: Whetstone's RINALDO AND GILETTA and Grange's THE GOLDEN APHRODITIS," in STUDIES IN HONOR OF A. H. R. FAIRCHILD, ed. C. T. Prouty. University of Missouri Press, 1946, pp. 133-50.

547. Whetstone, George. AN HEPTAMERON OF CIVILL DISCOURSES. London, 1582.

  Prose fiction in the guise of a courtesy book; the tales drawn largely from Giraldi Cinthio's HECATOMMITHI; the source of Shakespeare's MEASURE FOR MEASURE.

  a. Prouty, Charles T. "George Whetstone and the Sources of MEASURE FOR MEASURE," SQ, 15 (1964), 131-45.

  b. Izard, Thomas C. GEORGE WHETSTONE: MID-ELIZABETHAN GENTLEMAN OF LETTERS. Columbia University Press, 1952.

548. Grange, John. THE GOLDEN APHRODITIS. London, 1577.

  A quasi-classical story swathed in rhetoric; see also 546.a.

A. _____. THE GOLDEN APHRODITIS, AND GRANGE'S GARDEN, ed. Hyder E. Rollins. New York: Scholars' Facsimiles, 1939.

  a. Tilley, Morris P. "Borrowings in Grange's GOLDEN APHRODITIS," MLN, 53 (1938), 407-12.

549. Wotton, Henry, tr. A COURTLIE CONTROVERSIE OF CUPIDS CAUTELS. London, 1578.

  A collection of five tales in a framework reminiscent of Boccaccio; translated from the French of Jacques Yver.

550. Lyly, John. EUPHUES. THE ANATOMY OF WYT. London, 1578.

A frivolous tale of youthful peccadilloes told with weighti-
ness, stylistic as well as moral; immensely popular, with
at least eight editions by 1590; in VIII.H, VIII.I, VIII.L;
see also 382.

551. _____. EUPHUES AND HIS ENGLAND. London, 1580.

A sequel to EUPHUES, equally popular.

A. _____. THE COMPLETE WORKS, ed. R. W. Bond. 3 vols.
Oxford, 1902.

B. _____. EUPHUES: THE ANATOMY OF WIT; EUPHUES &
HIS ENGLAND, ed. M. W. Croll and Harry Clemons. London,
1916.

i. Tannenbaum, Samuel A. JOHN LYLY: A CONCISE BIBLIOG-
RAPHY. New York, 1940.

ii. Johnson, Robert C. ELIZABETHAN BIBLIOGRAPHIES SUPPLE-
MENTS, V: JOHN LYLY et al. London, 1968.

a. Ringler, William A. "The Immediate Source of Euphuism,"
PMLA, 53 (1938), 678-86.

b. Swart, J. "Lyly and Pettie," ES, 23 (1941), 9-18.

c. King, Walter N. "John Lyly and Elizabethan Rhetoric," SP,
52 (1955), 149-61.

d. Barish, Jonas A. "The Prose Style of John Lyly," ELH, 23
(1956), 14-35.

e. Borinski, Ludwig. "The Origin of the Euphuistic Novel and
Its Significance for Shakespeare," in STUDIES IN HONOR OF
T. W. BALDWIN, ed. D. C. Allen. University of Illinois
Press, 1958, pp. 38-52.

f. Zandvoort, R. W. "What is Euphuism?" in MELANGES DE
LINGUISTIQUE ET DE PHILOLOGIE: FERNAND MOSSE IN
MEMORIAM. Paris, 1959, 508-17.

g. Hunter, George K. JOHN LYLY; THE HUMANIST AS COURTIER.
Cambridge, 1962.

552. Munday, Anthony. ZELAUTO. THE FOUNTAINE OF FAME. London,

1580.

    Derivative fiction with a high moral content, riding on the coat-tails of EUPHUES; see also 740-741.

A.   _____. ZELAUTO: THE FOUNTAINE OF FAME, ed. Jack Stillinger. Southern Illinois University Press, 1963.

i.   Tannenbaum, Samuel A. ANTHONY MUNDAY: A CONCISE BIBLIOGRAPHY. New York, 1942.

ii.   Johnson, Robert C. ELIZABETHAN BIBLIOGRAPHIES SUPPLE-MENT, IX: MINOR ELIZABETHANS. [Anthony Munday et al.] London, 1968.

a.   Byrne, Muriel St. Clare. "Anthony Munday and His Books," LIBRARY, 4th series, 1 (1920-21), 225-56.

b.   Hayes, Gerald, R. "Anthony Munday's Romances of Chivalry," LIBRARY, 4th series, 6 (1925-26), 57-81.

c.   Turner, Celeste. ANTHONY MUNDAY: AN ELIZABETHAN MAN OF LETTERS. University of California Press, 1928.

d.   Creigh, Geoffrey. "ZELAUTO and Italian Comedy: A Study in Sources," MLQ, 29 (1968), 161-67.

553. Cartigny, Jean de. THE VOYAGE OF THE WANDERING KNIGHT, tr. William Goodyear. London, 1581.

    In the tradition of le pelerinage de la vie; at least six editions before the Restoration.

554. Rich, Barnabe. THE STRAUNGE AND WONDERFULL ADVENTURES OF DON SIMONIDES. London, 1581.

    Heroic fiction in the Spanish mode by a retired army captain; a second part in 1584; see also 402, 487, 739.

555.   _____. HIS FAREWELL TO MILITARIE PROFESSION. London, 1581.

    Eight bright tales from Belleforest and others; another edition in 1606.

A. Collier, John P., ed. EIGHT NOVELS EMPLOYED BY EN-GLISH DRAMATIC POETS OF THE REIGN OF QUEEN ELIZA-BETH. London: Shakespeare Society, 1846.

B. Rich, Barnabe. FAREWELL TO MILITARY PROFESSION, ed. Thomas M. Cranfill. University of Texas Press, 1959.

a. Starnes, DeWitt T. "Barnabe Riche's 'Sappho Duke of Mantona': A Study in Elizabethan Story-Making," SP, 30 (1933), 455-72.

b. Webb, Henry J. "Barnabe Rich--Sixteenth Century Military Critic," JEGP, 42 (1943), 240-52.

c. Cranfill, Thomas M., and Dorothy H. Bruce. BARNABY RICH: A SHORT BIOGRAPHY. University of Texas Press, 1953.

d. Jorgensen, Paul A. "Barnaby Rich: Soldierly Suitor and Honest Critic of Women," SQ, 7 (1956), 183-88.

e. Lievsay, John L. "A Word About Barnaby Rich," JEGP, 55 (1956), 381-92.

556. Rich, Barnabe. THE ADVENTURES OF BRUSANUS, PRINCE OF HUNGARIA. London, 1592.

Another heroic romance.

557. Anon. THE LIFE AND PRANKS OF LONG MEG OF WESTMINSTER. London, 1582.

A jest-book with a heroine instead of a hero; STC 17782.

558. Melbancke, Brian. PHILOTIMUS: THE WARRE BETWIXT NATURE AND FORTUNE. London, 1583.

A euphuistic trifle.

a. Rollins, Hyder E. "Notes on Brian Melbancke's PHILOTIMUS," SP, Extra Series 1 (1929), 40-57.

b. Tilley, Morris P. "Further Borrowings from Poems in PHILOTIMUS (1583)," SP, 27 (1930), 186-214.

c. Maud, Ralph. "The Date of Brian Melbancke's PHILOTIMUS," LIBRARY, 5th series, 11 (1956), 118-20.

559. Averell, William. A DYALL FOR DAINTY DARLINGS. London, 1584.

Stories told as moral exempla; another edition in 1590.

560. Warner, William. PAN HIS SYRINX, OR PIPE, COMPACT OF SEVEN REEDES. London, 1584.

Seven tales; another edition in 1597.

A. _____. SYRINX OR A SEVENFOLD HISTORY, ed. Wallace A. Bacon. Northwestern University Press, 1950.

561. Greene, Robert. MAMILLIA, A MIRROUR OR LOOKING GLASSE FOR THE LADIES OF ENGLANDE. London, 1583.

The first of Greene's many fictional romances, burdened with euphuistic mannerisms and an improbable plot; a second part in 1593; see also 397-401, 478-80.

562. _____. GWYDONIUS. THE CARDE OF FANCIE. London, 1584.

A listless reworking of the prodigal son motif; other editions in 1593 and 1608; in VIII.F.

a. Dent, Robert W. "Greene's GWYDONIUS: A Study in Elizabethan Plagiarism," HLQ, 24 (1960-61), 151-62.

563. Greene, Robert. ARBASTO, THE ANATOMIE OF FORTUNE. London, 1584.

An artless narrative of a luckless hero; other editions in 1589, 1594, 1617, and 1626.

564. _____. PLANETOMACHIA. London, 1585.

A collection of romantic "tragedies" set in the curious framework of a contentious dialogue among the seven planets.

a. Parr, Johnstone. "Sources of the Astrological Prefaces in Robert Greene's PLANETOMACHIA," SP, 46 (1949), 400-10.

565. Greene, Robert. EUPHUES HIS CENSURE TO PHILAUTUS. London, 1587.

A collection of stories exchanged between Greeks and Trojans during a truce in the war.

566. _____. PERIMEDES THE BLACKE-SMITH. London, 1588.

Still euphuistic in style and escapist in subject-matter.

567. _____. PANDOSTO. THE TRIUMPH OF TIME. London, 1588.

Perhaps the most popular of Greene's romances with at least ten editions by 1660; source of Shakespeare's WINTER'S TALE; in VIII.I, VIII.L.

A. _____. PANDOSTO, ed. P. G. Thomas. London, 1907.

a. Lawlor, John. "PANDOSTO and the Nature of Dramatic Romance," PQ, 41 (1962), 96-113.

568. Greene, Robert. MENAPHON, CAMILLAS ALARUM TO SLUMBERING EUPHUES. London, 1589.

> One of the most appealing of the pastoral romances in the tradition of Sidney's ARCADIA, with songs intermingled with the prose; other editions in 1599, 1610, and 1616.

A. _____. MENAPHON and Thomas Lodge, A MARGARITE OF AMERICA, ed. G. B. Harrison. Oxford: Bodley Head Quartos, 1927.

569. _____. CICERONIS AMOR. TULLIES LOVE. London, 1589.

> A complicated love-story with Cicero as matchmaker rather than rhetorician; at least nine editions by 1639.

A. _____. CICERONIS AMOR: TULLIES LOVE (1589) AND A QUIP FOR AN UPSTART COURTIER (1592), ed. E. H. Miller. Gainesville, Florida: Scholars' Facsimiles, 1954.

570. _____. GREENES MOURNING GARMENT. London, 1590.

> Thinly disguised autobiography in which Greene promises to turn from frivolous novelle to serious writing about contemporary issues, a promise realized in the cony-catching pamphlets (see 397-99).

571. _____. GREENES NEVER TOO LATE. London, 1590.

> A strange mixture of styles and of subjects, but again probably autobiographical; at least seven editions by 1631.

572. _____. FRANCESCOS FORTUNES. London, 1590.

> A popular sequel to GREENES NEVER TOO LATE.

573. _____. GREENES FAREWELL TO FOLLY. London, 1591.

> Moral tales told by ladies and gentlemen in a Boccaccio-like framework.

A. _____. THE LIFE AND COMPLETE WORKS IN PROSE AND VERSE, ed. Rev. A. B. Grosart. 15 vols. London: Huth Library, 1881-86.

i. Tannenbaum, Samuel A. ROBERT GREENE: A CONCISE BIBLI-
OGRAPHY. New York, 1939. SUPPLEMENT. New York, 1946.

ii. Johnson, Robert C. ELIZABETHAN BIBLIOGRAPHIES SUPPLE-
MENTS, V: ROBERT GREENE et al. London, 1968.

a. Pruvost, Rene. ROBERT GREENE ET SES ROMANS. Paris,
1938.

b. Allen, Don C. "Science and Invention in Greene's Prose,"
PMLA, 53 (1938), 1007-18.

c. Applegate, James. "The Classical Learning of Robert Greene,"
BHR, 28 (1966), 354-68.

574. Lodge, Thomas. THE DELECTABLE HISTORIE OF FORBONIUS AND
PRISCERIA, appended to AN ALARUM AGAINST USURERS. London,
1584.

An honest but unsuccessful attempt at aristocratic romance;
see also 374, 751-53.

a. Beaty, Frederick L. "Lodge's FORBONIUS AND PRISCERIA
and Sidney's ARCADIA," ES, 49 (1968), 38-45.

575. Lodge, Thomas. ROSALYNDE. EUPHUES GOLDEN LEGACIE. London,
1590.

One of the most successful pastoral romances, which
intersperses elegant prose with sonnets and eclogues;
adapted from the pseudo-Chaucerian TALE OF GAMELIN,
in the tradition of Sidney's ARCADIA, and the source of
Shakespeare's AS YOU LIKE IT; at least eight editions
by 1642; in VIII.L.

A. _____. ROSALYNDE, ed. W. W. Greg. London: Shakespeare Library, 1907.

B. _____. ROSALYNDE, ed. Thomas Maybank. London, 1928.

a. Davis, Walter R. "Masking in Arden: The Histrionics of
Lodge's ROSALYNDE," SEL, 5 (1965), 151-63.

576. Lodge, Thomas. THE LIFE AND DEATH OF WILLIAM LONG BEARD.
London, 1593.

An historical romance.

A. _____ . THE LIFE AND DEATH OF WILLIAM LONG BEARD, ed. John P. Collier. London, 1866.

577. _____ . A MARGUERITE OF AMERICA. London, 1596.

A sad tale about a girl of the not-so-golden West; in 568.A.

578. _____ . WITS MISERIE, AND THE WORLDS MADNESSE. London, 1596.

A medieval allegory of the seven deadly sins.

A. _____ . THE COMPLETE WORKS, ed. Sir Edmund Gosse. Glasgow: Hunterian Club, 1883.

i. Tannenbaum, Samuel A. THOMAS LODGE: A CONCISE BIBLIOGRAPHY. New York, 1940.

ii. Johnson, Robert C. ELIZABETHAN BIBLIOGRAPHIES SUPPLE-MENTS, V: THOMAS LODGE et al. London, 1968.

a. Paradise, N. Burton. THOMAS LODGE: THE HISTORY OF AN ELIZABETHAN. Yale University Press, 1931.

b. Sisson, Charles J., ed. THOMAS LODGE AND OTHER ELIZ-ABETHANS. Harvard University Press, 1933.

c. Tenney, Edward A. THOMAS LODGE. Cornell University Press, 1935.

d. Rae, Wesley D. THOMAS LODGE. New York: Twayne, 1967.

579. Anon. THE PLEASAUNT HISTORIE OF LAZARILLO DE TORMES, tr. David Rouland. London, 1586.

The Spanish classic of a picaresque rogue, sometimes attributed to Diego Hurtado de Mendoza; other editions in 1596, 1624, and 1639; a second part translated by W. Phiston (?) in 1596.

A. Anon. LAZARILLO DE TORMES, tr. David Rouland, ed. J. E. V. Crofts. Oxford: Percy Reprints, 1924.

580. Longus. DAPHNIS AND CHLOE, tr. Angel Day. London, 1587.

The prototype of pastoral romance; translated from the French of Amyot.

A. _____. DAPHNIS AND CHLOE, tr. Angel Day, ed. Joseph Jacobs. London, 1890.

581. Boccaccio. AMOROUS FIAMMETTA, tr. Bartholomew Young. London, 1587.

582. Sidney, Sir Philip. THE COUNTESSE OF PEMBROKES ARCADIA. London, 1590.

> The giant among pastoral romances, not only because it was the first in English, but because of Sidney's control in matters of plot and style, and because of the profundity of his thought in this artificial medium; written ca. 1580, but revised extensively before Sidney's death in 1586, so that two versions are extant, the "old" ARCADIA and the "new" ARCADIA; oft-reprinted; see also 194, 607, 618, 636.

A. _____. THE COUNTESS OF PEMBROKE'S ARCADIA, ed. H. O. Sommer. London, 1891.

B. _____. THE COUNTESS OF PEMBROKE'S ARCADIA, ed. Ernest A. Baker. London, 1921.

C. _____. THE COMPLETE WORKS, ed. Albert Feuillerat. 4 vols. Cambridge University Press, 1922-26.

D. _____. THE COUNTESS OF PEMBROKE'S ARCADIA (THE OLD ARCADIA), ed. Jean Robertson. Oxford, 1973.

i. Tannenbaum, Samuel A. SIR PHILIP SIDNEY: A CONCISE BIBLIOGRAPHY. New York, 1941.

ii. Guffey, George R. ELIZABETHAN BIBLIOGRAPHIES SUPPLE- MENTS, VII: SIR PHILIP SIDNEY et al. London, 1967.

a. Wallace, Malcolm W. THE LIFE OF SIR PHILIP SIDNEY. Cambridge University Press, 1915.

b. Genouy, Hector. L'ARCADIA. . .DANS SES RAPPORTS AVEC . . .SANNAZARO ET. . .MONTEMAYOR. Montpellier, 1928.

c. Zandvoort, Reinard W. SIDNEY'S ARCADIA: A COMPARISON BETWEEN THE TWO VERSIONS. Amsterdam, 1929.

d. Wilson, Mona. SIR PHILIP SIDNEY. London, 1931.

e. Myrick, Kenneth O. SIR PHILIP SIDNEY AS A LITERARY CRAFTSMAN. Harvard University Press, 1935. Rev. ed. University of Nebraska Press, 1965.

f. Wiles, A. G. D. "Parallel Analyses of the Two Versions of Sidney's ARCADIA," SP, 39 (1942), 167-206.

g. Duhamel, P. Albert. "Sidney's ARCADIA and Elizabethan Rhetoric," SP, 45 (1948), 134-50.

h. Ribner, Irving. "Machiavelli and Sidney: the ARCADIA of 1590," SP, 47 (1950), 152-72.

i. Danby, John F. POETS ON FORTUNE'S HILL: STUDIES IN SIDNEY, SHAKESPEARE, BEAUMONT & FLETCHER. London, 1952.

j. Buxton, John. SIR PHILIP SIDNEY AND THE ENGLISH RE-NAISSANCE. London, 1954.

k. Boas, Frederick S. SIR PHILIP SIDNEY, REPRESENTATIVE ELIZABETHAN. London, 1955.

l. Davis, Walter R. "Thematic Unity in the NEW ARCADIA," SP, 57 (1960), 123-43.

m. Heltzel, Virgil B. "The Arcadian Hero," PQ, 41 (1962), 173-80.

n. Davis, Walter R. "Actaeon in Arcadia," SEL, 2 (1962), 95-110.

o. Kaltstone, David. "The Transformation of Arcadia: Sannazaro and Sir Philip Sidney," CL, 15 (1963), 234-49.

p. Godshalk, William L. "Sidney's Revision of the ARCADIA, Books III-V," PQ, 43 (1964), 171-84.

q. Challis, Lorna. "The Use of Oratory in Sidney's ARCADIA," SP, 62 (1965), 561-76.

r. Davis, Walter R., and Richard A. Lanham. SIDNEY'S AR-CADIA. Yale University Press, 1965.

s. Rees, Joan. "Fulke Greville and the Revisions of ARCADIA,"

RES, 17 (1966), 54-57.

t. Lindheim, Nancy R. "Sidney's ARCADIA, Book II: Retrospective Narrative," SP, 64 (1967), 159-86.

u. Isler, Alan D. "Moral Philosophy and the Family in Sidney's ARCADIA," HLQ, 31 (1967-68), 359-71.

v. _____. "Heroic Poetry and Sidney's Two ARCADIAS," PMLA, 83 (1968), 368-79.

w. _____. "The Allegory of the Hero and Sidney's Two ARCADIAS," SP, 65 (1968), 171-91.

x. Dipple, Elizabeth. "Harmony and Pastoral in the OLD ARCADIA," ELH, 35 (1968), 309-28.

y. Howell, Roger. SIR PHILIP SIDNEY: THE SHEPHERD KNIGHT. London, 1968.

z. Rose, Mark. HEROIC LOVE: STUDIES IN SIDNEY AND SPENSER. Harvard University Press, 1968.

aa. Marenco, Franco. "Double Plot in Sidney's OLD ARCADIA," MLR, 64 (1969), 248-63.

bb. Turner, Myron. "The Heroic Ideal in Sidney's Revised ARCADIA," SEL, 10 (1970), 63-82.

cc. Dipple, Elizabeth. " 'Unjust Justice' in the OLD ARCADIA," SEL, 10 (1970), 83-101.

dd. Kimbrough, Robert. SIR PHILIP SIDNEY. New York: Twayne, 1971.

ee. Levy, F. J. "Philip Sidney Reconsidered," ELR, 2 (1972), 5-18.

ff. Hamilton, A. C. "Sidney's ARCADIA as Prose Fiction: Its Relation to Its Sources," ELR, 2 (1972), 29-60.

gg. Parker, Robert W. "Terentian Structure and Sidney's Original ARCADIA," ELR, 2 (1972), 61-78.

hh. Turner Myron. "The Disfigured Face of Nature: Image and Metaphor in the Revised ARCADIA," ELR, 2 (1972), 116-35.

ii. Lindheim, Nancy R. "Vision, Revision, and the 1593 Text of the ARCADIA," ELR, 2 (1972), 136-47.

jj. Osborn, James M. YOUNG PHILIP SIDNEY 1572-1577. Yale University Press, 1972.

kk. Lawry, Jon S. SIDNEY'S TWO "ARCADIAS": PATTERN AND PROCEEDING. Cornell University Press, 1972.

583. Colonna, Francesco. HYPNEROTOMACHIA: THE STRIFE OF LOVE IN A DREAME, tr. Sir Robert Dallington. London, 1592.

The erotic dream-vision from Italy via France; see also 239-240.

A. _____. THE STRIFE OF LOVE IN A DREAM, tr. Sir Robert Dallington, ed. Andrew Lang. London, 1890.

584. Nashe, Thomas. THE UNFORTUNATE TRAVELLER. OR, THE LIFE OF JACKE WILTON. London, 1594.

A classic in the picaresque tradition, combining the real-istic and the fantastic in a series of episodes that in-volves both the English and the Italians; in VIII.F, VIII.H, VIII.L; see also 383-84, 391-96.

A. _____. THE UNFORTUNATE TRAVELLER, ed. H. F. B. Brett-Smith. Boston: Percy Reprints, 1920.

B. _____. THE UNFORTUNATE TRAVELLER, ed. S. C. Chew. New York, 1926.

a. Bowers, Fredson T. "Thomas Nashe and the Picaresque Novel," in HUMANISTIC STUDIES IN HONOR OF JOHN CALVIN METCALF. Charlottesville, Virginia, 1941, pp. 12-27.

b. Croston, A. K. "The Use of Imagery in Nashe's THE UNFOR-TUNATE TRAVELLER," RES, 24 (1948), 90-101.

c. Latham, Agnes M. C. "Satire on Literary Themes and Modes in Nashe's UNFORTUNATE TRAVELLER, E&S, 1 (1948), 85-100.

d. Gibbons, Sister Marina. "Polemic, the Rhetorical Tradition, and THE UNFORTUNATE TRAVELLER," JEGP, 63 (1964), 408-21.

e. Kaula, David. "The Low Style in Nashe's THE UNFORTUNATE TRAVELER," SEL, 6 (1966), 43-57.

f. Lanham, Richard A. "Tom Nashe and Jack Wilton: Personality as Structure in THE UNFORTUNATE TRAVELLER," SSF, 4 (1966-67), 201-16.

g. Duncan-Jones, Katherine. "Nashe and Sidney: The Tournament in THE UNFORTUNATE TRAVELLER," MLR, 63 (1968), 3-6.

585. Twine, Laurence. THE PATTERNE OF PAINEFULL ADVENTURES. London, ca. 1594.

The famous history of Apollonius of Tyre once again; another edition in 1607; see also 520, 532.

A. _____. PATTERN OF PAINFUL ADVENTURES, ed. John P. Collier. London: Shakespeare's Library, 1875.

B. _____. THE PATTERNE OF PAINEFULL ADVENTURES, ed. Clarke Conwell. New Rochelle, New York, 1903.

586. Dickenson, John. ARISBAS, EUPHUES AMIDST HIS SLUMBERS. London, 1594.

Lyly's euphuism and Sidney's arcadianism wrought to the uttermost.

587. _____. GREENE IN CONCEIPT: NEW RAISED FROM HIS GRAVE TO THE TRAGIQUE HISTORIE OF FAIRE VALERIA OF LONDON. London, 1598.

Dickenson as amanuensis for a moral tale of marital woe urged by Robert Greene's ghost.

A. _____. PROSE AND VERSE, ed. Rev. A. B. Grosart. Manchester, 1878.

588. Forde, Emanuel. THE MOST PLEASANT HISTORIE OF ORNATUS AND ARTESIA. London, ca. 1595.

Other editions of this popular romance in 1607, 1619, 1634, 1650, etc.

589. _____. PARISMUS, THE RENOUMED PRINCE OF BOHEMIA. London, 1598.

One of the most popular romances throughout the seventeenth century.

Narrative Fiction

590. _____. PARISMENOS. London, 1599.

A sequel to PARISMUS (589).

591. _____. THE FAMOUS HISTORIE OF MONTELYON, KNIGHT OF THE ORACLE. London, 1633.

Earlier editions no longer extant; several later editions.

592. Chettle, Henry. PIERS PLAINNES SEAVEN YERES PRENTISHIP. London, 1595.

A kaleidoscope of scenes held together by a picaresque story no more improbable than most; in VIII.I; see also 403.

A. _____. PIERS PLAINNES SEVEN YERES PRENTISHIP, ed. Hermann Varnhagen. Erlangen, 1900.

593. Goodwine, Thomas Pope, tr. THE MOSTE PLEASAUNT HISTORYE OF BLANCHARDINE SONNE TO THE KING OF FRIZ; & THE FAIRE LADY EGLANTINE. London, 1595.

A paraphrase of an old medieval story printed by Caxton about 1489 (see 703); another edition of Godwine's translation in 1597.

594. Johnson, Richard. THE SEAVEN CHAMPIONS OF CHRISTENDOME. London, 1596.

A second part in 1597; oft-reprinted into the eighteenth century.

A. _____. THE SEVEN CHAMPIONS OF CHRISTENDOM, ed. F. J. Harvey Darton. London, 1913.

595. _____. THE HISTORY OF TOM THUMBE. London, 1621.

A prose version of a famous tale; attributed to Johnson; in 535: A.

596. Achilles Tatius. THE MOST DELECTABLE AND PLEASANT HISTORYE OF CLITOPHON AND LEUCIPPE, tr. William Burton. London, 1597.

A. _____. THE LOVES OF CLITOPHON AND LEUCIPPE, tr. William Burton, ed. Sir Stephen Gaselee and H. F. B. Brett-Smith. Oxford, 1923.

597. Marguerite d'Angouleme. THE QUEENE OF NAVARRES TALES, tr. A. B. London, 1597.

A collection of love stories written some fifty years earlier, modelled on Boccaccio and better known as the HEPTAMERON.

598. Deloney, Thomas. THE PLEASANT HISTORY OF JOHN WINCHECOMB . . .CALLED JACK OF NEWBURIE. London, 1597.

Deloney's first narrative, with a clothworker for its super-human hero; oft-reprinted; in VIII.F, VIII.H.

599. _____. THE GENTILE CRAFT. London, 1597.

Another success story aimed at the tradesman class, and the source of Dekker's SHOEMAKERS' HOLIDAY; another part in 1598, and oft-reprinted.

600. _____. THOMAS OF READING. London, 1598.

Middle-class morality--this time in the reign of Henry I; oft-reprinted; in VIII.F, VIII.L.

A. _____. THE WORKS, ed. Francis O. Mann. Oxford, 1912.

B. _____. NOVELS, ed. Merritt E. Lawlis. Indiana University Press, 1961.

a. Chevalley, Abel. THOMAS DELONEY, LE ROMAN DES METIERS AU TEMPS DE SHAKESPEARE. Paris, 1926.

b. Lawlis, Merritt E. APOLOGY FOR THE MIDDLE CLASS: THE DRAMATIC NOVELS OF THOMAS DELONEY. Indiana University Press, 1960.

601. Montemayor, Jorge de. DIANA, tr. Bartholomew Young. London, 1598.

The flamboyant Spanish romance.

A. _____. A CRITICAL EDITION OF YOUNG'S TRANSLATION OF MONTEMAYOR'S DIANA AND GIL POLO'S ENAMOURED DIANA, ed. Judith M. Kennedy. Oxford, 1968.

602. Breton, Nicholas. THE MISERIES OF MAVILLIA. London, 1599.

The tragedy of a virtuous maid told in first-person nar-rative; see also 411-12, 494-95.

603. _____. A POSTE WITH A MADDE PACKET OF LETTERS. London, 1602.

A gallimaufry of imaginary letters and replies; extremely

popular, with many later enlarged editions.

604. _____. A MERRIE DIALOGUE BETWIXT THE TAKER AND MISTAKER. London, 1603.

> Reprinted 1635 as A MAD WORLD MY MASTERS, and better known under that title.

A. _____. A MAD WORLD MY MASTERS AND OTHER PROSE WORKS, ed. Ursula Kentish-Wright. 2 vols. London, 1929.

605. _____. GRIMELLOS FORTUNES. London, 1604.

> A collection of stories told in a framework narrative about a young gentleman finding his place in the world.

A. _____. GRIMELLOS FORTUNES (1604), AN OLDE MANS LESSON (1605), ed. E. G. Morice. University of Bristol Press, 1936.

606. _____. CHOICE, CHANCE AND CHANGE. London, 1606.

> A tale of love among the country gentry, replete with realistic details.

A. _____. CHOICE, CHANCE AND CHANGE, ed. Rev. A. B. Grosart. Manchester, 1881.

B. _____. THE WORKS IN VERSE AND PROSE, ed. Rev. A. B. Grosart. 2 vols. Edinburgh: Chertsey Worthies' Library, 1879.

i. Tannenbaum, Samuel A. NICHOLAS BRETON: A CONCISE BIBLIOGRAPHY. New York, 1947.

607. Markham, Gervase. THE ENGLISH ARCADIA. London, 1607.

> An unworthy continuation of Sidney's ARCADIA (582); another installment in 1613.

608. Dobson, George. DOBSONS DRIE BOBBES. London, 1607.

> Spicy anecdotes from provincial and university life.

A. _____. DOBSONS DRIE BOBBES: A STORY OF SIXTEENTH CENTURY DURHAM, ed. E. A. Horsman. Oxford University Press, 1955.

a. Colgrave, Bertram. "Dobson's Drie Bobs," DURHAM UNIVERSITY

JOURNAL, 12 (1951), 77-85.

b. O'Brien, Avril S. "DOBSONS DRIE BOBBES: A Significant Contribution to the Development of Prose Fiction," SEL, 12 (1972), 55-70.

609. Anon. MERRIE CONCEITED JESTS OF GEORGE PEELE. London, 1607.

A fine collection of jests associated with a notorious sinner; other editions ca. 1620, 1627, 1657, and 1671.

610. Armin, Robert. A NEST OF NINNIES. London, 1608.

More jests.

A. Zall, Paul M., ed. A NEST OF NINNIES AND OTHER EN-GLISH JESTBOOKS OF THE SEVENTEENTH CENTURY. University of Nebraska Press, 1970.

a. Felver, Charles S. ROBERT ARMIN, SHAKESPEARE'S FOOL: A BIOGRAPHICAL ESSAY. Kent State University Press, 1961.

611. Bettie, W. THE HISTORIE OF TITANA, AND THESEUS. London, 1608.

A conventional romance in the manner of Sidney; another edition in 1636.

612. Hall, Joseph. THE DISCOVERY OF A NEW WORLD, tr. John Healey. London, ca. 1609.

A satiric allegory using the motif of the PELERINAGE DE LA VIE HUMAINE; the Latin text published ca. 1605 as MUNDUS ALTER ET IDEM; see also 80-83, 489, 756-57.

A. _____. THE DISCOVERY OF A NEW WORLD, tr. John Healey, ed. Huntington Brown. Harvard University Press, 1937.

613. Cervantes. THE HISTORY OF THE VALOROUS AND WITTIE KNIGHT-ERRANT, DON-QUIXOTE OF THE MANCHA, tr. Thomas Shelton. London, 1612.

Still a respected translation of Cervantes' masterpiece; Part I printed in 1612, Part II in 1620; see also 624.

A. _____. THE HISTORY OF DON QUIXOTE, tr. Thomas Shelton, ed. James Fitzmaurice-Kelly. 4 vols. London: Tudor Translations, 1896.

B. _____. DON QUIXOTE, tr. Thomas Shelton, ed. A. W. Pollard. 3 vols. London: English Classics, 1900.

a. Knowles, E. B., Jr. "The First and Second Editions of Shelton's DON QUIXOTE Part I: A Collation and Dating," HR, 9 (1941), 252-65.

614. Scoggin, John. SCOGGINS JESTES. London, 1613.

Undoubtedly there were earlier editions of this well-known jest-book; in the STATIONERS' REGISTER it is licensed to a printer in 1565-66.

615. Gainsford, Thomas. THE HISTORIE OF TREBIZOND. London, 1616.

Four books of romantic tales; see also 170-71.

616. Boccaccio. THE DECAMERON CONTAINING AN HUNDRED PLEASANT NOVELS, tr. anon. 2 vols. London, 1620.

The first complete translation of the DECAMERON, though it had been well-known in England since its composition; other editions in 1625, 1634, and 1655.

A. _____. THE DECAMERON, tr. anon., ed. Edward Hutton. 4 vols. London: Tudor Translations, 1909.

617. Urfe, Honore d'. THE HISTORY OF ASTREA, tr. anon. London, 1620.

The notorious roman a clef from France.

618. Wroth, Lady Mary. THE COUNTESSE OF MONTGOMERIES URANIA. London, 1621.

In the wake of Sidney's ARCADIA.

619. Aleman, Mateo. THE ROGUE: OR THE LIFE OF GUZMAN DE ALFARA-CHE, tr. James Mabbe. 2 pts. London, 1622.

The prototype of the picaresque novel; other editions in 1623, 1630, 1634, and 1655.

A. _____. THE ROGUE, tr. James Mabbe, ed. James Fitzmaurice-Kelly. 4 vols. London: Tudor Translations, 1924.

620. Achilles Tatius. THE LOVES OF CLITOPHON AND LEUCIPPE, tr. Anthony Hodges. Oxford, 1638.

A perennial favorite of Greek romance; see also 596.

621. Tarlton, Richard. TARLTONS JESTS. London, 1638.

   Anecodotes associated with one of the most gifted
   Elizabethan clowns; earlier editions of this popular
   collection no longer extant, though probably as early
   as 1592.

622. Godwin, Francis. THE MAN IN THE MOONE: OR A DISCOURSE OF
   A VOYAGE THITHER. London, 1638.

   An energetic forerunner of science fiction; another edition in 1657; in VIII.K.

   A. _____. THE MAN IN THE MOON, AND NUNCIUS INANI-
   MATUS, ed. Grant McColley. Northampton, Massachusetts,
   1937.

   B. _____. THE MAN IN THE MOONE, ed. Ivan Volkoff.
   Huntington Library, 1961.

   a. Nicolson, Marjorie H. A WORLD IN THE MOON: A STUDY
   OF THE CHANGING ATTITUDES TOWARD THE MOON IN
   THE SEVENTEENTH AND EIGHTEENTH CENTURIES. North-
   ampton, Massachusetts, 1936.

   b. _____. "Cosmic Voyages," ELH, 7 (1940), 83-107.

   c. Knowlson, James R. "A Note on Bishop Godwin's MAN IN
   THE MOONE: The East Indies Trade Route and a 'Language'
   of Musical Notes," MP, 65 (1967-68), 357-61.

623. Rivers, George. THE HEROINAE: OR THE LIVES OF ARRIA, PAULINA,
   LUCRECIA, DIDO, THEUTILLA, CYPRIANA, ARETAPHILA. London, 1639.

   A contribution to the fame of good women.

624. Cervantes. EXEMPLARIE NOVELLS, tr. James Mabbe. London, 1640.

   Cervantes' masterful novelle; see also 613.

   A. _____. EXEMPLARY NOVELS, tr. James Mabbe, ed. S. W.
   Orson. 2 vols. London, 1900.

625. Brathwaite, Richard. THE TWO LANCASHIRE LOVERS: OR THE EXCEL-
   LENT HISTORY OF PHILOCLES AND DORICLEA. London, 1640.

   A tale which rests upon romantic convention; see also
   498-99, 677-78.

626. _____. PANTHALIA: OR THE ROYAL ROMANCE. London, 1659.

    Seventeenth-century romance in full flower.

627. Sheppard, Samuel. THE LOVES OF AMANDUS AND SOPHRONIA. London, 1640.

    A romantic narrative enhanced with verses in the manner of Sidney.

628. Bayly, Thomas. HERBA PARIETIS: OR, THE WALL-FLOWER. London, 1650.

    A curious fantasy from the disturbed brain of a royalist divine imprisoned in Newgate.

629. Scudery, Madeleine de. IBRAHIM. OR THE ILLUSTRIOUS BASSA, tr. Henry Cogan. London, 1652.

    The first appearance in English of this famous French novelist.

630. Rabelais, Francois. THE WORKS, tr. Sir Thomas Urquhart. London, 1653.

    The first book only of Gargantua, with the second book of Pantagruel printed also in 1653, and the third book in 1693; the translation continued by Peter Motteux.

    A. _____. GARGANTUA AND PANTAGRUEL, tr. Sir Thomas Urquhart and Peter Le Motteaux, ed. Charles Whibley. 3 vols. London: Tudor Translations, 1900.

IX. LITERARY CRITICISM

IX. Literary Criticism

There is a surprising amount of critical writing in our period, the most interesting of which deals with the truth or fictitiousness of literature. But a wide range of issues was explored; and especially after the mid-sixteenth century, questions about prosody, language, and form were seriously debated. Most of the concern focused on poetry, of course, rather than on prose narrative or drama, except perhaps where the charge of immorality was made. There were no professional or even full-time critics, but there were plenty of practising poets and literate gentlemen to formulate a poetics for the English renaissance.

See also 315, VI.K, 365, 366-368, 372, 377, 391, 426, 439, 681.

A. Moulton, Charles W., ed. THE LIBRARY OF LITERARY CRITI-
    CISM. 8 vols. Buffalo, New York, 1901-10. Vols. I-II.

B. Collins, J. Churton, ed. CRITICAL ESSAYS AND LITERARY
    FRAGMENTS. Westminster: English Garner, 1903.

C. Smith, G. Gregory, ed. ELIZABETHAN CRITICAL ESSAYS.
    2 vols. Oxford University Press, 1904.

    The most extensive collection of critical treatises
    in English written between 1570 and 1603; contains
    the complete text of Gascoigne, CERTAYNE NOTES;
    Lodge, DEFENCE OF POETRY; Sidney, DEFENCE OF
    POESIE; Webbe, DISCOURSE OF ENGLISH POETRIE;
    Puttenham, ARTE OF ENGLISH POESIE; Campion,
    OBSERVATIONS IN THE ART OF ENGLISH POESIE;
    Daniel, DEFENCE OF RYME; and many shorter pieces.

D. Spingarn, Joel E., ed. CRITICAL ESSAYS OF THE SEVEN-
    TEENTH CENTURY. 3 vols. Oxford, 1908-09.

E. Hardison, O. B., Jr., ed. ENGLISH LITERARY CRITICISM:
    THE RENAISSANCE. New York, 1963.

A useful collection of critical statements in English from Caxton to Milton, with a valuable introduction; contains the complete texts of Gascoigne, CERTA-YNE NOTES; and Sidney, DEFENCE OF POESIE; and excerpts from many others.

F. Tayler, Edward W., ed. LITERARY CRITICISM OF SEVEN-TEENTH-CENTURY ENGLAND. New York, 1967.

a. Spingarn, Joel E. A HISTORY OF LITERARY CRITICISM IN THE RENAISSANCE. Columbia University Press, 1899. Rev. ed. Columbia University Press, 1954.

b. Sweeting, Elizabeth J. EARLY TUDOR CRITICISM: LINGUIS-TIC & LITERARY. Oxford, 1940.

c. Atkins, John W. H. ENGLISH LITERARY CRITICISM: THE RENASCENCE. 2nd ed. London, 1951.

d. _____. ENGLISH LITERARY CRITICISM: THE MEDIEVAL PHASE. 2nd ed. London, 1952.

631. Gascoigne, George. CERTAYNE NOTES OF INSTRUCTION CONCERN-ING THE MAKING OF VERSE OR RHYME IN ENGLISH, in THE POSIES. London, 1575.

Primarily a handbook on prosody, but with much sound advice on other poetical matters; in IX.C, IX.E; see also 544.

632. Lodge, Thomas. IN DEFENCE OF POETRY, MUSICK, AND STAGE PLAYS. London, ca. 1579.

An academic reply to Gosson's SCHOOL OF ABUSE (366), written with wit and learning; in IX.C; see also 374, 574-78, 751-53.

633. Harvey, Gabriel, and Edmund Spenser. THREE PROPER, AND WITTIE FAMILIAR LETTERS, LATELY PASSED BETWENE TWO UNIVERSITIE MEN. London, 1580.

Reformed English versifying and the London earthquake of 1580; see also 387-90.

634. Webbe, William. A DISCOURSE OF ENGLISH POETRIE. London, 1586.

A compendious and derivative discourse with many liter-ary judgments; in IX.C.

A. _____ . A DISCOURSE OF ENGLISH POETRIE, ed. Edward Arber. London, 1871.

635. Puttenham, George. THE ARTE OF ENGLISH POESIE. London, 1589.

The most comprehensive Elizabethan treatise on English poetry, especially instructive in its discussion of prosody and form; in IX.C, IX.E (selections).

A. _____ . THE ARTE OF ENGLISH POESIE, ed. Gladys D. Willcock and Alice Walker. Cambridge University Press, 1936.

636. Sidney, Sir Philip. THE DEFENCE OF POESIE. London: William Ponsonby, 1595.

The most intelligent and sensitive of the many treatises on literary art, combining a Platonic and an Aristotelian esthetics; written ca. 1580, and published in 1595 by two printers: William Ponsonby (authorized version) and Thomas Olney (with the title AN APOLOGIE FOR PO-ETRIE); in IXC, IX.E; see also 582.

A. _____ . THE DEFENCE OF POESY, ed. Albert S. Cook. Boston, 1890.

B. _____ . AN APOLOGIE FOR POETRIE, ed. J. C. Collins. Oxford, 1907.

C. _____ . AN APOLOGY FOR POETRY, ed. Geoffrey Shepherd. Edinburgh: Nelson's Medieval and Renaissance Library, 1965.

D. _____ . THE APOLOGY FOR POETRY, ed. Mary R. Mahl. San Fernando Valley State College, 1969.

An edition from a manuscript perhaps as early as 1585.

a. Maynadier, G. Howard. "The Areopagus of Sidney and Spenser," MLR, 4 (1908-09), 289-301.

b. Samuel, Irene. "The Influence of Plato on Sir Philip Sidney's DEFENSE OF POESY," MLQ, 1 (1940), 383-91.

c. Dowlin, Cornell M. "Sidney's Two Definitions of Poetry," MLQ, 3 (1942), 573-81.

d. Malloch, A. E. " 'Architectonic' Knowledge and Sidney's APOLOGIE," ELH, 20 (1953), 181-85.

e. Krouse, F. Michael. "Plato and Sidney's DEFENCE OF PO-
ESIE," CL, 6 (1954), 138-47.

f. Thorne, J. P. "A Ramistical Commentary on Sidney's AN
APOLOGIE FOR POETRIE," MP, 54 (1956-57), 158-64.

g. Hamilton, A. C. "Sidney's Idea of the 'Right Poet'," CL,
9 (1957), 51-59.

h. McIntyre, John P., S.J. "Sidney's 'Golden World'," CL, 14
(1962), 356-65.

i. Blackburn, Thomas H. "Edmund Bolton's THE CABANET ROYAL:
A Belated Reply to Sidney's APOLOGY FOR POETRY," SRen,
14 (1967), 159-71.

j. Hyman, Virginia R. "Sidney's Definition of Poetry," SEL, 10
(1970), 49-62.

k. Hardison, O. B., Jr. "The Two Voices of Sidney's APOLOGY
FOR POETRY," ELR, 2 (1972), 83-99.

l. Heninger, S. K., Jr. TOUCHES OF SWEET HARMONY: PY-
THAGOREAN COSMOLOGY AND RENAISSANCE POETICS.
Huntington Library, 1974. Part III.

637. Meres, Francis. PALLADIS TAMIA. WITS TREASURY. London, 1598.

As its title indicates, a storehouse of borrowed learning,
arranged by subjects; in IX.C (selections).

A. _____. PALLADIS TAMIA: WITS TREASURY, ed. Don C.
Allen. New York: Scholars' Facsimiles, 1938.

638. Cornwallis, Sir William. DISCOURSES UPON SENECA THE TRAGEDIAN.
London, 1601.

Annotation and interpretation of specific passages.

639. Campion, Thomas. OBSERVATIONS IN THE ART OF ENGLISH POESIE.
London, 1602.

A scrupulous treatment of prosody in English, most important for its advocacy that rime be abandoned in English
verse, preparing for the wave of neo-classicism; in IX.C,
IX.E (selections); see also 640.

a. MacDonagh, Thomas. THOMAS CAMPION AND THE ART OF ENGLISH POETRY. Dublin, 1913.

640. Daniel, Samuel. A DEFENCE OF RYME. AGAINST A PAMPHLET EN-TITULED: OBSERVATIONS IN THE ART OF ENGLISH POESIE, in A PANEGYRIKE CONGRATULATORIE. London, 1603.

A refutation of Campion's attack on rhyme (639) written with more charm than substance; in IX.C, IX.E (selections).

A. _____. A DEFENCE OF RYME. Thomas Campion, OBSERVA-TIONS IN THE ART OF ENGLISH POESIE, ed. G. B. Harrison. London: Bodley Head Quartos, 1925.

B. _____. POEMS AND A DEFENCE OF RYME, ed. Arthur C. Sprague. Harvard University Press, 1930.

641. Reynolds, Henry. MYTHOMYSTES, WHEREIN A SHORT SURVAY IS TAKEN OF THE NATURE AND VALUE OF TRUE POESY. London, 1632.

An imaginative treatise that allies poetry with mystical experience; in IX.D, IX.F.

a. Cinquemani, A. M. "Henry Reynolds' MYTHOMYSTES and the Continuity of Ancient Modes of Allegoresis in Seventeenth-Century England," PMLA, 85 (1970), 1041-49.

642. Jonson, Ben. TIMBER, OR DISCOVERIES MADE UPON MAN AND MAT-TER, in THE WORKES. London, 1640.

A commonplace book on a wide variety of topics, but most importantly with comments about literary practice; in IX.E (selections), IX.F.

A. _____. TIMBER; OR, DISCOVERIES MADE UPON MEN AND MATTER, ed. Felix E. Schelling. Boston, 1892.

B. _____. TIMBER, in BEN JONSON, ed. C. H. Herford and Percy Simpson. 11 vols. Oxford, 1925-52. Vol. VIII.

a. Fieler, Frank B. "The Impact of Bacon and the New Science upon Jonson's Critical Thought in TIMBER," RenP 1958, 1959, 1960. Durham, North Carolina, 1961, pp. 84-92.

643. Digby, Kenelm. OBSERVATIONS ON THE 22. STANZA IN THE 9th. CANTO OF THE 2d. BOOK OF SPENCERS FAERY QUEEN. London, 1643.

The first serious and sustained criticism of Spenser, written
in 1628; another edition in 1644.

644. Ross, Alexander. MYSTAGOGUS POETICUS: OR THE MUSES INTERPRET-
ER. London, 1647.

A handbook of mythology for the interpretation of poetry;
six editions by 1675; see also 124, 325, 333, 466.

X. WRITINGS ON EDUCATION

X. Writings on Education

During the Renaissance, education was in ferment, if not in crisis. The scholastic curriculum was modified by humanism, and later by empiricism. As always, there was heavy-handed instruction of the young, often laced with moral advice and admonition. Of particular interest in this section are the courtesy books, a genre imported from Italy which had a strong formative influence on all aspects of culture in England.

See also I.w, 10, 547, 644, 701, 711, 713, 714, 716, 720, 724, 726, 732, 747, 750, 756.

A. Pepper, Robert, ed. FOUR TUDOR BOOKS ON EDUCATION. Gainesville, Florida: Scholars' Facsimiles, 1966.

i. Noyes, Gertrude E. BIBLIOGRAPHY OF COURTESY AND CONDUCT BOOKS IN SEVENTEENTH-CENTURY ENGLAND. Yale University Press, 1937.

ii. Heltzel, Virgil B. A CHECK LIST OF COURTESY BOOKS IN THE NEWBERRY LIBRARY. Chicago, 1942.

iii. Watson, Foster. ENGLISH WRITERS ON EDUCATION, 1480-1603: A SOURCE BOOK. Gainesville, Florida: Scholars' Facsimiles, 1967.

   Notices of early writers on education.

a. Hazlitt, William C. SCHOOLS, SCHOOL-BOOKS AND SCHOOLMASTERS. London, 1888.

b. Woodward, W. H. "English Universities, Schools and Scholarship in the Sixteenth Century," in THE CAMBRIDGE HISTORY OF ENGLISH LITERATURE, ed. A. W. Ward and A. R. Waller. 15 vols. Cambridge University Press, 1907-27. III,418-38.

c. Watson, Foster. THE ENGLISH GRAMMAR SCHOOLS TO 1660: THEIR CURRICULUM AND PRACTICE. Cambridge University Press, 1908.

d. _____. THE BEGINNINGS OF THE TEACHING OF MODERN SUBJECTS IN ENGLAND. London, 1909.

e. Leach, Arthur F. THE SCHOOLS OF MEDIEVAL ENGLAND. London, 1915.

f. Kelso, Ruth. THE DOCTRINE OF THE ENGLISH GENTLEMAN IN THE SIXTEENTH CENTURY. University of Illinois Press, 1929.

g. Ustick, W. Lee. "Advice to a Son: A Type of Seventeenth Century Conduct Book," SP, 29 (1932), 409-41.

h. Mason, John E. GENTLEFOLK IN THE MAKING: STUDIES IN THE HISTORY OF ENGLISH COURTESY LITERATURE AND RELATED TOPICS FROM 1531 TO 1774. University of Pennsylvania Press, 1935.

i. Miller, Perry. THE NEW ENGLAND MIND: THE SEVENTEENTH CENTURY. New York, 1939.

j. Baldwin, Thomas W. WILLIAM SHAKESPERE'S PETTY SCHOOL. University of Illinois Press, 1943.

k. _____. WILLIAM SHAKESPERE'S SMALL LATINE & LESSE GREEKE. 2 vols. University of Illinois Press, 1944.

l. Pafort, Eloise. "A Group of Early Tudor School-Books," LIBRARY, 4th series, 26 (1945-46), 227-61.

m. McMahon, Clara P. EDUCATION IN FIFTEENTH-CENTURY ENGLAND. Johns Hopkins Press, 1947.

n. Thompson, Craig R. SCHOOLS IN TUDOR ENGLAND. Washington, D. C.: Folger Booklets, 1958.

o. Smith, Constance I. "Some Ideas on Education Before Locke," JHI, 23 (1962), 403-06.

p. Hamilton, Kenneth G. THE TWO HARMONIES: POETRY AND PROSE IN THE SEVENTEENTH CENTURY. Oxford, 1963.

A study of rhetoric in the renaissance.

q. Charlton, Kenneth. EDUCATION IN RENAISSANCE ENGLAND. London, 1965.

r. Simon, Joan. EDUCATION AND SOCIETY IN TUDOR ENGLAND. Cambridge University Press, 1966.

s. Ong, Walter J., S.J. "Tudor Writings on Rhetoric," SRen, 15 (1968), 39-69.

t. Mulder, John R. THE TEMPLE OF THE MIND: EDUCATION AND LITERARY TASTE IN SEVENTEENTH CENTURY ENGLAND. New York, 1969.

u. Armytage, Walter H. G. FOUR HUNDRED YEARS OF ENGLISH EDUCATION. 2nd ed. Cambridge University Press, 1970.

645. Aelfric. COLLOQUY. ca. 1000.

A fascinating document of medieval education which demonstrates actual classroom technique; see also 1-2.

A. _____. COLLOQUY, ed. G. N. Garmonsway. 2nd ed. London, 1947.

646. La Tour-Landry, Geoffroy de. THE BOOK WHICH THE KNIGHT OF THE TOWER MADE, tr. anon. ca. 1450.

A widower's moral instruction of his three young daughters, in large part through anecdote; printed by William Caxton in 1484.

A. _____. THE BOOK OF GEOFFREY DE LA TOUR-LANDRY, tr. anon., ed. Thomas Wright. EETS OS 33. London, 1868.

B. _____. THE BOOK OF THE KNIGHT OF LA TOUR-LANDRY, tr. anon., ed. G. S. Taylor. London, 1930.

C. _____. THE BOOK OF THE KNIGHT OF THE TOWER, ed. M. Y. Offord. Oxford University Press, 1971.

647. Anon. A GENERALL RULE TO TECHE EVERY MAN THAT IS WILLYNGE FOR TO LERNE, TO SERVE A LORDE OR MAYSTER. ca. 1450.

A. Anon. A FIFTEENTH-CENTURY COURTESY BOOK, ed. R. W. Chambers. EETS OS 148. London, 1914.

648. Wydeville, Anthony, Earl Rivers, tr. THE DICTES OR SAYENGIS OF THE PHILOSOPHRES. Westminster: William Caxton, 1477.

> An early instance of the humanists' interest in classical learning; other editions in 1480(?), 1489, and 1528.

649. Cox, Leonard. THE ARTE OR CRAFTE OF RHETHORYKE. London, 1524.

> The earliest rhetoric in English; another edition in 1532.

650. Vives, Juan Luis. THE INSTRUCTION OF A CHRISTEN WOMAN, tr. Richard Hyrde. London, ca. 1529.

> A tract on the education of women by the great Spanish humanist; at least eight editions of this translation by the end of the century.

    a. Watson, Foster. VIVES AND THE RENASCENCE EDUCATION OF WOMEN. London, 1912.

651. Vives, Juan Luis. AN INTRODUCTION TO WYSEDOME, tr. Richard Morysine. London, 1540.

> Education to inculcate humanistic values; other editions in 1544, 1550, ca. 1550, and 1564.

    A. _____. INTRODUCTION TO WISDOM, tr. Richard Morysine, ed. Marian L. Tobriner. New York: Classics in Education, 1968.

652. Elyot, Sir Thomas. THE BOKE NAMED THE GOVERNOUR. London, 1531.

> A moral treatise on politics and a courtesy book for the English courtier, specifically Henry VIII; at least eight editions by 1580; see also 286.

    A. _____. THE BOKE NAMED THE GOVERNOUR, ed. H. H. S. Croft. London, 1883.

    B. _____. THE BOOK NAMED THE GOVERNOR, ed. S. E. Lehmberg. London: Everyman's, 1962.

    a. Warren, Leslie C. HUMANISTIC DOCTRINES OF THE PRINCE FROM PETRARCH TO SIR THOMAS ELYOT. Chicago, 1939.

    b. Lehmberg, Stanford E. SIR THOMAS ELYOT: TUDOR HUMANIST. University of Texas Press, 1960.

c. Holmes, Elisabeth. "The Significance of Elyot's Revision of the GOVERNOUR," RES, 12 (1961), 352-63.

d. Hogrefe, Pearl. "Sir Thomas Elyot's Intention in the Opening Chapters of the GOVERNOR," SP, 60 (1963), 133-40.

e. Major, John M. SIR THOMAS ELYOT AND RENAISSANCE HUMANISM. University of Nebraska Press, 1964.

f. Hogrefe, Pearl. THE LIFE AND TIMES OF SIR THOMAS ELYOT. Iowa State University Press, 1967.

653. Elyot, Sir Thomas. OF THE KNOWLEDGE WHICHE MAKETH A WISE MAN. London, 1533.

A broad view of what constituted knowledge at the court of Henry VIII.

A. _____. OF THE KNOWLEDGE WHICH MAKETH A WISE MAN, ed. Edwin J. Howard. Oxford, Ohio, 1946.

654. Plutarch. THE EDUCATION OR BRINGINGE UP OF CHILDREN, tr. Sir Thomas Elyot. London, ca. 1535.

The classic from one of the great teachers of all time; in X.A; see also 652-53.

655. Erasmus. PROVERBES OR ADAGIES, tr. Richard Taverner. London, 1539.

A well-thumbed schoolbook derived from one of the most influential compendia of the humanistic movement; several editions throughout the sixteenth century; see also 773.

A. _____. PROVERBS OR ADAGIES, tr. Richard Taverner, ed. DeWitt T. Starnes. Gainesville, Florida: Scholars' Facsimilies, 1956.

656. _____. APOPHTHEGMES, tr. Nicholas Udall. London, 1542.

A translation by a famous educator and academic playwright (Ralph Roister Doister); another edition in 1564.

657. Ascham, Roger. TOXOPHILUS, THE SCHOLE OF SHOOTINGE. London, 1545.

A pseudo-classical dialogue between Philologus, "a lover of learning," and Toxophilus, "a lover of archery," which praises archery as essential to education; other editions in 1571 and 1589.

a. Greene, Thomas M. "Roger Ascham: The Perfect End of
Shooting," ELH, 36 (1969), 609-25.

658. Ascham, Roger. THE SCHOLEMASTER, OR PLAINE AND PERFITE WAY
OF TEACHYNG CHILDREN. . .THE LATIN TONG. London, 1570.

The fullest statement of humanist principles deployed in
education; at least three more editions in 1571, and another in 1589; in IX.E (selections).

A. _____. ENGLISH WORKS, ed. W. A. Wright. Cambridge
University Press, 1904.

B. _____. THE SCHOOLMASTER, ed. L. V. Ryan. Cornell
University Press: Folger Documents, 1967.

i. Tannenbaum, Samuel A. ROGER ASCHAM: A CONCISE
BIBLIOGRAPHY. New York, 1946.

ii. Johnson, Robert C. ELIZABETHAN BIBLIOGRAPHIES SUPPLE-
MENTS, IX: MINOR ELIZABETHANS. [Roger Ascham, et al.]
London, 1968.

a. Parks, George B. "The First Draft of Ascham's SCHOLEMASTER,"
HLQ, 1 (1938), 313-27.

b. Staton, Walter F., Jr. "Roger Ascham's Theory of History
Writing," SP, 56 (1959), 125-37.

c. Ryan, Lawrence V. ROGER ASCHAM. Stanford University
Press, 1963.

659. Baldwin, William. A TREATISE OF MORALL PHYLOSOPHIE, CONTAYN-
YNG THE SAYINGES OF THE WYSE. London, 1547.

A much used handbook of aphoristic wisdom that went
through at least thirty editions by 1650.

A. _____. A TREATISE OF MORALL PHILOSOPHIE, ed. Robert
H. Bowers. Gainesville, Florida: Scholars' Facsimiles, 1967.

a. Buhler, Curt F. "A Survival from the Middle Ages: William
Baldwin's Use of the DICTES AND SAYINGS," SPECULUM,
23 (1948), 76-80.

660. Wilson, Thomas. THE RULE OF REASON. London, 1551.

A textbook of logic; oft-reprinted until 1593.

661. _____. THE ARTE OF RHETORIQUE. London, 1553.

A manual for English style based on Latin rules with
much incidental literary criticism, oft-reprinted until
1585; in IX.E (selections).

A. _____. ARTE OF RHETORIQUE, ed. G. H. Mair. Oxford:
Tudor and Stuart Library, 1909.

B. _____. THE ARTE OF RHETORIQUE, ed. Robert H. Bowers.
Gainesville, Florida: Scholars' Facsimiles, 1962.

a. Schmidt, Albert J. "Thomas Wilson, Tudor Scholar-Statesman,"
HLQ, 20 (1956-57), 205-18.

b. _____. "Thomas Wilson and the Tudor Commonwealth: An
Essay in Civic Humanism," HLQ, 23 (1959-60), 49-60.

662. Rainolde, Richard. THE FOUNDACION OF RHETORIKE. London, 1563.

Another textbook, important for its thoroughness.

A. _____. THE FOUNDACION OF RHETORIKE, ed. Francis R.
Johnson. New York: Scholars' Facsimiles, 1945.

a. Johnson, Francis R. "Two Renaissance Textbooks of Rhetoric:
Aphthonius' PROGYMNASMATA and Rainolde's A BOOKE
CALLED THE FOUNDACION OF RHETORIKE," HLQ, 6 (1943),
427-44.

663. Casa, Giovanni della. GALATEO, tr. Robert Peterson. London, 1576.

With Castiglione's COURTIER (see 726), the most influential courtesy book of the renaissance.

A. _____. GALATEO, tr. Robert Peterson, ed. Herbert J. Reid.
London, 1892.

B. _____. GALATEO, tr. Robert Peterson, ed. Joel E. Spingarn.
Boston: Humanist's Library, 1914.

664. Peacham, Henry (the elder). THE GARDEN OF ELOQUENCE CONTEYN-
ING THE FIGURES OF GRAMMAR AND RHETORICK. London, 1577.

A useful textbook; another edition in 1593.

A. _____. THE GARDEN OF ELOQUENCE, ed. William G.
Crane. Gainesville, Florida: Scholars' Facsimiles, 1954.

665. Guazzo, Stefano. THE CIVILE CONVERSATION, tr. George Pettie. London, 1581.

>   An Italian work bearing strongly upon the renaissance concept of the gentleman; another edition in 1586.

A. _____. THE CIVILE CONVERSATION, tr. George Pettie, ed. Sir Edward Sullivan. 2 vols. London: Tudor Translations, 1925.

a. Lievsay, John L. STEFANO GUAZZO AND THE ENGLISH RENAISSANCE, 1575-1675. University of North Carolina Press, 1961.

666. Mulcaster, Richard. POSITIONS WHERIN THOSE PRIMITIVE CIRCUMSTANCES BE EXAMINED, WHICH ARE NECESSARIE FOR THE TRAINING UP OF CHILDREN. London, 1581.

>   A rigorous but intelligent statement from the man who was headmaster of the Merchant Taylors' School in London during Spenser's attendance there.

A. _____. POSITIONS, ed. Robert H. Quick. London, 1888.

B. _____. POSITIONS, ed. Richard L. De Molen. New York: Columbia Classics in Education, 1971.

667. _____. THE FIRST PART OF THE ELEMENTARIE WHICH ENTREATETH CHEFLIE OF THE RIGHT WRITING OF OUR ENGLISH TUNG. London, 1582.

A. _____. ELEMENTARIE, ed. E. T. Campagnac. Oxford: Tudor and Stuart Library, 1925.

B. _____. THE EDUCATIONAL WRITINGS, abridged by James Oliphant. Glasgow, 1903.

668. Day, Angel. THE ENGLISH SECRETORIE. London, 1586.

>   A handbook of rhetoric; several later editions.

669. Kempe, William. THE EDUCATION OF CHILDREN IN LEARNING. London, 1588.

>   A rationale for educating children by discipline to be good citizens and Christians; in X.A. [This William Kempe is not the famous clown.]

670. Fraunce, Abraham. THE ARCADIAN RHETORIKE. London, 1588.

   A pleasant textbook with examples from English as well
   as Greek and Latin authors.

   A. _____. THE ARCADIAN RHETORIKE, ed. Ethel Seaton.
   Oxford: Luttrell Society, 1950.

   a. Koller, Kathrine. "Abraham Fraunce and Edmund Spenser,"
   ELH, 7 (1940), 108-20.

671. Romei, Annibale. THE COURTIERS ACADEMIE, tr. John Kepers. London,
   1598.

   Another elegant courtesy book imported from Italy.

672. James I. BASILICON DORON. London, 1599.

   A royal father's advice to his son, Prince Henry; reprinted in several editions in 1603; see also 407.

   A. _____. THE BASILICON DORON, ed. James Craigie. 2
   vols. Edinburgh: Scottish Text Society, 1944-50.

673. Bacon, Francis. OF THE PROFICIENCE AND ADVANCEMENT OF
   LEARNING, DIVINE AND HUMANE. London, 1605.

   An astute survey of the state of knowledge at the end
   of Elizabeth's reign and practical recommendations for
   advancing it under the aegis of reason; reprinted 1629
   and 1633; complemented by Bacon's NEW ATLANTIS
   (316); see also 315, 482.

   A. _____. ADVANCEMENT OF LEARNING AND THE NEW
   ATLANTIS, ed. Thomas Case. Oxford University Press:
   World's Classics, 1906.

674. Brinsley, John. LUDUS LITERARIUS, OR THE GRAMMAR SCHOOLE.
   London, 1612.

   The early seventeenth-century curriculum.

   A. _____. LUDUS LITERARIUS, ed. E. T. Campagnac. University of Liverpool Press, 1917.

675. _____. A CONSOLATION FOR OUR GRAMMAR SCHOOLES. London,
   1622.

   A remedial course for slow learners.

A. _____ . A CONSOLATION FOR OUR GRAMMAR SCHOOLES, ed. Thomas C. Pollock. New York: Scholars' Facsimiles, 1943.

676. Peacham, Henry (the younger). THE COMPLEAT GENTLEMAN. London, 1622.

> The culmination of the courtesy book tradition; augmented in 1627 and 1634; see also 506.A.

A. _____ . COMPLEAT GENTLEMAN, ed. G. S. Gordon. Oxford: Tudor and Stuart Library, 1906.

677. Brathwaite, Richard. THE ENGLISH GENTLEMAN. London, 1630.

> A conduct book for young gentlemen; see also 498–99, 625–26.

678. _____ . THE ENGLISH GENTLEWOMAN. London, 1631.

> A conduct book for young ladies; oft-reprinted with Brathwaite's ENGLISH GENTLEMAN (677).

a. Black, Matthew W. RICHARD BRATHWAIT: AN ACCOUNT OF HIS LIFE AND WORKS. Philadelphia, 1928.

679. Raleigh, Sir Walter. INSTRUCTIONS TO HIS SONNE AND TO POST-ERITYE. London, 1632.

> A touching document, presumably written in 1618; see also 169, 229–30, 514.

680. Milton, John. OF EDUCATION. TO MASTER SAMUEL HARTLIB. London, 1644.

> A synthesis of humanistic ideals embodied in a staggering curriculum to produce the hypothetical well-rounded man; see also 443–53.

A. _____ . ON EDUCATION, ed. O. M. Ainsworth. Yale University Press, 1928.

a. Parker, William R. "Education: Milton's Ideas and Ours," CE, 24 (1962–63), 1–14.

681. Poole, Joshua. THE ENGLISH PARNASSUS: OR, A HELPE TO ENGLISH POESIE. London, 1657.

> A book of aids to help the neophyte poet.

682. Osborne, Francis. ADVICE TO A SON. Oxford, 1656.

   A hanger-on at court who enjoyed the fame this work
   brought him; second part in 1658; six editions by 1658;
   see also 518.

   A. _____. ADVICE TO A SON, ed. E. A. Parry. London,
      1896.

683. Hoole, Charles. A NEW DISCOVERY OF THE OLD ART OF TEACHING
   SCHOOLE. London, 1660.

   Written ca. 1637.

   A. _____. A NEW DISCOVERY OF THE OLD ART OF TEACH-
      ING SCHOOLE, ed. E. T. Campagnac. University of Liver-
      pool Press, 1913.

XI. TRANSLATIONS

XI. Translations

Translation flourished during this period. The English were eager to have in their own tongue the literary heritage of antiquity and the contemporary works of European neighbors. Some translators strove for elegance and polish, others for vitality and even raciness. Most took liberties with their text. But in an age when imitation often meant the reproduction of a model, translation was an art, not a menial exercise to be scorned.

See also I.1, 11, 17, 29, 31, 32, 53, 66, 86, 127, 134, 136, 143, 147, 150, 152, 159, 160, 165, 175, 200, 203, 207, 208, 210, 214, 216, 218, 223, 280, 282, 283, 285, 293, 297, 302, 306, 307, 315, 327, 328, VI.p, 342.c, 350, 351, 356, 410, 422, 437, 440, 520, 521, 522, 524, 525, 526, 527, 529, 530, 531, 532, 534, 536, 537, 538, 540, 541, 542, 543, 545, 547, 549, 553, 555, 579, 580, 581, 583, 593, 596, 597, 601, 612, 613, 616, 617, 619, 620, 624, 629, 630, 646, 648, 650, 651, 654, 655, 656, 663, 665, 671, 765-78.

A. Clements, Arthur F., ed. TUDOR TRANSLATIONS: AN ANTHOLOGY. Oxford, 1940.

> Short excerpts from a large number of translators from Lord Berners to Sir Thomas Urquhart.

B. Winny, James, ed. ELIZABETHAN PROSE TRANSLATION. Cambridge University Press, 1960.

> Excerpts from THE COURTIER, tr. Hoby; THE GOLDEN ASS, tr. Adlington; ETHIOPIAN HISTORY, tr. Underdowne; ROMAN HISTORY, tr. Holland; et al.

i. Palmer, Henrietta R. LIST OF ENGLISH EDITIONS AND TRANSLATIONS OF GREEK AND LATIN CLASSICS PRINTED BEFORE 1641. London, 1911.

ii. Pane, Remigio U. ENGLISH TRANSLATIONS FROM THE SPANISH, 1484-1943: A BIBLIOGRAPHY. Rutgers University Press, 1944.

iii. Farrar, Clarissa P., and Austin P. Evans. BIBLIOGRAPHY OF ENGLISH TRANSLATIONS FROM MEDIEVAL SOURCES. Columbia University Press, 1946.

a. Whibley, Charles. "Translators," in THE CAMBRIDGE HISTORY OF ENGLISH LITERATURE, ed. A. W. Ward and A. R. Waller. 15 vols. Cambridge University Press, 1907-27. IV, 1-25.

b. Harris, W. V. THE FIRST PRINTED TRANSLATION INTO ENGLISH OF THE GREAT FOREIGN CLASSICS. London, 1909.

c. Hatcher, O. L. "Aims and Methods of Elizabethan Translators," ENGLISCHE STUDIEN, 44 (1911-12), 174-92.

d. Scott, Mary A. ELIZABETHAN TRANSLATIONS FROM THE ITALIAN. Boston, 1916.

e. Amos, F. R. EARLY THEORIES OF TRANSLATION. New York, 1920.

f. Conley, Carey H. THE FIRST ENGLISH TRANSLATORS OF THE CLASSICS. Yale University Press, 1927.

g. Matthiessen, Francis O. TRANSLATION: AN ELIZABETHAN ART. Harvard University Press, 1931.

   Includes chapters on Hoby's COURTIER, North's Plutarch, Florio's Montaigne, and Philemon Holland.

h. Lathrop, Henry B. TRANSLATIONS FROM THE CLASSICS INTO ENGLISH FROM CAXTON TO CHAPMAN, 1477-1620. University of Wisconsin Press, 1933.

i. Bush, Douglas. "Popular Literature and Translations," in ENGLISH LITERATURE IN THE EARLIER SEVENTEENTH CENTURY 1600-1660. Oxford, 1945, pp. 39-75.

j. Wortham, James. "Sir Thomas Elyot and the Translation of Prose," HLQ, 11 (1947-48), 219-40.

k. Norgaard, Holger. "Translations of the Classics into English Before 1600," RES, 9 (1958), 164-72.

l. Randall, Dale B. THE GOLDEN TAPESTRY: A CRITICAL SURVEY OF NON-CHIVALRIC SPANISH FICTION IN ENGLISH TRANSLATION, 1543-1657. Duke University Press,

1963.

m. Speroni, Charles. WIT AND WISDOM OF THE ITALIAN RENAISSANCE. University of California Press, 1964.

n. Ebel, Julia G. "A Numerical Survey of Elizabethan Translations," LIBRARY, 5th series, 22 (1967), 104-27.

o. Devereux, James A., S.J. "The Collects of the First Book of Common Prayer as Works of Translation," SP, 66 (1969), 719-38.

684. Alfred the Great, tr. Bede, HISTORIA ECCLESIASTICA GENTIS ANG-LORUM. ca. 895.

Selections from Bede's important church history.

A. Bede. THE OLD ENGLISH VERSION OF BEDE'S ECCLESIAS-TICAL HISTORY, ed. Thomas Miller. EETS OS 95, 96, 110, 111. London, 1890-98.

a. Campbell, Jackson J. "The Dialect Vocabulary of the OE Bede," JEGP, 50 (1951), 349-72.

b. Kuhn, S. M. "Synonyms in the Old English Bede," JEGP, 46 (1947), 168-76.

c. Whitelock, Dorothy. "The Old English Bede," PBA, 48 (1962), 57-90.

685. Alfred the Great, tr. Pope Gregory I, DURA PASTORALIS. ca. 895.

A handbook on pastoral duties distributed among the clergy. In a preface, Alfred argues for use of the vernacular.

A. Pope Gregory I. KING ALFRED'S WEST-SAXON VERSION OF GREGORY'S PASTORAL CARE, ed. Henry Sweet. EETS OS 45, 50. London, 1871-72.

B. _____. THE PASTORAL CARE: KING ALFRED'S TRANSLA-TION OF ST. GREGORY'S REGULA PASTORALIS, ed. N. R. Ker. Copenhagen, 1956.

C. _____. THE OLD ENGLISH PROSE AND VERSE PREFACES TO KING ALFRED'S TRANSLATION OF GREGORY'S PASTO-RAL CARE, ed. Dorothy Whitelock. Oxford University Press, 1967.

a. Brown, William H., Jr. "Method and Style in the Old English PASTORAL CARE," JEGP, 68 (1969), 666-84.

686. Alfred the Great, tr. Paulus Orosius, HISTORIA ADVERSUS PAGANOS. ca. 895.

A paraphrase with significant additions of the history written by Orosius, a fifth century Spanish priest.

A. Paulus Orosius. KING ALFRED'S OROSIUS, ed. Henry Sweet. EETS OS 79. London, 1883.

a. Potter, Simeon. "Commentary on King Alfred's Orosius," ANGLIA, 71 (1953), 385-437.

b. Bately, Janet M. "King Alfred and the Latin Manuscripts of Orosius' History," C&M, 22 (1961), 69-105.

687. Alfred the Great, tr. Boethius, DE CONSOLATIONE PHILOSOPHIAE. ca. 895.

An inspired translation of Boethius' masterwork on fate and free will.

A. Boethius. KING ALFRED'S ANGLO-SAXON VERSION OF BOETHIUS' DE CONSOLATIONE PHILOSOPHIAE, ed. Rev. Samuel Fox. London: Bohn's, 1864.

B. _____. KING ALFRED'S OLD ENGLISH VERSION OF BOETHIUS' DE CONSOLATIONE PHILOSOPHIAE, ed. Walter J. Sedgefield. Oxford, 1899. Tr. Walter J. Sedgefield. Oxford, 1900.

a. Donaghey, Brian S. "The Sources of King Alfred's Translation of Boethius's DE CONSOLATIONE PHILOSOPHIAE," ANGLIA, 82 (1962), 23-57.

b. Otten, Kurt. KONIG ALFREDS BOETHIUS. Tubingen, 1964.

c. Payne, Frances A. KING ALFRED & BOETHIUS, AN ANALYSIS OF THE OLD ENGLISH VERSION OF THE CONSOLATION OF PHILOSOPHY. University of Wisconsin Press, 1968.

688. Alfred the Great, tr. St. Augustine, SOLILOQUIAE. ca. 895.

A. St. Augustine. KING ALFRED'S VERSION OF ST. AUGUSTINE'S SOLILOQUIES, ed. T. A. Carnicelli. Harvard University Press, 1969.

B. Alfred the Great. THE WHOLE WORKS, ed. J. A. Giles.
3 vols. Oxford and Cambridge, 1852-53.

a. Brooke, Stopford A. KING ALFRED AS EDUCATOR OF HIS
PEOPLE AND MAN OF LETTERS. London, 1901.

b. Plummer, Charles. THE LIFE AND TIMES OF ALFRED THE
GREAT. Oxford, 1902.

c. Thomas, P. G. "Alfred and the Old English Prose of His
Reign," in THE CAMBRIDGE HISTORY OF ENGLISH LITERA-
TURE, ed. A. W. Ward and A. R. Waller. 15 vols. Cam-
bridge University Press, 1907-27. I,88-107.

d. Browne, Rev. G. F. KING ALFRED'S BOOKS. London,
1920.

e. Duckett, Eleanor S. ALFRED THE GREAT. University of
Chicago Press, 1956.

689. Chaucer, Geoffrey, tr. Boethius. DE CONSOLATIONE PHILOSOPHIAE.
ca. 1380.

A reverential version of Boethius' much admired classic;
printed by William Caxton ca. 1478.

A. Boethius. CHAUCER'S TRANSLATION OF BOETHIUS'S "DE
CONSOLATIONE PHILOSOPHIAE", ed. Rev. Richard Morris.
EETS ES 5. London, 1868.

B. _____. CHAUCER'S "BOECE", ed. Rev. Richard Morris.
London: Chaucer Society, 1886.

690. Trevisa, John, tr. Ranulph Higden, POLYCHRONICON. ca. 1380.

A seminal translation made from an important item in
the medieval chronicle tradition.

A. Higden, Ranulph. POLYCHRONICON, tr. John Trevisa, ed.
Rev. J. R. Lumby. Rolls Series. 9 vols. London, 1865-86.

691. Trevisa, John, tr. Bartholomaeus Anglicus, DE PROPRIETATIBUS RERUM.
1398.

A translation of Bartholomaeus' fourteenth century encyclopedia which remained a reference work throughout

the sixteenth century; published by Wynken de Worde
in 1495 and by Thomas Berthelet in 1535; see also 306.

A. Bartholomaeus Anglicus. MEDIEVAL LORE, ed. Robert Steele.
London, 1893.

Selections from John Trevisa's translation of
Bartholomaeus.

a. Wilkins, Henry J. JOHN DE TREVISA: HIS LIFE AND WORK.
London, 1915.

b. Fowler, David C. "John Trevisa and the English Bible," MP,
58 (1960-61), 81-98.

c. _____. "New Light on John Trevisa," TRADITIO, 18 (1962),
289-317.

692. Love, Nicholas, tr. THE MIRROUR OF THE BLESSED LYF OF JESU
CHRIST. ca. 1410.

The life of Christ with moral interpretation, freely
translated from a Latin text wrongly attributed to St.
Bonaventura; printed by William Caxton in 1486, with
other editions in 1490, 1494, and 1506.

A. THE MIRROUR OF THE BLESSED LYF OF JESU CHRIST, tr.
Nicholas Love, ed. Lawrence F. Powell. Oxford: Roxburghe
Club, 1908.

693. Caxton, William, tr. Raoul Lefevre. RECUYELL OF THE HISTORYES OF
TROY. Bruges, ca. 1475.

The first book printed in English, significantly a Continental version of classical material; kept in print
throughout the sixteenth and seventeenth centuries.

A. Lefevre, Raoul. THE RECUYELL OF THE HISTORYES OF
TROYE. Kelmscott Press, 1892.

B. _____. THE RECUYELL OF THE HISTORYES OF TROYE, tr.
William Caxton, ed. H. O. Sommer. 2 vols. London, 1894.

694. Caxton, William, tr. Anon., THE HISTORYE OF REYNART THE FOXE.
Westminster, 1481.

Translated from a Dutch source; other editions in 1489,
1494, ca. 1515, 1550, 1620, 1629, and 1640.

A. Anon. THE HISTORY OF REYNARD THE FOX, tr. William Caxton, ed. Edward Arber. London: English Scholar's Library, 1878.

B. Anon. THE HISTORY OF REYNARD THE FOX, tr. William Caxton, ed. Edmund Goldsmid. Edinburgh, 1884.

C. Anon. THE HISTORY OF REYNARD THE FOX, tr. William Caxton. Kelmscott Press, 1892.

D. Anon. THE HISTORY OF REYNARD THE FOX, tr. William Caxton, ed. D. B. Sands. Harvard University Press, 1960.

E. Anon. THE HISTORY OF REYNARD THE FOX, tr. William Caxton, ed. Norman F. Blake. EETS OS 263. London, 1970.

a. Blake, Norman F. "William Caxton's REYNARD THE FOX and His Dutch Original," BJRL, 46 (1963-64), 298-325.

b. _____. "English Versions of Reynard the Fox in the Fifteenth and Sixteenth Centuries," SP, 62 (1965), 63-77.

695. Caxton, William, tr. Guilelmus, Archbishop of Tyre, GODFREY OF BOLOYNE. Westminster, 1481.

A. Guilelmus, Archbishop of Tyre. GODEFFROY OF BOLOYNE, tr. William Caxton, ed. Mary N. Colvin. EETS ES 64. London, 1893.

B. _____. GODDEFROY OF BOLOYNE, tr. William Caxton. Kelmscott Press, 1893.

696. Caxton, William, tr. Gossouin, THE MYRROUR OF THE WORLDE. Westminster, 1481.

A fourteenth century encyclopedia wrongly attributed to Vincent de Beauvais.

A. Gossouin. MIRROUR OF THE WORLD, tr. William Caxton, ed. Oliver H. Prior. EETS ES 110. London, 1913.

697. Caxton, William, tr. Jacobus de Voragine, LEGENDA AUREA. Westminster, 1483.

A popular collection of simple lives of the saints; other editions ca. 1487, 1493, 1498, 1503, ca. 1510, 1512, and 1527.

A. Voragine, Jacobus de. THE GOLDEN LEGEND, tr. William Caxton, ed. F. S. Ellis. Kelmscott Press, 1892.

B. ____. THE GOLDEN LEGEND, tr. William Caxton. 7 vols. London: Temple Classics, 1900-1931.

a. Butler, Pierce. A STUDY OF CAXTON'S GOLDEN LEGEND. Baltimore, 1899.

b. Jeremy, Sister Mary. "Caxton's GOLDEN LEGEND and Voragine's LEGENDA AUREA," SPECULUM, 21 (1946), 212-21.

c. Kurvinen, Auvo. "Caxton's GOLDEN LEGEND and the Manuscripts of the GILTE LEGENDE," NM, 60 (1959), 353-75.

698. Caxton, William, tr. Aesop, THE SUBTYL HISTORYES AND FABLES. Westminster, 1484.

The classic collection of fables illustrated with an outstanding series of woodcuts.

A. Aesop. THE FABLES, tr. William Caxton, ed. Joseph Jacobs. London, 1889.

B. ____. CAXTON'S AESOP, ed. R. T. Lenaghan. Harvard University Press, 1967.

699. Caxton, William, tr. Ramon Lull, THE BOOKE OF THE ORDRE OF CHYVALRY OR KNYGHTHODE. Westminster, ca. 1484.

A relatively minor work by the notorious mystic and alchemist from Catalonia.

A. Lull, Ramon. THE ORDER OF CHIVALRY, tr. William Caxton, ed. F. S. Ellis. Kelmscott Press, 1893.

B. ____. THE BOOK OF THE ORDRE OF CHYVALRY, tr. William Caxton, ed. A. T. P. Byles. EETS OS 168. London, 1926.

700. Caxton, William, tr. Anon., THYSTORYE OF THE NOBLE KNYGHT PARYS AND OF THE FAYRE VYENNE. Westminster, 1485.

An engaging romance translated from a late medieval text; other editions in 1492, 1502, and 1510.

A. Anon. PARIS AND VIENNE, tr. William Caxton, ed. Mac-Edward Leach. EETS OS 234. London, 1957.

a. Finlayson, John. "The Source of Caxton's PARIS AND VIENNE," PQ, 46 (1967), 130-35.

701. Caxton, William, tr. Lorens d'Orleans, THE ROYAL BOOK OR BOOK FOR A KING. Westminster, 1486.

Caxton's rendition of Lorens d'Orleans LA SOMME DES VICES ET DES VERTUS.

702. _____. anon., THE FOUR SONS OF AYMON. London, 1489.

A literal rendition of an ancient French Chanson De Geste; other editions in 1504 and 1554.

A. Anon. THE RIGHT PLESAUNT AND GOODLY HISTORIE OF THE FOURE SONNES OF AYMON, tr. William Caxton, ed. Octavia Richardson. EETS ES 44, 45. London, 1884.

703. Caxton, William, tr. anon., BLANCHARDYN AND EGLANTINE. London, ca. 1489.

A sentimental French romance; continued by Thomas Pope Goodwine (see 593).

A. Anon. CAXTON'S BLANCHARDYN AND EGLANTINE, ed. Leon Kellner. EETS ES 58. London, 1890.

B. Caxton, William. THE PROLOGUES AND EPILOGUES, ed. W. J. B. Crotch. EETS OS 176. London, 1928.

a. Plomer, Henry R. WILLIAM CAXTON, 1424-1491. London, 1925.

b. Aurner, Nellie S. CAXTON: A STUDY OF THE LITERATURE OF THE FIRST ENGLISH PRESS. London, 1926.

c. Roberts, William W. WILLIAM CAXTON, WRITER AND CRITIC. Manchester, 1930.

d. Byles, A. T. P. "William Caxton as a Man of Letters," LIBRARY, 4th series 15 (1934-35), 1-25.

e. Sands, Donald B. "Caxton as a Literary Critic," PBSA, 51 (1957), 312-18.

    f.   Buhler, Curt F. WILLIAM CAXTON AND HIS CRITICS.
        Syracuse University Press, 1960.

    g.   Blake, Norman F. "Investigations into the Prologues and
        Epilogues by William Caxton," BJRL, 49 (1966-67), 17-46.

    h.   _____. "Caxton and Courtly Style," E&S, 21 (1968), 29-45.

    i.   Bennett, Henry S. ENGLISH BOOKS & READERS, 1475-1557.
        2nd ed. Cambridge University Press, 1969.

    j.   Blake, Norman F. CAXTON AND HIS WORLD. London,
        1969.

704. Bourchier, Sir John, Lord Berners, tr. anon., THE BOKE HUON DE
      BORDEUXE. London: Wynken de Worde, ca. 1534.

        The famous French romance; another edition in 1601;
        see also 134.

    A. Anon. THE BOKE OF DUKE HUON OF BURDEUX, tr. Sir
       John Bourchier, Lord Berners, ed. S. L. Lee. EETS ES 40,
       41, 44, 50. London, 1882-87.

    B. Anon. HUON OF BORDEAUX: DONE INTO ENGLISH BY
       SIR JOHN BOURCHIER, LORD BERNERS, ed. Robert Steele.
       London, 1895.

705. Bourchier, Sir John, Lord Berners, tr. anon., ARTHUR OF LYTELL BRY-
      TAYNE. London, ca. 1555.

        Another French romance in translation; another edition
        in 1582.

    A. Anon. ARTHUR OF LITTLE BRITAIN, tr. Sir John Bourchier,
       Lord Berners, ed. E. V. Utterson. London, 1814.

706. Bourchier, Sir John, Lord Berners, tr. Antonio de Guevara, THE GOLD-
      EN BOOK OF MARCUS AURELIUS. London, 1535.

        At least twelve more editions by 1586; see also 720.

707. Barclay, Alexander, tr. Sallust, THE FAMOUS CRONYCLE OF THE
      WARRE WHICH THE ROMAYNS HAD AGAYNST JUGURTH. London,
      ca. 1520.

708. Tiptoft, John, tr. Julius Caesar, COMMENTARYES. London, 1530.

A. Webb, Henry J. "English Translations of Caesar's COMMEN-
TARIES in the Sixteenth Century," PQ, 28 (1949), 490-95.

709. Tiptoft, John, tr. Cicero, TULLIUS DE AMICICIA. London, ca. 1530.

a. Lathrop, H. B. "The Translations of John Tiptoft," MLN, 41
(1926), 496-501.

b. Mitchell, Rosamond J. JOHN TIPTOFT (1427-1470). London,
1938.

710. Poyntz, Sir Francis, tr. Cebes, THE TABLE. London, ca. 1530.

The first English translation of a well-known Neoplatonic
allegory about the life of man; several other renderings
of this text in the sixteenth and seventeenth centuries.

711. Whittington, Robert, tr. Cicero, THE THRE BOOKES OF TULLYES OF-
FYCES. London: Wynken de Worde, 1534.

Another edition in 1540.

712. _____. Seneca, DE REMEDIIS FORTUITORUM. London, 1547.

a. Espiner-Scott, Janet. "Seneque dans la prose anglaise
de More a Lyly (1500-1580)," RLC, 34 (1960), 177-95.

713. Wilkinson, John, tr. Aristotle, THE ETHIQUES. London, 1547.

714. Chaloner, Sir Thomas, tr. Erasmus, THE PRAISE OF FOLIE. London,
1549.

The masterful spoof of the classical encomium and renaissance values; other editions ca. 1560 and 1577.

A. Erasmus. THE PRAISE OF FOLLIE, tr. Sir Thomas Chaloner,
ed. Clarence H. Miller. EETS OS 257. London, 1965.

715. Nicolls, Thomas, tr. Thucydides, THE HYSTORY. London, 1550.

From the French of C. de Seyssel.

716. Grimald, Nicholas, tr. Cicero, THRE BOKES OF DUETIES. London,
1553.

A schoolbook with parallel Latin and English texts, kept
in print throughout the century.

717. Paynell, Thomas, tr. Guido delle Colonne, THE DESTRUCTION OF TROYE COMPYLED BY DARES PHRIGIUS. London, 1553.

> A prose version of the pseudo-Homeric material made popular in English by Lydgate.

718. _____. anon., THE TREASURIE OF AMADIS OF FRAUNCE. London, 1567.

719. Colville, George, tr. Boethius, THE COMFORTE OF PHILOSOPHYE. London, 1556.

> One of the most popular and influential books in the late middle ages and still in demand.

A. Boethius. CONSOLATION OF PHILOSOPHY, tr. George Colville, ed. Ernest B. Bax. London: Tudor Library, 1897.

720. North, Sir Thomas, tr. Antonio de Guevara, THE DIALL OF PRINCES, WITH THE FAMOUS BOOKE OF MARCUS AURELIUS. London, 1557.

> A popular translation of a famous treatise which is part historical anecdote, part moral admonition, and part courtesy book; written in an elaborate style that prepared for euphuism; other editions in 1568, 1582, and 1619; see also 706.

A. Guevara, Antonio de. THE DIALL OF PRINCES, tr. Sir Thomas North, ed. K. N. Colvile. London: Scholars' Library, 1919.

721. North, Sir Thomas, tr. Bidpai, THE MORALL PHILOSOPHIE OF DONI. London, 1570.

> A collection of moral fables originally from India, belonging somewhere between Aesop and THE ARABIAN NIGHTS.

A. Bidpai. THE FABLES OF BIDPAI, tr. Sir Thomas North, ed. Joseph Jacobs. London, 1888.

722. North, Sir Thomas, tr. Plutarch, THE LIVES OF THE NOBLE GRECIANS AND ROMANES. London, 1579.

> A famous translation (from the French of Jacques Amyot) of a much-revered collection of ancient biographies, rifled by Shakespeare and others for characterizations, incidents, and even dialogue; other editions in 1595, 1603, 1612, 1631, and 1656.

A. Plutarch. LIVES OF THE NOBLE GRECIANS AND ROMANS,

tr. Sir Thomas North, ed. George Wyndham. 6 vols. London: Tudor Translations, 1895-96.

B. _____. THE LIVES OF THE NOBLE GRECIANS AND ROMANS, ed. Roland Baughman. New York: Limited Editions Club, 1941.

C. _____. SELECTED LIVES, tr. Sir Thomas North, ed. Paul Turner. 2 vols. Southern Illinois University Press, 1963.

723. Morwyng, Peter, tr. Joseph ben Gorion, A COMPENDIOUS HISTORY OF THE JEWES COMMUNE WEALE. London, 1558.

At least ten other editions by 1615; see also 297.

724. Barker, William, tr. Xenophon, THE BOOKES OF XENOPHON, CON-TAYNING THE DISCIPLINE, SCHOLE, AND EDUCATION OF CYRUS. London, ca. 1560.

The best known education of a prince from classical times; another edition in 1567.

a. Parks, George B. "William Barker, Tudor Translator," PBSA, 51 (1957), 126-40.

725. Dolman, John, tr. Cicero, THOSE FYVE QUESTIONS, WHICH MARKE TULLYE CICERO, DISPUTED IN HIS MANOR OF TUSCULANUM. London, 1561.

726. Hoby, Sir Thomas, tr. Baldassare Castiglione, THE COURTYER. London, 1561.

The courtesy book sans pareil in a worthy translation; other editions in 1577, 1588, and 1603; excerpts in XI.B.

A. Castiglione, Baldassare. THE BOOK OF THE COURTIER, tr. Sir Thomas Hoby, ed. Sir Walter A. Raleigh. London: Tudor Translations, 1900.

B. _____. THE BOOK OF THE COURTIER, tr. Sir Thomas Hoby, ed. Drayton Henderson. London: Everyman's, 1928.

a. Hoby, Sir Thomas. THE TRAVELS AND LIFE OF SIR THOMAS HOBY, KT. OF BISHAM ABBEY, WRITTEN BY HIMSELF, 1547-1564, ed. Edgar Powell. London: Camden Society, 1902.

b. Trafton, Dain A. "Structure and Meaning in THE COURTIER," ELR, 2 (1972), 283-97.

727. Eden, Richard, tr. Martin Cortes, THE ARTE OF NAVIGATION. London, 1561.

> The standard manual of navigation; kept in print until well into the seventeenth century; see also 207-08.

728. Golding, Arthur, tr. Aretino, THE HISTORIE. . .CONCERNING THE WARRES BETWENE THE IMPERIALLES AND THE GOTHES FOR THE POSSESSION OF ITALY. London, 1563.

729. _____. Julius Caesar, THE EYGHT BOOKES OF CAIUS JULIUS CAESAR CONTEYNING HIS MARTIALL EXPLOYTES IN GALLIA AND THE COUNTRIES BORDERING. London, 1565.

730. _____. Seneca, THE WOORKE. . .CONCERNING BENEFYTING. London, 1578.

731. _____. Pomponius Mela, THE SITUATION OF THE WORLD. London, 1585.

> A popular cosmography that had survived from classical times.

a. Golding, Louis Thorn. AN ELIZABETHAN PURITAN: ARTHUR GOLDING. New York, 1937.

b. Wortham, James. "Arthur Golding and the Translation of Prose," HLQ, 12 (1948-49), 339-67.

732. Sanford, James, tr. Epictetus, THE MANUELL. London, 1567.

> The earliest English translation of this late classical moral treatise which enjoyed its greatest popularity during the renaissance; see also 543.

733. _____. Heinrich Cornelius Agrippa, OF THE VANITIE AND UNCERTAINTIE OF ARTES AND SCIENCES. London, 1569.

> The masterwork of the master skeptic, calling all disciplines into doubt; another edition in 1575.

734. Watson, Christopher, tr. Polybius, THE HYSTORIES. . .DISCOURSING OF THE WARRES BETWIXT THE ROMANES & CARTHAGINENSES. London, 1568.

735. Newton, Thomas, tr. Cicero, PARADOXA STOICORUM. WHEREUNTO IS ANNEXED SCIPIO HYS DREAME. London, 1569.

736. Wilson, Thomas, tr. Demosthenes, THE THREE ORATIONS. . .IN FA-
VOUR OF THE OLYNTHIANS. . .WITH. . .FOWER ORATIONS AGAINST
KING PHILIP. London, 1570.

See also 660-61.

737. Fleming, Abraham, tr. A PANOPLIE OF EPISTLES. London, 1576.

Translations of letters (a literary form that the renaissance uncommonly admired) by Cicero, Pliny the Younger,
et al.

738. _____. Aelianus, A REGISTRE OF HYSTORIES. London, 1576.

739. Rich, Barnabe, tr. Herodotus, THE FAMOUS HYSTORY. London, 1584.

Questionably attributed to Rich on the basis of the
initials "B. R."; see also 554-56.

A. Herodotus, THE FAMOUS HYSTORY, tr. B. R., ed. Leonard
Whibley. London: Tudor Translations, 1924.

740. Munday, Anthony, tr. anon., PALMERIN D'OLIVA. London, 1588.

A Spanish romance of extraordinary persistence; other
editions in 1597, 1615, 1616, and 1637; see also 552.

a. Patchell, Mary. THE PALMERIN ROMANCES IN ELIZABETHAN
PROSE FICTION. New York, 1947.

741. Munday, Anthony, tr. anon., THE FIRST BOOK OF AMADIS OF GAULE.
London, ca. 1590.

The medieval classic; a second part published in 1595,
and other editions in 1618 and 1619.

742. Savile, Sir Henry, tr. Tacitus, FOWER BOOKES OF THE HISTORIES.
Oxford, 1591.

At least six editions by 1640.

743. Greneway, Richard, tr. Tacitus, THE ANNALES. . .THE DESCRIPTION
OF GERMANIE. London, 1598.

Later printed with Savile's translation of Tacitus (742).

744. Elizabeth I, tr. QUEEN ELIZABETH'S ENGLISHINGS, ed. Caroline
Pemberton. EETS OS 113. London, 1899.

Elizabeth's translations from Boethius, Plutarch, and
Horace, done 1593-98.

745. Holland, Philemon, tr. Livy, THE ROMANE HISTORIE. London, 1600.

The first major translation by this indefatigable classicist who rendered Greek and Latin into highly readable English; excerpts in XI.B; see also 165.

746. _____. Pliny, HISTORIE OF THE WORLD. London, 1601.

A. Pliny, SELECTIONS FROM THE HISTORY OF THE WORLD, tr. Philemon Holland, ed. Paul Turner. Southern Illinois University Press, 1962.

747. Holland, Philemon, tr. Plutarch, THE MORALS. London, 1603.

748. _____. Suetonius, THE HISTORIE OF TWELVE CAESARS. London, 1606.

A. Suetonius. HISTORY OF TWELVE CAESARS, tr. Philemon Holland, ed. Charles Whibley. 2 vols. London: Tudor Translations, 1899.

B. _____. THE HISTORIE OF TWELVE CAESARS, tr. Philemon Holland. London, 1931.

749. Holland, Philemon, tr. Ammianus Marcellinus, THE ROMAN HISTORIE. London, 1609.

750. _____. Xenophon, CYRUPAEDIA. London, 1632.

i. Silvette, Herbert. CATALOGUE OF THE WORKS OF PHILEMON HOLLAND. University of Virginia Press, 1940.

751. Lodge, Thomas, tr. Josephus, THE FAMOUS AND MEMORABLE WORKES. London, 1602.

The JEWISH HISTORY and other works; see also 574-78, 632.

752. _____. Seneca, THE WORKES. . .BOTH MORRALL AND NATURALL. London, 1614.

Revised 1620.

a. Sorensen, Knud. "Thomas Lodge's 'Seneca'," ARCHIV, 199 (1962-63), 313-24.

753. Lodge, Thomas, tr. Simon Goulart, A LEARNED SUMMARY UPON THE FAMOUS POEME OF WILLIAM OF SALUSTE LORD OF BARTAS. London,

1621.

An informative commentary on Du Bartas' major work,
LA SEPMAINE, which Joshua Sylvester had translated
into English verse with the title, DEVINE WEEKES AND
WORKES.

754. Florio, John, tr. Montaigne, THE ESSAYES OR MORALL, POLITIKE AND
MILITARIE DISCOURSES. London, 1603.

A. Montaigne. ESSAYS, tr. John Florio, ed. George Saintsbury.
3 vols. London: Tudor Translations, 1892-93.

B. _____. ESSAYS, tr. John Florio, ed. J. I. M. Stewart.
2 vols. London, 1931.

C. _____. SELECTED ESSAYS, tr. John Florio, ed. Walter
Kaiser. Boston: Riverside Editions, 1964.

a. Yates, Frances A. JOHN FLORIO: THE LIFE OF AN ITAL-
IAN IN SHAKESPEARE'S ENGLAND. Cambridge University
Press, 1934.

755. Heywood, Thomas, tr. Sallust, THE CONSPIRACIE OF CATELINE. . .
AND THE WARRE WHICH JUGURTH FOR MANY YEARES MAINTAINED.
2 pts. London, 1608-09.

A translation by one of the busiest writers of the early
seventeenth century; see also 173-74, 426.

A. Sallust. THE CONSPIRACY OF CATILINE AND THE WAR OF
JUGURTHA, tr. Thomas Heywood, ed. Charles Whibley. London: Tudor Translations, 1924.

756. Healey, John, tr. Epictetus, EPICTETUS HIS MANUALL. AND CEBES
HIS TABLE. London, 1610.

Two moral tracts of enduring popularity; Healey's translation of Theophrastus' CHARACTERS added to this in
the 1616 edition; other editions in 1616 and 1636;
see also 612.

757. _____. St. Augustine, OF THE CITIE OF GOD. London, 1610.

A. St. Augustine. OF THE CITIE OF GOD, tr. John Healey,
ed. Ernest Barker and R. V. G. Tasker. 2 vols. London:
Everyman's, 1945.

758. Bingham, John, tr. Xenophon, THE HISTORIE. [ANABASIS]. London, 1623.

759. Hobbes, Thomas, tr. Thucydides, EIGHT BOOKES OF THE PELOPON-NESIAN WARRE. London, 1629.

> A youthful exercise by the great political philosopher; the first eight books only, but completed by Hobbes in 1650; see also 463-65.

760. Crosse, William, tr. Sallust, THE WORKES. London, 1629.

761. Grimstone, Edward, tr. Polybius, THE HISTORY. London, 1633.

762. Casaubon, Meric, tr. Marcus Aurelius, HIS MEDITATIONS CONCERN-ING HIMSELFE. London, 1634.

> Another edition in 1635.

A. Marcus Aurelius. THE GOLDEN BOOK, tr. Meric Casaubon, ed. W. H. D. Rowse. London: Temple Classics, 1898.

763. Wither, George, tr. Nemesius, THE NATURE OF MAN. London, 1636.

764. Cogan, Henry, tr. Diodorus Siculus, THE HISTORY. London, 1653.

XII. TRANSLATIONS OF THE BIBLE

XII. Translations of the Bible

Translations of the Bible have a separate history and tradition, and therefore English versions of it are listed together in this section. It is impossible to calculate the influence that these translations exerted on English prose. Some of them were the most familiar literary prose in the language.

a. Cook, Albert S. THE BIBLE AND ENGLISH PROSE STYLE. New York, 1892.

b. Westcott, B. F. A GENERAL VIEW OF THE HISTORY OF THE ENGLISH BIBLE, rev. W. A. Wright. 3rd ed. London, 1905.

c. Lovett, Richard. THE PRINTED ENGLISH BIBLE 1525-1885. London: Religious Tract Society, 1909.

d. Lowes, John L. "The Noblest Monument of English Prose," in ESSAYS IN APPRECIATION   Boston, 1936.

e. Robinson, H. Wheeler, ed. THE BIBLE IN ITS ANCIENT AND MODERN ENGLISH VERSIONS. Rev. ed. Oxford, 1954.

f. Thompson, Craig R. THE BIBLE IN ENGLISH, 1525-1611. Washington, D. C.: Folger Booklets, 1958.

g. Bruce, Frederick F. THE ENGLISH BIBLE: A HISTORY OF TRANSLATION. Oxford University Press, 1961.

h. Hargreaves, Henry. "From Bede to Wyclif: Medieval English Bible Translations," BJRL, 48 (1965-66), 118-40.

765. Aelfric, tr. HEPTATEUCH. ca. 1000.

An Anglo-Saxon rendition of the first seven books of the OLD TESTAMENT.

A. _____. THE OLD ENGLISH VERSION OF THE HEPTATEUCH, ed. S. J. Crawford. EETS OS 160. London, 1922.

766. Wyclif, John, tr. BIBLE. ca. 1384.

The earliest rendition of the entire Old and New Testaments into English, translated from the Latin vulgate text of St. Jerome, though probably not by Wyclif; see also 16, 21.

A. _____. THE HOLY BIBLE, ed. Rev. Josiah Forshall and Sir Frederic Madden. 4 vols. Oxford University Press, 1850.

767. Tyndale, William, tr. NEW TESTAMENT. Cologne, 1525.

The first English translation from a Greek text (of Erasmus); see also 36-39, 340.

A. _____. THE BEGINNING OF THE NEW TESTAMENT TRANSLATED BY WILLIAM TYNDALE, 1525, ed. Alfred W. Pollard. Oxford, 1926.

a. Maveety, Stanley R. "Doctrine in Tyndale's New Testament: Translation as a Tendentious Art," SEL, 6 (1966), 151-58.

768. Tyndale, William, tr. THE FYRST BOKE OF MOSES CALLED GENESIS, etc. [THE PENTATEUCH.] Antwerp, 1531.

A translation from the Hebrew; first printed in London in 1551.

A. _____. FIVE BOOKS OF MOSES, CALLED THE PENTATEUCH, ed. Rev. J. I. Mombert. New York, ca. 1884.

B. _____. FIVE BOOKS OF MOSES CALLED THE PENTATEUCH, ed. Rev. J. I. Mombert, rev. F. F. Bruce. Southern Illinois University Press, 1967.

769. _____. THE PROPHETE JONAS. Antwerp, ca. 1531.

Another translation from the Hebrew of the OLD TESTAMENT.

770. Coverdale, Miles, tr. THE BIBLE. London, 1535.

The first complete translation of the Bible printed in English, drawing heavily upon Tyndale's translations (767-69); see also 46-47, 772.

A. _____. THE BIBLE, ed. Francis Fry. London, 1867.

771. Rogers, John (alias Thomas Matthew), tr. THE BYBLE. London, 1537.

Largely a redaction of the translations by Tyndale, completed by that of Coverdale; with a strongly Protestant bias; called the MATTHEW'S BIBLE.

772. Coverdale, Miles, ed., THE BYBLE. London, 1539.

Prepared as an official text to be placed in every church at the direction of Archbishop Cromwell; a revision of the MATTHEW'S BIBLE (771); called the GREAT BIBLE.

a. Mozley, James F. COVERDALE AND HIS BIBLES. London, 1953.

773. Taverner, Richard, tr. THE MOST SACRED BIBLE. London, 1539.

Another revision of the MATTHEW'S BIBLE (771); see also 655.

774. Cranmer, Thomas, ed. THE BYBLE. London, 1540.

A second edition of the GREAT BIBLE (772) with a preface by Archbishop Cranmer; see also 48-49.

a. Willoughby, Harold R. THE FIRST AUTHORIZED ENGLISH BIBLE, AND THE CRANMER PREFACE. University of Chicago Press, 1942.

775. Whittingham, William, et al., tr. THE BIBLE AND HOLY SCRIPTURES. Geneva, 1560.

Prepared by Protestant exiles in Geneva during the persecution of Mary Tudor, and therefore with a Calvinistic flavor, especially in the notes; sometimes called the BREECHES BIBLE because of its translation of Genesis iii.7; based on Tyndale's translations (767-68).

776. THE HOLIE BIBLE. London, 1568.

A cooperative revision of the GREAT BIBLE (772), undertaken by several Anglican bishops under the encouragement of Archbishop Parker, and therefore known as the BISHOPS' BIBLE.

777. THE NEW TESTAMENT OF JESUS CHRIST. Rheims, 1582. THE HOLIE BIBLE. Douai, 1609.

A papist version prepared by English exiles at Catholic centers in France; called the DOUAI BIBLE.

778. THE HOLY BIBLE. London, 1611.

The enduring "authorized version" prepared by forty-seven learned divines; based on the BISHOPS' BIBLE (776) and sponsored by James I; therefore called the KING JAMES' BIBLE.

a. Butterworth, Charles C. THE LITERARY LINEAGE OF THE KING JAMES BIBLE, 1340-1611. University of Pennsylvania Press, 1941.

INDEX

Index

A

Abbott, G.   233

Achilles Tatius   596, 620

Adams, J.Q.   248.A

Adams, R.G.   224.A

Adams, R.P.   342.a, VIII.u, 544.c

Addison, W.   180.b

Adlington, W.   536

Adolph, R.   I.oo

Aelfric   1-2, 277, 645, 765

Aelianus   738

Aesop   698

Agrippa, H.C.   328, 733

Ainsworth, O.M.   680.A

Alcock, J.   30

Aleman, M.   619

Alfred the Great   I.i, 684-88

Allen, D.C.   I.p, 384.a, 483.A, 573.b, 637.A

Allen, H.E.   10.a, 10.b, 12.C, 12.c, 473.A

Allen, H.M.   476.A

Allen, P.R.   342.k

Allen, P.S.   476.A

Allestree, R.   128

Allison, C.F.   II.cc

Alston, L.   371.A

Alter, R.   VIII.aa

Amadis of Gaul   741

Ames, R.A.   342.d

Ammianus Marcellinus   749

Amos, F.R.   XI.e

Anderau, A.   544.e

Anderson, G.   134.B

Anderson, W.   134.B

Andreasen, N.N.C.   90.c

Andrewes, L.   76-77, 126

Anselment, R.A.   382.d

Index

Apollonius of Tyre   520, 532, 585

Applegate, J.   573.c

Apuleius   536

Arber, E.   50.A, 187.A, 208.A, 227.A, 229.A, 247.A, 270.A, 338.B, 366.A, 416.A, 502.A, 634.A, 694.A

Aretino   728

Aristotle   285, 713

Armin, R.   610

Armytage, W.H.G.   X.u

Arnold, T.   16.A

Arrowood, C.F.   336.a

Ascham, R.   657-58

Ashbee, E.W.   532.A

Ashley, R.   VIII.H

Ashley, Robert   481

Ashton, J.   VIII.D

Atkins, J.W.H.   VIII.f, IX.c, IX.d

Atkynson, W.   31

Aubert, D.   530

Augustine, St.   86, 130, 688, 757

Aurner, N.S.   528.c, 703.b

Averell, W.   559

Awdeley, J.   354

Axon, W.E.A.   102.A

Aydelotte, F.   VI.c

Aylmer, J.   349

Ayre, J.   58.B

B

Babb, L.   317.C, 317.b, 317.e

Babington, C.   27.A

Bacon, Lady Ann   351

Bacon, Sir F.   I.s, I.ss, 172, 194.a, 315-16, 482, 673

Bacon, W.A.   560.A

Bailey, J.E.   102.A

Baker, Father A.   13.C

Baker, E.A.   VIII.k, 582.B

Baker, Herschel   III.p

Baker, Humphrey   301

Baker, Sir R.   188

Bald, R.C.   91.d

Baldwin, T.W.   X.j, X.k

Baldwin, W.   659

Bale, J.   137-38, 344-45

Bandinel, B.   202.A

Banks, M.M.   525.A

Barclay, A.   707

Barclay, J.   437

Barish, J.A.   I.ee, 551.d

Barker, A.E.   453.c

Barker, E.   757.A

Barker, W.   724

Barrett, W.P.   239.A

Bartholomaeus Anglicus   306, 691

Bashe, E.J.   I.i

Bately, J.M.   686.b

Batman, S.   306

Battles, F.L.   53.A

Baugh, A.C.   10.C, 528.b

Baughan, D.E.   211.A

Baughman, R.   722.B

Bax, E.B.   719.A

Baxter, R.   114-15

Bayly, L.   84

Bayly, T.   628

Baynes, W.E.C.   440.B

Beaty, N.L.   43.a

Beazley, C.R.   IV.B

Becher, R.   3.i

Bede   143, 684

Bedingfield, T.   159

Beeching, H.C.   52.B

Belfour, A.O.   7

Bellenden, J.   136

Benbow, R.M.   149.b

Bennett, H.S.   I.n, I.o, 703.i, 28.a

Bennett, J.   511.e

Bennett, J.A.W.   528.l

Bennett, J.R.   I.ii

Bennett, J.W.   200.c

Benson, L.D.   134.a

Bent, J.T.   IV.A

Berman, R.   94.a

Berners, Dame J.   337

Berners, Lord   134, 704-06

Berry, L.O.   IV.F

Best, G.   215

Bethurum, D.   2.c, 3.B

Bettie, W.   611

Beum, R.   I.hh

Bevington, D.M.   342.h

Bible   765-78

Bidpai   721

Bigges, W.   225

Billingsley, H.   302

Binder, J.   342.c

Bingham, J.   758

Birch, T.   230.C, 335.A

Black, M.W.   678.a

Blackburn, T.H.   636.i

Blacker, I.R.R.   221.D

Blackie, E.M.   28.a, 204.A

Blake, N.F.   II.E, 694.E, 694.a, 694.b, 703.g, 703.h, 703.j

Blench, J.W.   II.y

Bliss, J.   77.A, 116.A

Index

Blitzer, C. 468.b

Blount, Sir H. 268

Blundeville, T. 309

Blunt, J.H. 35.A

Boas, F.S. 426.a, 582.k

Boccaccio, G. 537, 581, 616

Bodin, J. 422

Boece, H. 136

Boethius 687, 689, 719, 744

Bogholm, N. 10.c

Bolton, E. 636.h

Bolton, F.R. 113.c

Bond, R.W. 551.A

Bonheim, H. VIII.iv

Boorde, A. 205, 292, 306.a, 535

Booth, S. 149.c

Booty, J.E. 351.A, 352.a

Borinski, L. 551.e

Bosanquet, E.F. VI.d, VI.e

Botero, G. 235

Boughner, D.C. 405.c

Bourchier, Sir J. 134, 704-06

Bowers, F.T. 584.a

Bowers, R.H. 486.A, 659.A, 661.B

Bowes, T. 307

Boxer, C.R. IV.E

Boyce, B. VII.g, VII.h, VIII.v

Boyle, R. 335

Braaksma, M.H. IV.i

Bradbrook, M.C. 528.f

Bradley, A.G. 247.A

Bradner, L. 544.a, 544.d

Brandeis, A. 23.A

Brathwaite, R. 498-99, 625-26,
677-78

Brende, J. 534

Breton, N. 411-12, 494-95,
602-06

Brett-Smith, H.F.B. 416.B,
584.A, 596.A

Brewer, D.S. 528.e

Brewer, J.S. 179.A

Brie, F.W.D. 133.A

Bright, T. 308

Brinkley, R.F. I.I

Brinsley, J. 105

Brinsley, John 674-75

Brockdorff, Baron C. von 465.A

Bromiley, G.W. 49.a

Brooke, S.A. 688.a

Brown, C.C. 121.a

Brown, H. 612.A

Brown, J. 118.A

Brown, W.H. 685.a

Browne, G.F.   688.d

Browne, R.M.   317.c

Browne, Sir T.   I.dd, I.ss, 326,
333, 509-11

Bruce, D.H.   555.c

Bruce, F.F.   XII.g

Brugis, T.   323

Brushfield, T.N.   230.i

Buchan, J.   515.B

Buchert, J.R.   538.e

Buckeridge, J.   77

Buford, A.H.   III.l

Buhler, C.F.   595.A, 659.a, 703.f

Bullein, W.   353

Bullen, A.H.   353.A

Bullett, G.W.   II.p

Burton, H.   95

Burton, R.   I.dd, I.ss, 317

Burton, W.   596

Bush, D.   I.G, II.n, III.h, IV.l,
V.e, VI.p, VII.e, 538.a, 545.a,
XI.i

Butler, P.   697.a

Butler-Bowden, W.   473.B

Butterworth, C.C.   778.a

Buxton, J.   582.j

Byles, A.T.P.   699.B, 703.d

Byrhtferth   278

Byrne, M. St.C.   314.a, 552.a

C

Caius, J.   295

Calvin, J.   53

Camden, C.   VI.i, 414.a

Camden, W.   164-65, 175

Campagnac, E.T.   667.A, 674.A,
683.A

Campbell, J.J.   684.a

Campbell, W.E.   341.a, 342.D,
476.B

Campion, T.   639

Capgrave, J.   130-32, 201

Caradog of Llancarvan   152

Carew, R.   237

Carey, J.   I.pp

Carlson, L.H.   358.A

Carnicelli, T.A.   688.A

Carrithers, G.H.   89.i

Carter, J.   511.B

Cartier, J.   218

Cartigny, J. de   553

Cartwright, T.   358

Cary, L.   457

Casa, G. della   663

Casaubon, M.   762

Case, T.   673.A

Index

Castiglione, B. 726

Catherine, St., of Sienna 32

Cattley, S.R. 54.A

Cavendish, G. 142

Cawley, R.R. IV.j, 505.A

Caxton, W. 20, 524, 528, 593, 646, 648, XI.h, 689, 692, 693-703

Cebes 710

Cervantes 613, 624

Challis, L. 582.q

Chaloner, Sir T. 714

Chambers, P.F. 472.a

Chambers, R.W. I.i, VI.J. 647.A

Chandler, F.W. VI.b, VIII.d

Chapman, C.O. 520.a

Charles I 462

Charlton, K. X.q

Chaucer 281, 689

Cheke, Sir J. 346

Chester, A.G. 52.C, 52.b

Chettle, H. 403, 592

Chevalley, A. 600.a

Chew, S.C. IV.h, 584.B

Chillingworth, W. 104

Cholmeley, K. 473.a

Christmas, H. 345.A

Christophers, R.A. 233.i

Church, R. 148.A

Cicero 709, 711, 725, 735, 737

Cinquemani, A.M. 641.a

Clancy, T.H. VI.z

Clark, A.C. I.e

Clark, C. 129.G

Clarke, S. 274

Clausen, W. VII.f

Clements, A.F. XI.A

Clemons, H. 551.B

Coffin, C.M. 425.A

Cogan, H. 764

Coleman, T.W. II.i

Colet, J. 40-41

Colgrave, B. 608.a

Colie, R.L. I.mm, 123.a

Colledge, E. II.A

Collier, J.P. 236.A, VI.A, VI.C, 365.A, 384.A, 555.A, 576.A, 585.A

Collingwood, R.G. 464.a

Collins, J.C. IX.B, 636.B

Collinson, R. 215.A

Collis, L. 473.b

Colonna, F. 583

Colonne, G. delle 717

Colvile, K.N. 720.A

Colville, G.   719

Colvin, M.N.   695.A

Commines, P. de   160

Conley, C.H.   XI.f

Conwell, C.   585.B

Cook, A.S.   I.D, 636.A, XII.A

Cooper, J.R.   515.c

Cooper, T.   385

Cope, J.I.   I.qq

Copland, R.   285, 532

Cornwallis, Sir W.   483-85, 638

Corrie, G.E.   52.A

Cortes, M.   727

Coryate, T.   249

Cosin, J.   93

Cotta, J.   428

Cotton, R.   395.a

Coverdale, M.   46-47, 770, 772

Cox, J.E.   49.A

Cox, L.   649

Craig, H.   308.A

Craigie, J.   672.A

Craik, H.   I.C

Crane, R.S.   482.a, VIII.j

Crane, W.G.   I.k, 664.A

Cranfill, T.M.   555.B, 555.c

Cranmer, T.   48-49, 774

Crawford, S.J.   278.A, 765.A

Creeth, E.H.   I.T

Creigh, C.   552.d

Croft, H.H.S.   652.A

Crofts, J.E.V.   579.A

Croll, M.W.   I.g, I.h, I.kk, 551.B

Cross, J.E.   1.c

Crosse, H.   413

Crosse, W.   760

Croston, A.K.   584.b

Crotch, W.J.B.   703.B

Crummey, R.O.   IV.F

Cudworth, R.   106, 123.i

Cuffe, H.   488

Culpeper, N.   334

Culpeper, Sir T.   516

Culverwel, N.   117-18, 123.i

Cuningham, W.   298

Cunliffe, J.W.   544.A

Curtius Rufus, Q.   534

Cust, H.   159.A, 440.A

D

Dacres, E.   440

Dallington, Sir R.   239-40, 583

Danby, J.F.   382.i

Danett, T.   160

Daniel, S.   640

Index

Daniells, R.   I.m

Darby, H.S.   52.a

Darcy, A.   175

Darton, F.J.H.   594.A

Darwin, F.D.S.   II.m

Daunt, M.   VI.J

Davies, D.W.   243.a

Davies, E.T.   405.e

Davies, G.   VI.O

Davies, R.T.   528.g

Davies, W.H.   299.A

Davies, W.T.   345.i

Davis, J.   232

Davis, N.   I.ff

Davis, W.R.   VIII.ee, 575.a, 582.l, 582.n, 582.r

Davy, N.   V.A

Day, A.   580, 668

Day, J.   242

Deacon, R.   303.b

Dean, L.F.   III.i

Deane, C.   244.A

Dee, J.   302, 303

Deguileville, G. de   524

Dekker, T.   VI.Q, 414-19, 421, 599

Delany, P.   III.q

Dell, F.   317.A

Deloney, T.   598-600

DeMolen, R.L.   666.B

Demosthenes   736

Denonain, J.-J.   509.A

Dent, A.   60-63

Dent, R.W.   562.a

DePorte, M.V.   122.A

Devereux, J.A.   XI.o

Devereux, R.   226

Dewar, M.   371.a

Dick, H.G.   482.C

Dickenson, J.   586-87

Dickinson, W.C.   153.A

Dickson, A.   531.A, 531.a

Digby, Sir K.   324, 325, 510, 643

Digges, L.   296

Digges, T.   296, 305

Dillenberger, J.   53.B

Diodorus Siculus   764

Dionysius Periegetes   210

Dipple, E.   582.x, 582.cc

Dobson, E.J.   10.f

Dobson, G.   608

Dolman, J.   725

Donaghey, B.S.   687.a

Donald, A.K.   529.A

Donne, J.   I.ss, 89-91, 183, 184.A, 424-25, 492, 515.A

Donner, H.W.   342.b

Donno, E.S.   406.A

Donovan, D.   I.v, 317.i, 317.ii, 419.i, 426.ii, 511.ii, 511.iii, 515.i

Dorsch, T.S.   151.a, 342.o

Douglas, R.L.   540.A

Dowlin, C.M.   636.c

Drake, Sir F.   225, 263-64

Drummond, W.   497

Dubois, M.-M.   2.d

Duckett, E.S.   688.e

Duffield, G.E.   39.D, 49.C

Dugdale, Sir W.   198-99

Duhamel, P.A.   41.a, 342.f, 382.g

Duncan-Jones, K.   584.g

Dunham, W.H.   VI.M

Duvall, R.F.   443.a

Dyson, H.   408

E

Eames, W.   247.i

Earle, J.   I.a

Earle, John   502

Ebel, J.G.   XI.n

Edelen, G.   154.A, 154.a

Eden, C.P.   113.B

Eden, R.   207-08, 727

Edward, Lord Herbert of Cherbury   192

Edwards, T.   461

Eliot, T.S.   77.a

Elizabeth I   744

Elliott, R.C.   342.i

Ellis, F.S.   697.A, 699.A

Ellis, Sir H.   135.A, 139.A, 145.A, 149.A

Ellis, R.L.   482.A

Ellrodt, R.   497.A

Elmen, P.   113.b, 128.a

Elyot, Sir T.   286, 306.a, 652-53, 654, XI.j

Emerson, E.H.   28.c

Endicott, N.   511.D

Engel, S.M.   464.b

Epictetus   732, 756

Erasmus   655, 656, 714

Erbe, T.   20.A

Esdaile, A.   VIII.i

Espiner-Scott, J.   712.a

Essex, Earl of, see Devereux, R.

Etienne de Besancon   525

Euclid   302

Evans, A.P.   XI.iii

Evans, J.   279

Index

Evans, J.X.   449.b

Everard, J.   327

F

Fabyan, R.   135

Farrar, C.P.   XI.iii

Fellheimer, J.   149.a

Fell-Smith, C.   303.a

Felltham, O.   501

Felver, C.S.   610.a

Fenton, G.   150, 540

Ferguson, A.B.   28.d, VI.t

Ferry, A.D.   II.D

Feuillerat, A.   582.C

Field, P.J.C.   528.r, 528.s

Fieler, F.B.   642.a

Finlayson, J.   700.a

Firth, C.H.   VI.F

Fisch, H.   I.t

Fish, S.   338

Fish, S.E.   I.ss

Fisher, St. J.   33-34

Fisher, J.H.   10.e

Fitzmaurice-Kelly, J.   613.A, 619.A

Flecknoe, R.   517

Fleischhacker, R. von   280.A

Fleming, A.   737-38

Fletcher, G.   228

Fletcher, P.   100-01

Florio, J.   218, 754

Floyd, T.   409

Foakes-Jackson, F.J.   405.b

Forde, E.   588-91

Forsey, G.F.   278.a

Forshall, J.   766.A

Fortescue, J.   336, 356

Fortescue, T.   542

Fowler, D.C.   691.b, 691.c

Fox, S.   687.A

Foxe, J.   39.A, 54-55

Frampton, J.   214, 216

Francis, W.N.   11.B

Frank, J.   VI.x

Franklin, J.H.   422.a

Fraunce, A.   670

Freake, J.   328

Frobisher, M.   215

Froissart, J.   134

Fry, F.   770.A

Fuller, T.   72.A

Fuller, Thomas   102, 177-80, 273, 507-08

Funke, O.   3.f

Furnivall, F.J.   205.A, 283.A,
304.A, 338.A, 354.A, 355.A,
372.A, 436.A, 530.A

Furnivall, P.   304.A

G

Gainsford, T.   170-71, 615

Gardner, H.L.   13.a, 18.a, 91.B

Garmonsway, G.N.   129.E, 645.A

Gascoigne, G.   364, 544, 631

Gaselee, Sir S.   214.A, 536.B,
596.A

Gatch, M. McC.   II.z

Gathorne-Hardy, R.   113.i

Gauden, J.   462

Gauthier, D.P.   464.g

Gebert, C.   VI.K

Gee, J.A.   45.A

Genouy, H.   582.b

Gentillet, I.   410

Gerard, J.   310

Gerould, G.H.   2.b

Gesner, C.   297, 313-14

Gesta romanorum   526

Gibbons, Sister M.   584.d

Gibson, R.W.   342.i, 482.i

Gibson, S.   180.i

Gifford, G.   378-79

Gifford, W.   89.g

Gilbert, Sir H.   213, 217

Giles, J.A.   688.B

Gill, A.   103

Godden, M.R.   1.d

Godshalk, W.M.   582.p

Godwin, F.   622

Godwin, T.   255

Goepp, P.H.   520.b

Golding, A.   66, 728-31

Golding, L.T.   731.a

Goldsmid, E.   694.B

Gollancz, I.   545.A

Goodman, G.   85,88

Goodwin, J.   454-55

Goodwine, T.P.   593, 703

Goodyear, W.   553

Goolden, P.   520.A

Gordon, G.S.   676

Gordon, I.A.   I.II

Gorges, Sir A.   315

Gorion, J. ben   723

Gosse, Sir E.   421.A, 578.A

Gosson, S.   366-69, 426

Gossouin   696

Gottfried, R.B.   150.a

Gottlieb, S.A.   540.a

Index

Gough, A.B.   316.A

Gough, R.   165.A

Goulart, S.   753

Grafton, R.   145

Grange, J.   546.a, 548

Grantham, H.   537

Green, A.W.   482.c, 482.f

Green, V.H.H.   28.b

Greenblatt, S.J.   230.e

Greene, R.   VI.Q, 386, 387, 390.a, 392, 396.c, 397–401, 402, 403, 411, 420, 478–80, VIII.G, 561–73, 587

Greene, T.M.   657.a

Greenslade, S.L.   39.C

Greenwood, A.D.   I.c

Greet, W.C.   24.A

Greg, W.W.   575.A

Gregg, K.L.   419.a

Gregory I, Pope   685

Grein, C.W.M.   I.A

Greneway, R.   743

Greville, F.   189, 194, 582.s

Grigson, G.   482.B

Grimald, N.   716

Grimestone, E.   166, 761

Grislis, E.   405.k

Grosart, A.B.   99.A, 194.B, 390.A,

413.A, 419.B, 573.A, 587.A, 606.A, 606.B

Guazzo, S.   665

Guevara, A. de   706, 720

Guffey, G.R.   123.i, 582.ii

Guicciardini, F.   150

Guicciardini, L.   543

Gulielmus of Tyre   695

Gunther, R.T.   281.B

Guy de Chauliac   282

H

Habington, W.   185–86

Hake, E.   359

Hakewill, G.   87–88

Hakluyt, R.   219–21, 223, 253

Hall, E.   139

Hall, John   127, 513

Hall, Joseph   80–83, 126, 447, 489, 612

Haller, W.   54.b, VI.L, VI.O, VI.I

Hallett, P.E.   342.C

Halvorson, N.O.   I.a

Hamelius, P.   200.B

Hamilton, A.C.   582.ff, 636.g

Hamilton, K.G.   I.ii, 453.e, X.p

Hanning, R.W.   III.o

Harding, D.P.   142.B, 176.B

Harding, D.W.   90.d

Hardison, O.B., Jr.   IX.E, 636.k

Hargreaves, H.   16.d, XII.h

Hargreaves, M.   465.i

Harington, Sir J.   406

Harlow, C.G.   395.a, 396.e

Harlow, V.T.   230.B

Harman, T.   355

Harrell, J.G.   12.D

Harrington, J.   467-68

Harriot, T.   224

Harris, J.W.   345.a

Harris, V.   I.Q, I.z

Harris, W.V.   XI.b

Harrison, G.B.   234.A, VI.H, 370.A, 387.A, 397.A, 397.B, 400.A, 403.A, 407.A, 414.A, 479.A, 568.A, 640.A

Harrison, W.   154

Hartlib, S.   442, 680

Hartman, H.   545.B

Harvey, G.   382, 387-90, 391-93, 633

Harvey, Ralph   22.A

Harvey, Richard   155, 373, 386, 391-93

Hasleton, R.   231

Haslewood, J.   337.A

Hatcher, O.L.   XI.c

Hawkins, Sir J.   209

Hawkins, Sir R.   262

Hayes, G.R.   552.b

Hayward, Sir J.   161-62

Hazlitt, W.C.   VI.B, VIII.B, VIII.C, 533.A, X.a

Head, R.   VI.g

Healey, J.   612, 756-57

Healy, T.S.   91.B, 425.B

Hearne, T.   138.A

Heath, D.D.   482.A

Heath, T.G.   141.a

Hebel, J.W.   I.J, 492.A

Heideman, M.A.   511.a

Heidler, J.B.   VIII.1

Heiserman, A.R.   342.j

Heliodorus   541

Heltzel, V.B.   477.A, 477.a, 481, 481.a, 506.A, 582.m, X.ii

Henderson, D.   726.B

Henel, H.   277.A

Heninger, S.K.   19.b, V.j, 636.1

Hepburn, R.W.   85.b

Herbert, G.   119, 184.A, 515.A

Herbert, J.A.   525.a

Herbert, Sir T.   267

Herford, C.H.   642.B

Index

Hermes Trismegistus   283, 327

Herodotus   739

Heron, H.   477

Herr, A.F.   II.j

Herrtage, S.J.   343.a, 526.A

Heusinkveld, A.H.   I.i

Heuston, R.F.V.   I.gg

Hexter, J.H.   342.E, 342.e

Heylyn, P.   261

Heywood, T.   173-74, 426, 755

Hibbard, G.R.   VI.Q, 296.d

Hierocles   127

Higden, R.   690

Higginson, F.   265

Hill, W.S.   405.i, 405.l, 405.m

Hilton, W.   II.dd, 18, 471

Hindley, C.   435.A

Hingeston, F.C.   131.A

Hitchcock, E.V.   25.A, 26.A, 176.A

Hobbes, T.   120, 463-65, 466, 467, 759

Hodges, A.   620

Hodgson, G.E.   12.b

Hodgson, P.   II.dd, 13.A, 13.B, 13.b, 32.A

Hogrefe, P.   652.d, 652.f

Holden, W.P.   VI.s

Holinshed, R.   149, 154

Holland, P.   165, 745-50

Hollingsworth, G.E.   264.A

Holmes, E.   652.c

Holmes, M.   139.b

Holmstedt, G.   17.A

Holthausen, F.   9.A

Holzknecht, K.J.   I.K

Hood, F.C.   464.d

Hooker, R.   184.A, 405, 515.A

Hoole, C.   683

Horsman, E.A.   608.A

Horstman, C.   12.B, 522.A

Hosley, R.   149.C

Houghton, W.E., Jr.   507.a

Houk, R.A.   405.B

Howard, C.M.   IV.d

Howard, E.J.   369.A, 653.A

Howell, J.   270, 441, 470, 512

Howell, R.   582.y

Howell, W.S.   I.w

Hudson, W.S.   347.a

Hughes, H.S.   VIII.m

Hughes, H.T.   113.d

Hughes, M.Y.   452.a, 453.A

Hunt, E.W.   41.b

Hunter, G.K.   551.g

Huntley, F.L.   113.e, 509.a, 511.c, 511.f

Hurley, M.   16.b

Husain, I.   I.Q

Hussey, M.   61.a

Hussey, S.S.   18.b

Hutchinson, F.E.   II.c

Huth, A.N.   29.A

Hutton, E.   616.A

Hyman, V.R.   636.j

Hyrde, R.   650

I

Inge, W.R.   II.a

Ingram, J.K.   31.A

Irwin, M.   230.c

Isler, A.D.   582.u, 582.v, 582.w

Izard, T.C.   547.b

J

Jackson, H.   317.B

Jacob, E.F.   28.e

Jacobs, J.   512.B, 538.A, 580.A, 698.A, 721.A

James, E.   I.L

James, I.   407, 672

Janelle, P.   II.v

Jayne, S.   41.d

Jean d'Arras   529

Jenkins, H.   403.a, 479.a

Jeremy, Sister M.   697.b

Jewel, J.   58, 351–52

Jewkes, W.T.   IV.r, VIII.w

Joannes de Hildesheim   522

Johnson, E.   195

Johnson, F.R.   V.d, 397.a, 662.A, 662.a

Johnson, Richard   594–95

Johnson, Robbin S.   342.s

Johnson, Robert   235, 486

Johnson, Robert C.   396.ii, 544.ii, 551.ii, 552.ii, 573.ii, 578.ii, 658.ii

Johnson, Ronald C.   544.h

Jones, C.W.   II.A

Jones, D.   471.A

Jones, E.D.   IV.x

Jones, H.W.   V.g

Jones, J.W.   219.A

Jones, R.F.   II.f

Jones-Davies, M.T.   419.c

Jonson, B.   642

Jordan-Smith, P.   317.A

Jorgensen, P.A.   555.d

Josephus   751

Jost, K.T.   3.d

Index

Judges, A.V.   VI.I

Julian of Norwich   472

Julius Caesar   708, 729

Jusserand, J.J.   IV.a, VIII.e

K

Kahrl, S.J.   VIII.bb, VIII.cc, 535.A

Kaiser, W.   754.C

Kalstone, D.   582.o

Kaula, D.   584.e

Keble, J.   405.A

Kellner, L.   703.A

Kelso, R.   X.f

Kemp, W.   234

Kempe, M.   473

Kempe, W.   669

Kendall, W.   449.a

Kennedy, J.M.   601.A

Kentish-Wright, U.   604.A

Kepers, J.   671

Kepler, T.S.   109.A

Ker, N.R.   685.B

Ker, W.P.   134.A

Keynes, Sir G.L.   91.i, 308.a,
510.A, 511.i, 515.A

Kimbrough, R.   582.dd

Kimmelman, E.   538.c

Kinard, J.P.   3.a

King, H.   94

King, W.N.   551.c

Kingsford, C.L.   III.c, 408.B

Kinloch, T.F.   83.a

Kinney, A.F.   366.b

Kirk, R.   81.A, 489.A

Kirkman, F.   VI.g

Kirkwood, J.J.   172.d

Knachel, P.A.   462.A

Knights, L.C.   I.j, VIII.n

Knolles, R.   238, 422

Knowles, D.   II.w

Knowles, E.B.   613.a

Knowlson, J.R.   622.c

Knox, J.   153, 348, 349

Kocher, P.H.   V.f

Koller, K.   VIII.s, 670.a

Kranidas, T.   446.a, 453.d

Krapp, G.P.   I.f

Krouse, F.M.   636.e

Krueger, R.   89.e

Kuhn, S.M.   684.b

Kuriyagawa, F.   18.D

Kurvinen, A.   697.c

L

Ladell, A.R.   115.a

Lambarde, W.   148

Lambert, R.S.   IV.g

Lanfranco of Milan   280

Lang, A.   583.A

Langdale, A.B.   101.a

Langton, R.   204

Lanham, R.A.   544.g, 582.r, 584.f

LaPrimaudaye, P. de   307

Latham, A.M.C.   584.c

Lathrop, H.B.   XI.h, 709.a

Latimer, H.   50-52

La Tour-Landry, G. de   646

Laud, W.   77, 116

Laudonniere, R. de   223

Lavynham, R.   15

Lawler, T.M.C.   18.c

Lawlis, M.E.   VIII.L, 600.B, 600.b

Lawlor, J.   567.a

Lawry, J.S.   582.kk

Leach, A.F.   X.e

Leach, M.   700.A

LeComte, E.   91.c

Lee, S.L.   704.A

Lefevre, R.   693

Lefranc, P.   230.d

Lehmberg, S.E.   652.B, 652.b

Leland, J.   138, 151.a

Lenaghan, R.T.   698.B

Lenton, F.   504

Leo   521

Letts, M.H.I.   200.C, 200.b

Levin, S.R.   3.e

Levy, F.J.   165.c, 582.ee

Lewis, C.S.   I.u

Lewis, G.   92.b

Lichtenstein, A.   123.b

Lieb, M.   453.g

Liegey, G.M.   32.A

Lievsay, J.L.   I.vii, 72.a, IV.t, VI.n, 491.A, 491.a, 555.e, 665.a

Liljegren, S.B.   467.A

Lilly, W.   329, 458-60

Lindheim, N.R.   582.t, 582.ii

Lindsay, A.D.   464.B

Lipp, F.R.   2.f

Lithgow, W.   254

Livy   745

Llwyd, H.   146, 152

Lodge, T.   374, 574-78, 632, 751-53

Long, M. McD.   20.a

Longus   580

Loomis, R.S.   VIII.x, 528.h

Lorens d'Orleans 11, 701

Love, N. 692

Lovett, Richard 37.A, XII.c

Lovett, Robert M. VIII.m

Lowe, I. 89.c

Lowes, J.L. XII.d

Lull, R. 699

Lumby, J.R. 690.A

Lumiansky, R.M. 528.m

Lupset, T. 40, 42–45

Lupton, D. 181, 275, 438

Lupton, J.H. 342.A

Lyly, J. 382, 383, 385, VIII.r,
550–51

Lyman, D.B. 180.a

M

Mabbe, J. 619, 624

McCann, J. 13.C

Macchiavelli, N. 159, 350, 410,
440

McColley, G. 622.A

McCollum, J.I. 154.b, 169.b

McCrea, H. 501.b

McCutcheon, E. 77.e

MacDonagh, T. 639.A

Macdonald, H. 465.i

MacDonald, W.L. VII.a

McGinn, D.J. 358.b, 382.c,
391.a, 396.a

McGrade, A.S. 405.i

McIntosh, A. 3.c

McIntyre, J.P. 636.h

Mackenzie, N. 511.h, 511.i

McKerrow, R.B. 396.A, 402.A,
419.A

MacKinnon, F.I. 123.A

McLean, A. V.1

Maclean, H.N. 194.a

Maclure, M. II.u

McMahon, C.P. X.m

McNeill, J.T. 53.A

McNeilly, F.S. 464.f

McRae, K.D. 422.A

Madden, Sir F. 766.A

Maguire, J. 176.a

Mahl, M.R. I.S, 636.D

Mair, G.H. 661.A

Maitland, F.W. 371.A

Major, J.M. 453.f, 652.e

Malloch, A. 295.A

Malloch, A.E. 636.d

Malone, K. I.q

Malory, Sir T. 528

Mandeville, Sir J. 200

Mann, F.O.   600.A

Maplet, J.   299-300

Marc'hadour, G.   52.c, 476.a

Marcus Aurelius   706, 720, 762

Marenco, F.   582.aa

Marguerite d'Angouleme   597

Markham, C.R.   209.A

Markham, G.   404, 607

Marsh, T.N.   VI.v

Marshall, J.S.   405.j

Martin, H.   115.b

Martin, L.C.   511.C

Martz, L.L.   342.E, 475.c

Mary Denise, Sister   32.a

Mascall, L.   380

Masefield, J.   221.B

Mason, J.E.   X.h

Mason, W.   500

Matthew, F.D.   16.B

Matthews, A.G.   115.i

Matthews, T.   86

Matthews, W.   I.P, I.vi, 528.o

Matthiessen, F.O.   XI.g

Maud, R.   558.c

Maveety, S.R.   767.a

May, T.   191, 437

Maybank, T.   575.B

Maynadier, G.H.   636.a

Mayor, J.E.B.   34.A

Meadows, A.J.   V.k

Meech, S.B.   473.A

Melbancke, B.   558

Meres, F.   637

Mexia, P.   542

Meyer, C.S.   41.i, 49.B

Miles, L.   41.c, 41.e, 475.B, 475.a, 475.b

Miles, W.   538.B

Miller, C.H.   714.A

Miller, E.H.   I.cc, 396.c, 401.a, 401.b, 401.c, 569.A

Miller, P.   456.A, X.i

Miller, T.   684.A

Mills, C.A.   201.A

Milosh, J.   18.d

Milton, J.   I.ss, 443-53, 680

Miner, E.   I.rr

Mintz, S.I.   464.c

Mirk, J.   20

Mish, C.C.   VIII.K, VIII.iii, VIII.t

Misyn, R.   22

Mitchell, R.J.   709.b

Mitchell, W.F.   II.g

Index

Mitchell, W.S.   353.a

Moir, E.   III.n

Molesworth, Sir W.   465.B

Molinari, P.   472.c

Moloney, M.F.   511.d

Mombert, J.I.   768.A, 768.B

Monardes, N.   214

Monroe, N.E.   412.a

Montaigne   754

Montemayor, J. de   601

Moore, C.A.   I.G

Moorman, C.   528.j, 528.k, 528.n

More, H.   120-23

More, Sir T.   I.i, 52.c, 141, 172.a, 176, 339-42, 474-76

Morgan, C.E.   VIII.h

Morgan, M.M.   II.r

Morice, E.G.   606.A

Morison, J.L.   28.A

Morison, S.   II.l, VI.j

Morley, H.   VIII.E

Mornay, P. de   66

Morris, R.   6, 8, 11.A, 689.A, 689.B

Morton, J.   10.A, 10.B

Morwyng, P.   297, 723

Morysine, R.   651

Moryson, F.   257

Moseley, E.M.   VIII.H

Mosher, J.A.   VIII.g

Mott, A.S.   221.C

Motteux, P.   630

Moulton, C.W.   IX.A

Mozley, J.F.   39.a, 54.a, 772.a

Mueller, W.R.   89.d, 317.d

Muir, K.   I.M

Mulcaster, R.   356, 666-67

Mulder, J.R.   X.t

Mun, T.   430

Munday, A.   370, 408, 552, 740-41

Munro, J.J.   130.A

Munz, P.   405.g

Murphy, G.   VII.A, VII.i

Murphy, J.J.   II.aa

Mynshul, G.   429

Myrick, K.O.   582.e

N

Napier, A.S.   3.A

Napier, J.   78

Napier, M.   196.A

Nashe, T.   VI.Q, 383-84, 386, 388-90, 391-96, 415-16, 584

Nathanson, L.   511.j

Naunton, Sir R. 187

Needham, G.I. 2.B

Nelson, W. VIII.dd

Nemesius 763

New, J.F.H. VI.y

Newton, A.P. IV.f

Newton, T. 735

Nichols, P. 263

Nichols, W. 178.A

Nicoll, A. 149.B

Nicolls, T. 715

Nicolson, M.H. 622.a, 622.b

Norden, J. 64–65, 156–58

Nørgaard, H. XI.k

Norris, J. 123.i

North, Sir T. 720–22

Northbrooke, J. 56–57, 365

Norton, T. 53

Novarr, D. I.R, 184.a

Noyes, G.E. X.i.

Nugent, E.M. I.N

Nuttall, G.F. 115.c

Nuttall, P.A. 180.A

O

Oakeshott, M. 464.C

O'Brien, A.S. 608.b

O'Brien, E.J. VIII.G

O'Dell, S. VIII.ii

Oesterley, H. 526.a

Offord, M.Y. 646.C

Ogden, M.S. 282.A

Ohmann, R. I.aa

Oldys, W. 230.C

Oliphant, J. 667.B

Oliver, H.J. 515.a, 515.b

O'Malley, C.D. V.i

Ong, W. I.jj, X.s

Orosius, P. 686

Orr, R.R. 104.a

Orson, S.W. 624.A

Orton, H. I.iii

Orwell, G. VI.P

Osborn, J.M. IV.s, 582.jj

Osborne, F. 518, 682

Otten, K. 687.b

Overbury, Sir T. 493

Owst, G.R. II.d, II.h

P

Pafort, E. X.l

Painter, W. VIII.G, 538

Palmer, H.R. XI.i, 703.a

Palmerin d'Oliva 740

Index

Pane, R.U. XI.ii

Paradise, N.B. 578.a

Pargellis, S. VI.M

Parish, V. 306.a

Parker, H. 523

Parker, M. 147

Parker, R.B. 401.d

Parker, R.W. 582.gg

Parker, W.R. 680.a

Parkes, J. IV.e

Parks, G.B. IV.o, IV.p, IV.w,
  206.A, 221.a, VIII.r, 658.a, 724.a

Parr, J. 564.a

Parry, E.A. 682.A

Parry, W. 236

Parsons, R. 59

Patchell, M. 740.a

Patericke, S. 410

Patrick, J.M. 317.a, 453.C, 482.d

Patrides, C.A. III.r, 169.A

Patterson, L.D. 290.a

Paylor, W.J. 493.B

Payne, F.A. 687.c

Payne, J.F. V.a

Paynell, T. 717-18

Peacham, H. (the elder) 664

Peacham, H. 505-06, 676

Peacock, W. I.E

Pearson, A.F.S. 358.a

Pearson, G. 47.A, 47.B

Pearson, T.P. 372.a

Peckham, Sir G. 217

Pecock, R. 24-28

Peel, A. 358.A

Peele, G. 609

Pemberton, C. 744

Pendry, E.D. 419.C

Penrose, B. IV.k, IV.m, IV.q

Pepler, C. II.t

Pepper, R.D. X.A

Perkins, D. 393.a

Perkins, W. 423

Perkinson, R.H. 426.A

Perry, G.G. 12.A

Person, D. 319

Peter, J. VI.u

Peter Martyr (Anglerius) 207-08

Peters, R. 41.f

Peterson, R. 663

Peterson, S. VI.R

Petti, A.G. 391.c

Pettie, G. VIII.G, 545, 551.b,
  665

Pfander, H.G. 523.a

Pierce, W.   382.A, 382.b

Piggott, S.   165.b

Pineas, Rainer   39.b, 341.b, 341.c, 342.l, 342.r, 345.b, 345.c

Pipes, R.   228.A

Pliny   746

Pliny the Younger   737

Plummer, C.   129.B, 336.A, 688.b

Plutarch   654, 722, 744, 747

Pollard, A.F.   VI.E

Pollard, A.W.   613.B, 676.A

Pollock, T.C.   675.A

Polo, Marco   216

Polybius   734, 761

Pomponius Mela   731

Ponet, J.   347

Poole, J.   681

Pope, J.C.   1.C

Porter, T.   276

Potter, G.R.   89.A

Potter, S.   686.a

Powell, E.   726.a

Powell, L.F.   692.A

Powell, T.   436

Powicke, Sir M.   165.a

Poyntz, Sir F.   710

Pratt, J.   54.B

Price, G.R.   419.d

Prior, O.H.   696.A

Proclus   293

Proctor, J.   140

Prouty, C.T.   544.b, 546.a, 547.a

Pruvost, R.   VIII.o, 573.a

Prynne, W.   116.a, 439

Purchas, S.   251-53

Puttenham, G.   635

Pynson, R.   200, 523, 707

Q

Quick, R.H.   666.A

Quinn, D.B.   213.A, 220.A, 221.b

R

Raab, F.   440.a

Rabelais, F.   630

Racin, J.   169.a

Rae, W.D.   578.d

Rainolde, R.   662

Raleigh, Sir W.   169, 229-30, 514, 679

Raleigh, W.A.   IV.b, VIII.a, 726.A

Randall, D.B.   XI.I

Rankins, W.   377

Rastell, J.   357, 533

Rastell, W.   476

Ratcliff, E.C.   II.o

Index

Rawlinson, H.G. 253.B

Raymond, J. 272

Read, C. III.i

Recorde, R. 287-91

Reed, A.W. 476.B

Rees, J. 194.b, 582.s

Reid, H.J. 663.A

Reidy, M.F. 77.b

Reiss, E. 528.p

Renwick, W.L. I.iii

Reszkiewicz, A. 2.e

Reynolds, Sister A.M. 472.A

Reynolds, E.E. 342.n

Reynolds, H. 641

Reynolds, J. 431

Reynolds, R. VI.P

Rhys, E. 408.A

Ribner, I. 382.h

Rich, B. 402, 487, VIII.G, 554-56, 739

Richardson, H.G. 523.b

Richardson, O. 702.A

Rimbault, E.F. 493.A

Ringler, W.A., Jr. 366.a, 369.a, 551.a

Rivers, G. 623

Roberts, J.R. II.C

Roberts, M. I.H

Roberts, W.W. 703.c

Robertson, J. 501.a, 582.D

Robinson, C.N. IV.c

Robinson, F.C. I.viii

Robinson, F.G. 66.a

Robinson, H.W. XII.e

Robson, J.A. 16.c

Robynson, R. 342

Rogers, J. 771

Rohde, E.S. V.c

Rolle, R. II.dd, 12, 22

Rollins, H.E. 548.A, 558.a

Romei, A. 671

Roper, W. 176

Rose, M. 582.z

Rositzke, H.A. 129.D

Ross, A. 124, 325, 333, 466, 644

Ross, W.O. 14

Rossi, P. 482.h

Rouland, D. 579

Rous, F. 269

Routh, H.V. VI.a

Rowe, F.A. 89.f

Rowlands, R. 212

Rowlands, S. 420-21

Rowse, W.H.D.   762.A

Rumble, T.C.   528.i

Russell, K.F.   V.i

Russell, M.   196.A

Russell-Smith, H.F.   468.a

Rust, G.   123.i

Ryan, L.V.   658.B, 658.c

S

Saintsbury, G.   I.B, I.d, III.b,
   184.A, VI.D, VIII.F, VIII.b, 754.A

Sallust   707, 755, 760

Saltonstall, W.   503

Salu, M.B.   10.E

Salusbury, W.   293

Samuel, I.   636.b

Sanders, C.   390.a

Sanderson, R.   92, 184.A, 515.A

Sands, D.B.   694.D, 703.e

Sandys, Sir E.   79

Sandys, G.   256

Sanford, J.   543, 732-33

Sasek, L.   VI.w

Saunders, T.   222

Savage, J.E.   493.C

Savile, Sir H.   742

Schaar, C.   19.a

Schelling, F.E.   642.A

Schlauch, M.   VIII.y

Schleiner, W.   89.h

Schmidt, A.J.   228.B, 661.a, 661.b

Schneider, J.P.   12.a

Schoeck, R.J.   342.m

Schomburgk, Sir R.H.   230.A

Schueler, D.G.   528.q

Schuster, Sister M.F.   172.a

Scoggin, J.   614

Scot, R.   360-61

Scott, M.A.   XI.d

Scott, W.   116.A

Scudery, M. de   629

Seaton, E.   670.A

Sedgefield, W.J.   I.F, 687.B

Selden, J.   427

Sells, A.L.   IV.u

Seneca   712, 712.a, 730, 752

Serjeantson, M.S.   279

Seymour, M.C.   200.D, 200.e

Shaaber, M.A.   I.O, VI.h

Shakespeare, W.   403, 547, 575,
   582.i

Shapiro, I.A.   90.a, 398.a, 401.e

Shaw, P.   419.b

Shawcross, J.T.   452.b, 453.g

Shelton, T.   613

Shepherd, G.   636.C

Sheppard, S.   627

Sherley, Sir A.   236, 242, 243

Sherley, T.   242, 243.a

Sherley-Price, L.   18.C

Shirley, F.J.   405.f

Sibbes, R.   96-99

Sidney, Sir P.   66, 194, 366, 574.a,
   582, 607, 618, 636

Silvester, J.   248

Silvette, H.   750.i

Simon, J.R.   317.f

Simon, Joan   X.r

Simpson, E.M.   89.A, 91.A, 91.a

Simpson, P.   642.B

Sisson, C.J.   405.d, 578.b

Sitwell, G.   18.B

Skeat, W.W.   2.A, 19.A, 281.A

Skelton, J.   539

Skelton, R.A.   220.A

Smeaton, O.   501.A

Smetana, C.L.   1.b

Smith, A.H.   129.C

Smith, C.I.   X.o

Smith, C.S.   544.f

Smith, D.E.   V.b

Smith, D.N.   III.d

Smith, G.G.   IX.C

Smith, H.   67-72

Smith, Capt. John   244-47

Smith, John   123.i, 519

Smith, L.P.   113.A

Smith, L.T.   138.B, IV.a

Smith, N.   194.A

Smith, R.M.   139.a

Smith, Sir T.   241, 371

Snortum, N.K.   391.b

Soden, G.I.   85.a

Sola Pinto, V. de   I.iv, III.k

Sommer, H.O.   528.A, 582.A,
   693.B

Somner, W.   182

Sorenson, K.   752.a

Sorley, W.R.   465.a

Southern, A.C.   VI.q

Southwell, R.   74-75

Sparrow, J.   90.A

Spedding, J.   482.A

Speed, J.   167-68

Spenser, E.   266, 582.z, 633,
   636.a, 643

Speroni, C.   XI.m

Spingarn, J.E.   IX.D, IX.a, 663.B

Spottiswood, J.   196

Sprague, A.C.   640.B

Stanley, T.   197

Stanwood, P.G.   93.A

Stapleton, T.   143

Starkey, T.   343

Starnes, D.T.   555.a, 655.A

Staton, W.F.   I.y, 658.b

Stauffer, D.A.   III.e

Steadman, J.M.   464.e

Stedmond, J.M.   I.r

Steele, R.   284, 285.A, 342.B,
   691.A, 704.B

Stefansson, V.   215.B

Steiner, A.   200.a

Stephens, J.   496

Sterry, P.   123.i

Stevens, M.   475.A

Stewart, J.I.M.   754.B

Stillinger, J.   552

Stone, R.K.   472.d

Story, G.M.   77.B

Stow, J.   144, 151, 408

Stoye, J.W.   IV.n

Strachan, M.   249.a

Stranks, C.J.   113.a

Strathmann, E.A.   230.a

Stubbes, P.   73, 372, 384

Stubs, J.   147

Stueber, Sister M.S.   405.h

Suetonius   748

Summers, R.   361.A

Summersgill, T.L.   396.b

Surtz, E.L.   34.a, 34.b, 342.E,
   342.g

Sutherland, J.   I.x

Svendsen, K.   448.a

Swan, J.   320

Swart, J.   551.b

Sweet, H.   1.A, 685.A, 686.A

Sweeting, E.J.   IX.b

Swinburn, L.M.   21.A

Sylvester, R.S.   141.A, 142.A,
   142.B, 142b, 176.B, 342.E, 342.p,
   342.q

T

Tacitus   742, 743

Taft, A.I.   474.A

Tannenbaum, S.A.   286.A, 396.i,
   419.i, 426.i, 544.i, 551.i, 552.i,
   573.i, 578.i, 582.i, 606.i, 658.i

Tarlton, R.   621

Tasker, R.V.G.   757.A

Taverner, R.   655, 773

Tayler, E.W.   IX.F

Taylor, G.S.   646.B

Taylor, Jeremy   109-13

Taylor, John   258-60, 432-35

Teets, B.E.   VIII.z

Tenney, E.A.   578.c

Thomas a Kempis   31

Thomas, J.D.   200.d

Thomas, P.G.   567.A, 688.c

Thomas, S.   403.b

Thomas, W.   206

Thompson, C.R.   X.n, XII.f

Thompson, E.N.S.   453.a, VII.c, VII.d

Thompson, J.A.K.   I.v

Thompson, J.W.   III.g

Thoms, W.J.   VIII.A

Thorne, J.P.   636.f

Thorpe, B.   129.A

Thucydides   715, 759

Tilley, M.P.   548.a, 558.b

Tinker, C.B.   I.D

Tiptoft, J.   708-09

Tobriner, M.L.   651.A

Tolkien, J.R.R.   10.D

Tonkin, H.   230.ii

Topsell, E.   313-14

Townsend, G.   54.A

Trafton, D.A.   726.b

Traherne, T.   123.i

Trease, G.   IV.v

Trevisa, J.   690-91

Trevor-Roper, H.R.   116.b

Trimble, W.R.   III.j

Trinterud, L.J.   VI.S

Tupper, J.W.   I.b

Turberville, G.   362-63

Turler, J.   211

Turner, C.   552.c

Turner, M.   582.bb, 582.hh

Turner, P.   722.C, 746.A

Turner, W.   294

Tuvill, D.   490-91

Twine, L.   585

Twyne, T.   210

Tyndale, W.   36-39, 340-41, 767-69

U

Udall, J.   381

Udall, N.   656

Umbach, H.H.   89.a, 89.b

Underdowne, T.   541

Underhill, E.   18.A

Underhill, J.G.   VIII.c

Upcott, J.D.   263.A

Urfe, H. d'   617

Urquhart, T.   630

Usk, T.   19

Ustick, W.L.   X.g

Utley, F.L.   10.d

Utterson, E.V.   705.A

V

Vane, Sir H.   125

Vann, W.H.   512.a

Varnhagen, H.   592.A

Vaughan, T.   330-32

Vaughan, W.   311

Verstegen, R.   163

Vicary, T.   304

Vickers, B.   482.i

Viles, E.   354.A, 355.A

Vinaver, E.   528.B, 528.a, 528.i

Vives, J.L.   650, 651

Volkoff, I.   622.B

Voragine, J. de   697

W

Wagner, H.R.   208.a

Waite, A.E.   332.A

Wakelin, M.F.   20.b

Walker, A.   635.A

Walker, Henry   340.A

Walker, Hugh   VII.b

Walkington, T.   312

Wallace, K.R.   482.g

Wallace, M.W.   582.a

Wallace, W.M.   230.b

Wallenberg, J.K.   11.a

Waller, A.R.   464.A

Walsh, J.   II.bb

Walten, M.G.   507.A

Walter, H.   38.A, 39.B

Walters, H.B.   III.f

Walton, I.   90.a, 92.a, 183-84, 405.a, 515

Ware, Sir J.   266

Warner, G.F.   200.A

Warner, R.D.-N.   1.B, 5

Warner, W.   560

Warrack, G.   472.B

Warren, A.   511.b

Warren, L.C.   652.a

Watson, C.   734

Watson, F.   X.iii, X.c, X.d, 650.a

Watson, H.   531

Webb, H.J.   V.h, 555.b, 708.a

Webbe, E.   227

Webbe, W.   634

Webber, J.   I.nn, 77.d, 90.b, 91.b

Weber, K.   457.a

Webster, C.   442.A

Weldon, Sir A.   193, 271

Wells, S.   396.B

Welsby, P.A.   77.c

Westcott, B.F.   XII.b

Westlake, J.S.   521.A

Wey, W.   202

Wheatley, H.B.   527.A

Wheeler, T.   III.m, 172.b, 172.c

Whetstone, G.   375-76, VIII.G,
546-47

Whibley, C.   III.a, 160.A, 536.A,
540.A, 630.A, XI.a, 748.A, 755.A

Whibley, L.   739.A

Whichcote, B.   123.i

Whitaker, A.   250

Whitaker, V.K.   482.e

White, B.   379.A, 493.a

White, C.L.   2.a

White, H.C.   II.e, II.k, II.q,
II.x, VI.o

Whitehorne, P.   350

Whitelock, D.   3.b, 4.A, 129.F,
684.c, 685.C

Whitlock, R.   469

Whitney, J.P.   II.b

Whittingham, W.   775

Whittington, R.   711-12

Wiles, A.G.D.   582.f

Wiley, P.L.   142.a

Wilkins, H.J.   691.a

Wilkins, J.   107-08, 321-22

Wilkinson, C.H.   503.A

Wilkinson, J.   713

Wilkinson, J.T.   114.B

Willcock, G.D.   635.A

Williams, C.   528.d

Williams, C.H.   39.c

Williams, R.   456

Williamson, G.   I.s, 511.g

Williamson, H.R.   361.B

Williamson, J.A.   209.a, 262.A

Willoughby, H.R.   774.a

Wills, R.   208

Wilson, A.   189-90

Wilson, F.P.   I.dd, VI.f, VI.m,
396.A, 414.B, VIII.p

Wilson, H.S.   390.b

Wilson, J.D.   VI.G, 382.a

Wilson, J.P.   77.A

Wilson, Mona   582.d

Wilson, R.M.   I.bb, 472.b

Wilson, T.   660-61, 736

Winn, H.E.   16.C

Winny, J.   IV.C, VIII.I, XI.B

Wither, G.   763

Withington, R.   VII.B

Wittreich, J.A.   449.C

Wolf, M.H.   487.A

Wolfe, D.M.   453.B, 453.b

Wolff, S.L.   VIII.i

Wolters, C.   13.D

Wood, J.O.   508.A

Woodhouse, A.S.P.   VI.N

Woodward, W.H.   X.b

Worde, Wynken de   18, 30, 32,
203, 473, 522, 526, 531, 532,
691, 704, 711

Wordsworth, C.   82.A

Workman, H.B.   16.a

Workman, S.K.   I.l

Wortham, J.   XI.j, 731.b

Worthington, J.   123.i

Wotton, Sir H.   184, 318, 515.A

Wotton, H.   549

Wright, A.   126

Wright, C.E.   VIII.q

Wright, H.G.   VI.r, 538.d

Wright, L.B.   IV.D, VI.k, 538.b

Wright, T.   646.A

Wright, W.A.   524.A, 658.A

Wroth, Lady M.   618

Wulfstan   3-4

Wulker, R.P.   I.A

Wyclif, J.   16, 21, 766

Wydeville, A.   648

Wyer, Robert   293

Wyndham, G.   722.A

X

Xenophon   724, 750, 758

Y

Yates, F.A.   754.a

Young, B.   581, 601

Young, W.   114.A

Z

Zall, P.M.   VIII.J, 533.B, 610.A

Zandvoort, R.W.   551.f, 582.c

Zeeman, E.   II.s

Zeitlin, J.   482.b

Zutphen, J.P.W.M. van   15.A

WITHDRAWAL